# crossing jordan

### Joshua, Holy War, and God's Unfailing Promises

Other books by this author:
  *The Nature of Christ*

To order, call **1-800-765-6955.**

Visit us at **www.reviewandherald.com** for information on other Review and Herald® products.

# crossing jordan

Joshua, Holy War, and God's Unfailing Promises

Roy Adams

REVIEW AND HERALD® PUBLISHING ASSOCIATION
HAGERSTOWN, MD 21740

The author assumes full responsibility for the accuracy of all facts and quotations as cited in this book.

Unless otherwise noted, Bible texts in this book are from the *Holy Bible, New International Version.* Copyright © 1973, 1978, 1984, International Bible Society. Used by permission of Zondervan Bible Publishers.

Scripture quotations marked NASB are from the *New American Standard Bible,* copyright © 1960, 1962, 1963, 1968, 1971, 1972, 1973, 1975, 1977, 1994 by The Lockman Foundation. Used by permission.

Texts credited to NEB are from *The New English Bible.* © The Delegates of the Oxford University Press and the Syndics of the Cambridge University Press 1961, 1970. Reprinted by permission.

Texts credited to NKJV are from the New King James Version. Copyright © 1979, 1980, 1982 by Thomas Nelson, Inc. Used by permission. All rights reserved.

Bible texts credited to NRSV are from the New Revised Standard Version of the Bible, copyright © 1989 by the Division of Christian Education of the National Council of the Churches of Christ in the U.S.A. Used by permission.

Bible texts credited to RSV are from the Revised Standard Version of the Bible, copyright © 1946, 1952, 1971, by the Division of Christian Education of the National Council of the Churches of Christ in the U.S.A. Used by permission.

This book was
Edited by Gerald Wheeler
Copyedited by James Cavil and Delma Miller
Cover designed by Bryan Gray/Genesis Design
Cover images by: Robert Hunt/portrait, Bettmann/CORBIS/engraving,
    Photos.com/water photo
Electronic makeup by Shirley M. Bolivar
Typeset: Bembo 12/14

PRINTED IN U.S.A.

09 08 07 06 05          5 4 3 2 1

**R&H Cataloging Service**
Adams, Roy, 1941-
    Crossing Jordan: Joshua, holy war,
and God's unfailing promises.

    1. Bible. O.T. Joshua—Study and teaching.   2. H.

                        222.2

ISBN 0-8280-1845-6

To George W. Brown and G. Ralph Thompson,

who introduced me to theology,

and whose contined affirmation

has profoundly influenced my entire ministry

# Acknowledgments

It was with considerable trepidation that I decided to make the book of Joshua a subject for protracted study. I was afraid my enthusiasm for it at the moment might wane upon closer examination.

But exactly the opposite happened: my interest deepened. And I see more clearly now than ever its fundamental relevance for modern Christians facing obstacles in their personal lives and struggling with the perennial issues of violence, justice, and faith.

To obtain the maximum benefit from this book, you should read it along with the book of Joshua and a map of ancient Palestine. This book is designed for both personal reading and group study.

Several individuals deserve gratitude for their role in this project—George Knight, for his invaluable editorial input in the early stages; and Bill Shea, for his critique of the original draft. I also thank Nicole Bolder Mattox, Mary Maxson, and Ruth Wright, each of whom lent secretarial and computer skills to the work.

I'm grateful also to the Review and Herald for pushing the book through a tight schedule; and to acquisitions editor Jeannette Johnson for bringing it to their attention. Gerald Wheeler, as he edited the document, kept in touch with me, and shared many valuable suggestions.

I thank my wife, Celia, and our children, Dwayne and Kim, for putting up with a virtual recluse, as I devoted to the book quality time that I might have spent with them.

Finally, thanks be to God for His sustaining grace. My hope is that the reader will come to share my excitement for Joshua. Its message—strong, fresh, timely—speaks both directly and indirectly to foot-weary modern pilgrims on the verge of the Promised Land.

# Contents

# Introduction

For as long as I can remember, I've been fascinated with the book of Joshua. Something about its first chapter in particular has always intrigued me. On countless occasions I've found myself repeating God's assurances and instructions to the soldier-prophet as though the Lord had spoken them directly to me. "I will give you every place where you set your foot. . . . No one will be able to stand up against you all the days of your life. As I was with Moses, so I will be with you; I will never leave you nor forsake you" (Joshua 1:3-5).

Meditating on the passage, my mind would move beyond the literal historical setting and apply the promises to whatever obstacles (human or otherwise) that stood in my way. And the conditions stipulated with the promises have always challenged me: "Be strong and very courageous. Be careful to obey all the law my servant Moses gave you; do not turn from it to the right or to the left, that you may be successful wherever you go" (verse 7; see also verses 8, 9).

I suspect that not everyone shares my enthusiasm for the book. Some probably find large sections of it—especially the middle portion (with its interminable listings of unfamiliar territory allotments)—forbidding, difficult, and boring. Moreover, the book seems dwarfed by the Pentateuch (the five books of Moses) preceding it.

But those five books, notwithstanding their size, represent unfinished business. God's people have not yet reached Canaan. They are not yet home. Thus Joshua comes at a logical spot, completing, as it does, a turbulent saga that reaches all the way back to the days of Abraham.

The task facing the book's chief character was a formidable one. Having no formal military experience to write home about, Joshua was nevertheless assigned to lead a ragtag army against the fortified towns and cities of Canaan, overthrow their rulers, take possession of their territories—and all this with a motley band of men, women, and children in tow.

But God had long been preparing the soldier-prophet for his difficult mission. He'd participated in the Exodus from Egypt and had ascended Mount Sinai with Moses (perhaps of all the other leaders going the furthest with him [see Ex. 24:13, 14]). Besides enduring the wilderness experience, he was one of only two (nonpriestly) persons (Caleb being the other) to come out of Egypt as adults and make it to the very border of the Promised Land, ready to enter (see Num. 26:63-65). Moreover, his reputation and stature had been growing ever since he joined Caleb in presenting that courageous minority report on the prospect of conquering Canaan (see Num. 13:30-33; 14:1-10, 36-38). Now, through events shortly to occur, it was God's purpose to build up his stature even more (see Joshua 1:5; 3:7; 4:14) so as to fill the vacuum left by the death of Moses.

One more item needs mentioning at this point. It concerns the mission itself. And the question is: Was it "ethnic cleansing"? And what are its implications for how we view the character of God? It's an issue of immense philosophical and theological importance, and I will devote an entire chapter (chapter 8) to addressing it.

## Purpose of Joshua

Perhaps *the most basic purpose* of Joshua was to fill what would otherwise have been a historical gap between the period of the Pentateuch and the subsequent history of Israel. Without Joshua, neither the Pentateuch nor the books that follow it in the canon would be completely intelligible. It serves as a complement to the Pentateuch, "related to the five books of Moses," observes *The Seventh-day Adventist Bible Commentary,* "in somewhat the same way as the book of Acts is related to the four Gospels."[1] It supplies, so to speak, "the rest of the story" in a way no other book of the Old Testament does. Without it, the voluminous Pentateuch would remain incomplete and, to a large extent, pointless. Joshua bridges that critical historical gap.

A *second* purpose of the book—one of immediate value to the

# Introduction

people of the time—was to provide a formal record of the allocation of the land. For these erstwhile slaves, this was of critical importance—historically, economically, and politically.

*Third,* the document emphasized God's faithfulness. When God once threatened to destroy Israel and raise up another people, Moses had worried about what the Egyptians might say. They will claim, he had argued, that Yahweh had purposely led the people out so that He might destroy them in the desert (Ex. 32:11, 12). Or worse, that "the Lord was not able to bring [them] into the land he promised them on oath; so he slaughtered them in the desert" (Num. 14:16).

Now Israel had arrived at the point at which not only the entire generation in question had perished, but the great Moses himself was gone. And the logical question on the minds of many was whether God's promises stood on the brink of failure, His program on the verge of collapse. It was at this critical moment that God came to Joshua with the forthright directive we find in Joshua 1:2: "Moses my servant is dead. Now then, you and all these people, get ready to cross the Jordan River into the land I am about to give to them" (cf. verses 1-9).

In these powerful lines God sought to make it crystal clear that He had no intention of abandoning His people. "I will never leave you nor forsake you," He said to the new leader and, by extension, to the rest of Israel (verse 5). Under Joshua's management the people would, indeed, "inherit the land [God] swore to their forefathers to give them" (verse 6).

And near the end of the book Joshua solemnly affirmed God's faithfulness in fulfilling the covenant promises made to Israel: "You know with all your heart and soul that not one of all the good promises the Lord . . . gave you has failed" (Joshua 23:14).

A *fourth* purpose of the book was to demonstrate God's permanence in the midst of transition and change. And what transition! What change! The face of the whole nation was different. As God had decreed, an entire generation had perished in the desert (Num. 32:13; Deut. 1:35; 2:14). Even Moses was gone. Of all the (non-priestly) adults who left Egypt, only Caleb and Joshua remained.

But God was still there! That's the purpose of the book of Joshua. In the words of the book of Hebrews more than a thousand years later, He is "the same yesterday and today and forever" (Heb. 13:8).

## Major Teachings of the Book of Joshua

1. *Surrendered, consecrated leadership is essential for the fulfillment of God's plan and purpose.* This idea, which runs through the entire book, is announced at its very beginning—and in a most unusual way: "Moses my servant is dead" (Joshua 1:2).

The references to Moses (11 times in the first chapter alone) recall the indomitable leadership of this intrepid giant of the Exodus. And they remind the reader of God's ability to take timid, hesitant individuals, transform them into bold, fearless leaders, and use them to fulfill His purpose.

"Moses my servant." The expression says indirectly that God, great being that He is, nevertheless uses people—"servants"—such as Moses to accomplish His work effectively.

2. *No human leader, however powerful or gifted, is indispensable.* That's the other side of God's need for consecrated leaders. God's overall purpose transcends even the greatest human leader. That's the meaning of the directive following the reference to Moses' death. "Moses my servant is dead. *Now then, you and all these people, get ready to cross . . .*" (Joshua 1:2).

Dale R. Davis captures the meaning of the interesting juxtaposition: "'Moses my servant has died, so you must wait'? No. 'You must weep'? No. But, 'Rise, cross over . . . into the land.' Moses may die; God's promise lives on. There is the passing of an era yet the endurance of the promise. Yahweh's fidelity does not hinge on the achievements of men, however gifted they may be, nor does it evaporate in the face of funerals."[2]

The way Joshua received the passing of the torch demonstrated, moreover, that God would tolerate no cult mentality among His people. The success of the divine enterprise must not get wrapped up in one charismatic person. God must remain Israel's only supreme leader, independent of any human instrument.

3. *Yahweh owns the land.* In any human economic or political revolution, the toughest and stickiest problem usually has to do with distribution of land. Who gets to own the real estate? And one of the messages of the book of Joshua, a point implied in God's original

promise to Abraham, is that God is the supreme landlord. Yahweh owns the land. As He would say through the psalmist hundreds of years later, "every animal of the forest is mine, and the cattle on a thousand hills" (Ps. 50:10). As the supreme landlord, God has the intrinsic right to bequeath the land to whomsoever He pleases.

Were it not for this fact, the entire operation described in Joshua would be illegal and immoral. The divine sanction must undergird the Israelite action, for it would lead to the shedding of blood and dispossessing of people. Hence the appearance of the Divine Warrior in Joshua 5:13-15. The Lord assured Joshua that he was not acting on his own. God was with him and would take responsibility for the operation.

Herein lies, however, one of the most critical questions involving God's character. At the command of Yahweh, human beings, including youth and little children, would perish at the hands of Joshua and Israel. And contemporary people have a right to question what kind of God would issue such directives and by what logic we might distinguish Israel's action from the atrocities we've witnessed in more recent times at the hands of religious fundamentalists and fanatics. (The importance and urgency of such questions give rise to the central chapter of this work—chapter 8.)

4. *Loyalty and surrender to Yahweh constitute the basis of success—both for individuals and nations.* This comes through clearly in God's charge to Joshua at the beginning of the book (Joshua 1:1-9), and in Joshua's farewell address to Israel's leaders at the end, in which he admonishes them in language similar to that used by the Lord in His own commissioning (see Joshua 23:7-13). For continued prosperity, Israel must keep faith with Yahweh, not forming alliances with the surrounding nations to serve their gods. Joshua's strongest challenge in this regard comes in Joshua 24:15: "But if serving the Lord seems undesirable to you, then choose for yourselves this day whom you will serve . . ."

5. *God is omnipotent (all-powerful).* This idea underlies the divine command at the beginning of the book: "Now then, . . . get ready to cross" (Joshua 1:2). The indirect message here is that a swollen Jordan is no obstacle for the Lord (see Joshua 3:14-17), nor the walled city of Jericho (Joshua 6), nor the powerful Canaanite confederacy.

# Crossing Jordan

The Lord would stop the sun in the heavens (Joshua 10) if that was necessary to accomplish His purpose. The concept of God's power finds explicit mention in Joshua 4:24: "He did this so that all the peoples of the earth may know that the hand of the Lord is powerful."

6. *Yahweh keeps His promises.* Here is what I believe is the most fundamental message of the book.

On a cloudless, moonless night hundreds of years before, God had promised Abraham a large posterity—one as numerous as the stars in the sky above him (Gen. 15:1-21; 17:1-8). Now, after hundreds of years of slavery and wandering, Israel would see the fulfillment of that vow, a fact emphasized by Joshua at several strategic points in the book (see Joshua 11:23; 21:43-45; 23:9, 14; 24:5-13).

And because Yahweh keeps His promises to us, we must also honor ours to Him and to our fellow humans—even to conniving pretenders such as the Gibeonites (Joshua 9:1-10:7) or to public prostitutes such as Rahab (Joshua 2:1-21; 6:22-25).

We cannot overemphasize this sixth point. It is a reaffirmation of God's faithfulness. If only in this respect, the book of Joshua should have particular relevance to contemporary Adventist Christians. Like ancient Israel, we stand today—after years of wilderness wanderings—on the very verge of the heavenly Canaan. The message of Joshua seeks to strengthen faith that, notwithstanding the passage of time, God is faithful, His promises are sure.

---

[1] *The Seventh-day Adventist Bible Commentary* (Washington, D.C.: Review and Herald Pub. Assn., 1953-1957, 1976-1980), vol. 2, p. 172.

[2] Dale Ralph Davis, *No Falling Words: Expositions of the Book of Joshua* (Grand Rapids: Baker Book House, 1988), pp. 17, 18.

# Chapter 1

# The Big Event Tomorrow

## Joshua 1:1-3:13

During Israel's rebellion in the Desert of Paran following the return of the spies, God had vowed that those who left Egypt as adults (the perpetrators and adult witnesses to that uprising) would never set foot in Canaan. He exempted only Caleb and Joshua, the two spies who gave a favorable report and who had not lost faith during the ensuing revolt (see Num. 13:26-14:35). Even Moses and Aaron eventually fell under the divine proscription—for their failure to give due reverence to the Lord during another rebellious incident at Meribah Kadesh (see Deut. 32:48-52).

Forty years had now elapsed since the crisis at Paran. A new generation had come of age. Moses, who earlier that very year had witnessed the death of his brother, Aaron (see Num. 33:38), was now himself dead (Joshua 1:1). The time to cross the Jordan had finally come. And Joshua was God's person of the hour.

Thus the account in the book of Joshua builds upon and completes the unfinished business of the Pentateuch. The first part of the book (Joshua 1-3:13) describes the crucial final preparations now set in motion to cross the river. After years of frustrating meanderings through inhospitable country, Israel now stood on the brink of the big event.

### Passing the Torch

The transition from Deuteronomy to Joshua is perhaps the smoothest between any two books of the Bible, except perhaps for that between 2 Chronicles and Ezra, in which the last words of one are the first words of the other. The two books connect their events in regard both to time and place.

15

# Crossing Jordan

In respect to time, Moses' formal recounting of Israel's desert history (as recorded in the book of Deuteronomy) took place "in the fortieth year [of their wilderness experience], on the first day of the eleventh month" (Deut. 1:3). And Joshua reports that the crossing of Jordan occurred on or about "the tenth day of the first month" of (as seems evident) the forty-first year (see Joshua 4:19). *This means that the time between Moses' final address and the fording of the Jordan was only about 70 days.*

The setting of Moses' speech to the nation was the plains of Moab. And that's the same place Joshua was—at Shittim—when God addressed him in the words that begin his book.

The plains of Moab had seen some of the most significant events of Israel's checkered desert history. It was here that Balaam, on the urging of Balak, king of Moab, sought to curse the budding nation (Num. 22-24). Here a new generation of Israelites renewed their covenant with God before entering the Promised Land (Deut. 29; 30). Here their 40 years of wanderings ended (Joshua 3:1). And here God gave that final, poignant call to Moses: "Go up . . . to Mount Nebo in Moab, across from Jericho. . . . There on the mountain . . . you will die" (Deut. 32:49, 50).

Moses obeyed, ascending the heights of Nebo, never again to return to the camp of Israel (Deut. 34:1-6). He was now dead, and a new leader took his place at the helm. "After the death of Moses . . . the Lord said to Joshua son of Nun, Moses' aide: 'Moses my servant is dead'" (Joshua 1:1, 2).

The pronouncement, if we may call it that, provides a commentary on the entire human race—on the fragility of human existence.

> "The boast of heraldry, the pomp of power,
>     And all that beauty, all that wealth e'er gave,
>     Awaits alike the inevitable hour:
>     The paths of glory lead but to the grave."[1]

Moses' journey, however, had not been one of glory in the worldly sense. He was "mistreated along with the people of God" (Heb. 11:25). But when the day was done, God honored him in spectacular fashion—showing that the path he'd chosen, "the road less traveled," led not to the grave, as Thomas Gray suggested in the poetic lines above, but to Canaan—indeed, the heavenly Canaan!

His life reminds us that however difficult the road, however perilous the journey, we have a pillar of cloud to lead the way, a pillar of fire to guide us through the darkness. Only later do we see the full picture. Said Sophocles, "One must wait until the evening to see how splendid the day has been."

"Moses my servant is dead. Now then, you and all these people, get ready to cross" (Joshua 1:2). God's command to Joshua was not a sudden "laying on of hands." No, the preparation for this hour had been 40 years in process.

Not long after Israel's departure from Egypt, Joshua had taken up position as Moses' military commander. And while Aaron and Hur stood atop a hill supporting Moses' hands, Joshua was in the valley below, leading the charge against the Amalekites (Ex. 17:8-14). A member of the group of 70 elders (see Num. 11:16, 17, 26-28), he had the supreme privilege (with the others) of approaching (albeit "at a distance") the living presence of God on Mount Sinai (Ex. 24:1, 2, 9-11). We even find a vague hint that he'd been permitted to approach closer than the rest (see Ex. 24:13, 14).

Joshua had stood by Moses' side when the great leader had descended from God's presence to find a nation in the thralldom of rebellious idolatry (Ex. 32:15-17). And he was usually with Moses as the latter would go to inquire of God in the (temporary) "tent of meeting" pitched outside the desert camp (Ex. 33:7-11)—a most sacred responsibility.

But perhaps the role for which we generally best remember Joshua was his inclusion among the 12 military agents sent out just after the Exodus to assess the state of affairs across the river in Canaan, in preparation for an immediate entry into the land (see Num. 13). In that assignment Joshua performed his duty with distinction, standing solid with the redoubtable Caleb in presenting a faith-centered minority report, one calculated to bolster the flagging zeal of an apprehensive nation (Num. 14:6-9). Pleased with Joshua's work in all its phases, the Lord selected him to inherit Moses' mantle (see Num. 27:18-23; cf. Deut. 3:28).

And so, in his farewell address to Israel, Moses "summoned Joshua and said to him in the presence of those assembled, 'Be strong and courageous, for you must go with this people into the land that the Lord swore to their forefathers to give them. . . . The Lord himself goes before you and will be with you; he will never leave you nor forsake you. Do not be afraid; do not be discouraged'" (Deut. 31:7, 8).

## Time to Advance

Joshua was eminently conscious of his divine grooming to assume the mantle of leadership at Moses' death—but only at Moses' death. And there being no human eyewitness to the historic event (see Deut. 34:5, 6), the word of God came to the soldier-prophet as confirmation of the passing of an era: "Moses my servant is dead" (Joshua 1:2).

The announcement occurred, we may reasonably assume, sometime following the period of national mourning (Deut. 34:8) for the great leader, and suggested the time to advance had arrived.

"Moses my servant is dead. Now then. . . ." The Lord hardly needed to finish the sentence, for Joshua already knew (in view of what we find in Numbers 27:12-14; Deuteronomy 3:23-28; 32:50-52) that Moses' death, however painful, was the last remaining obstacle to the long-awaited crossing. The people were now to "get ready to cross the Jordan" (Joshua 1:2).

God issued His directive here with a sense of urgency. There was to be no more delay. Suddenly the moment for the actual crossing had come.

That's how it frequently is in salvation history. After protracted delay, the time of deliverance usually occurs suddenly. The Israelites had been waiting hundreds of years in Egyptian bondage. Hope had well-nigh dissipated, and the arrival of Moses and Aaron only seemed to make things worse. But then the word went out by relay across the Hebrew community: *Time to leave! The Passover has arrived. Eat it in all haste—with sandaled feet! Deliverance is at midnight* (see Ex. 11:4-6; 12:11).

In the thralldom of sin following the Exile, Israel went through another spiritual nightmare—a nearly 490-year probationary period (see Dan. 9:24) filled with national calamity and disappointment. But just when the situation seemed most hopeless,[2] deliverance arrived. Said the angel messenger to humble shepherds on a hillside outside

Bethlehem: *"Today in the town of David a Savior has been born to you; he is Christ the Lord"* (Luke 2:11).

And so it was that after languishing in a hot and barren desert 40 years—with no knowledge of when the end would come—these foot-weary pilgrims suddenly received the word: *"Get ready to cross"* *"three days from now"* (Joshua 1:2, 11). What a thrill! And what a challenge!

Thus it will be at the end of time. "Therefore keep watch," said Jesus, "because you do not know when the owner of the house will come back—whether in the evening, or at midnight, or when the rooster crows, or at dawn. If he comes *suddenly,* do not let him find you sleeping" (Mark 13:35, 36).

## Was It Fair? The "Scandal" of Dispossession

As Israel prepared to cross the Jordan, God reiterated His ancient promise of the land of Palestine: "I will give you every place where you set your foot, as I promised Moses" (Joshua 1:3). They were to dispossess the Hittites, occupy the land "from the [Judean] desert to Lebanon, and from . . . the Euphrates [River] . . . to the . . . [Mediterranean] Sea on the west" (verse 4).

From our distance in both time and space, most of us read these words without skipping a beat. But we'd have been struck with terror had we been among the inhabitants of those territories back then, with a sense of the supernatural occurrences associated with this strange desert people fresh in our minds. And we'd also have been outraged. On the basis of what kind of logic could anyone explain this impending takeover?

Across the centuries and among all people, few things have been regarded with more intense sacredness than the right to the land. And we see this still today—in the Middle East, for example, the very region under discussion here in the book of Joshua. The sticking point for decades now has been the competing claims for the land. For the Jewish people, Palestine is their ancestral land. For the Palestinians, it is their homeland. The Syrians insist that the Golan Heights belongs to them and must return. The Arabs claim Jerusalem as rightfully theirs. The Jews see it as their eternal city.

And all over the world the claim to the land has been a source of tension among peoples and nations—between Russia and Japan (over Sakhalin Island); between European settlers and nationals in Zimbabwe; between Indonesia and Irian Jaya; between Tamils and Singhalese in Sri Lanka; between India and Pakistan in Kashmir; between the Australian government and the country's Aboriginal peoples.

But the book of Joshua flies smack in the face of all human legal claims and conventions and takes as an absolute given God's sovereignty over the land, His ownership of all property. As we will see in succeeding chapters, land is taken from its long-established occupants and given to the people of Israel. From a human standpoint, it was nothing short of "scandalous."

Yet Yahweh ordered it.

Later (chapter 8) we will grapple more fully with this issue. But for now we may observe that, however "outrageous" it might seem to us, it stands as a reminder that as humans, we have no inherent ownership claim to anything. We're stewards only. Ultimately, everything belongs to God—"every animal of the forest . . . and the cattle on a thousand hills" (Ps. 50:10). As the great cosmic landlord, God has absolute right to give, to withhold, to transfer, or to confiscate.

The "scandal" seems even worse because of Israel's history up to that point. It was not the portrait of a people eminently deserving of such favors—a fact that reminds us of grace, God's unmerited favor that defies human logic. "The Lord," Moses told Israel, "did not set his affection on you and choose you because you were more numerous than other peoples, for you were the fewest of all peoples. But it was because the Lord loved you and kept the oath he swore to your forefathers that he brought you out with a mighty hand and redeemed you from the land of slavery" (Deut. 7:7, 8).

Patently unfair! And scandalous! How can human logic possibly explain this?

It cannot. Nor can we explain grace.

And note that God is *giving* them the land—not selling it to them. They could do nothing to pay for it or deserve it—further hints about unmerited favor, of grace.

The nations that Israel was to displace Scripture described under the generic name of Canaanites (Gen. 12:6) and sometimes under the term Amorites (Gen. 15:16). But in other passages (see Gen. 13:7; 34:30; Ex. 23:28; 33:2; Deut. 20:17) and in Joshua 3:10 we have a detailed listing of the complex ethnic population of ancient western Palestine as "Canaanites, Hittites, Hivites, Perizzites, Girgashites, Amorites and Jebusites" (Joshua 3:10).[3]

We should keep in mind that these nations do not represent independently existing entities with unknown origins. By whatever route, each one traces back to Noah and was originally part of God's one family. But gradually through the centuries each had abandoned their roots and rebelled against the God of their ancestors, the one true God. They not only had turned their backs on Yahweh, but had descended into the grossest forms of idolatry, until there was no remedy. The cup of their iniquity was now full (cf. Gen. 15:16), and the time for their destruction had arrived. We must, therefore, assume no arbitrariness on God's part in their displacement. Divine patience had borne long with them—for some 300-400 years, ever since the time of Abraham.

Even so, God does not give Israel the whole world. Other people have a right to live as much as they. The Lord permitted dispossession only in one region—an area whose inhabitants, because of their iniquity and hundreds of years of neglected divine opportunities, had forfeited their right to the land.

Indeed, when we come right down to it, God's supreme purpose for giving Israel that territory was precisely for the sake of the world. As the Lord later said through Ezekiel: "This is Jerusalem, which I have set in the center of the nations, with countries all around her" (Eze. 5:5). The implications are obvious. It was God's intention that Israel should become a blessing to the entire world community. Far from being an afterthought, that concept was already embedded in the promise made to Abraham: "All peoples on earth will be blessed through you" (Gen. 12:3).

## Pepping Up Joshua

However thoroughly prepared for the assignment before him, Joshua, like all of us, needed a pep talk—a final word of affirmation and assurance. And God was there to provide it: "As I was with Moses, so I will be with you" (Joshua 1:5).

# Crossing Jordan

The passage (verses 5-9) is one of the most encouraging and powerful in the Bible. It's for leaders (or anyone) feeling apprehensive, discouraged, and wondering how they could possibly carry on against the odds. And it's for the individual facing seemingly insurmountable obstacles and difficulties. For those struggling with the sense that every human help has vanished. And it's particularly for the leader taking up the reins laid down by a stellar predecessor and wondering: *How can I ever follow that act?*

God says to the apprehensive Joshua: "No one will be able to stand up against you all the days of your life" (verse 5). All who seek your embarrassment or defeat will fail. You will be victorious in every conflict. Don't worry about the prospect of following Moses' brilliant legacy. I will be with you just as I was with him. "I will never leave you nor forsake you" (verse 5).

While we may each find encouragement in these words, we should all remember also that none of us has exclusive rights to the promise. This means that while the promise is true for me, it's also true for the other person. If as a leader I'm tempted to "stand up against" another person (or another leader, whom God has also called), I should remember that God also made the same promise to them, and that in opposing them I may find myself standing up against the Lord Himself.

So while the passage gives personal impetus for courageous leadership, it also teaches us to be solicitous and respectful of our fellow leaders, remembering that they have as much right to the promise as we.

It is utterly important to keep in mind the stipulations that accompany God's special promises and assurances to Joshua. He was to walk strictly according to "all the law," turning neither left nor right (see verses 7, 8). The "Book of the Law" (the things Moses had committed to writing under divine inspiration) was to be Joshua's source of wisdom and instruction.

This "Book of the Law" that Joshua knew ("the Bible in embryo," as it were), combined with the sacred text that has followed in succeeding centuries, still guides our feet today. "The secret of success in both the material and moral spheres [is] obedience, which was enjoined upon Israel as the highest form of divine service (Joshua 22:5)."[4]

And God had one more stipulation. However severe the pressure (indeed, *because of it*), Joshua was to take time to "meditate on . . . [the law] day and night" (Joshua 1:8).

Meditation—a lost spiritual art in our hectic times. "Hastiness and superficiality are the psychic diseases of the twentieth century," observed the Russian writer Alexander Solzhenitsyn.[5] If we would become channels of spiritual power, clear conduits of God's message for these confusing times, we'll need to recapture the art of meditation and prayer. Moral giants are not born helter-skelter in frantic restlessness. "But they that wait upon the Lord shall renew their strength" (Isa. 40:31, KJV).

## United Action

In the final section of Joshua 1 (verses 12-18) Joshua addresses the tribes of Reuben, Gad, and the half tribe of Manasseh and reiterates the understanding and agreement Moses had negotiated with them. Under its terms these two and a half tribes (sometimes called the Transjordan tribes) were to stand shoulder to shoulder with the rest of Israel in the conquest of western Canaan.

The context indicates that it was an extremely sensitive issue for the young nation. When the two and a half tribes first broached the question of a homeland for themselves east of the Jordan, and before they could explain their full intentions, Moses, suspecting a move to secede, had launched into a withering tirade, excoriating them for what he perceived as cowardly abandonment. "Shall your countrymen go to war while you sit here [east of the Jordan]? Why do you discourage the Israelites from going over into the land the Lord has given them?" (Num. 32:6, 7).

In stunned silence the tribal representatives listened as the great leader recounted the history of Israel's rebellion, ending with an expression of deepest outrage: "And here you are," he said, "a brood of sinners, standing in the place of your fathers and making the Lord even more angry with Israel. If you turn away from following him, he will again leave all this people in the desert, and *you* [I can see his finger pointing]—*you* will be the cause of their destruction" (verse 14).

We are too far removed from the scene to judge whether or to what extent Moses might have overreacted. But if his suspicions were valid, the tribal leaders standing before him made one of the quickest turnabouts in history. They had no intention of reneging on their responsibility, they assured the great leader. The two and a half tribes intended to be full participants and "will not return to [their] homes until every Israelite has received his inheritance" (verse 18). Mollified by the strong pledge of support on their part, Moses granted their request (verses 20-22). Now, on the eve of the crossing, Joshua reminded them of that pledge and of Moses' stipulations.

If we think that such caution was unnecessary, we need only go back and notice the strong conditions attached to the original agreement (verses 23-33). The possibility of a radical change of mind was always present—a development of enormous proportions, and a potential nightmare for the budding nation. To Joshua's great relief, and that of Israel, the Transjordan tribes reaffirmed their commitment (Joshua 1:16, 18).

Like ancient Israel, the church today can ill afford to lose the contribution of even a single "tribe." For the corporate body such a loss is always a severe blow. For the "tribe" it is often fatal. Joshua (like Moses before him) wanted the whole nation to move together. And today, as was the case then, unity is fundamental for the accomplishment of the church's final mission. "If Christians were to act in concert, moving forward as one, under the direction of one Power, for the accomplishment of one purpose, they would move the world."[6]

### Espionage Mission to Jericho

It was not the first time that the advancing Hebrews had sent out spies. A major exploratory mission had occurred under Moses from the camp at Kadesh in the Desert of Paran, involving 12 men (Num. 13). But that was some 40 years earlier, and Joshua evidently felt it necessary to update the intelligence.

Still we may wonder why Joshua, who'd so recently been in direct contact with the Lord, would feel the need for such a mission. Hadn't the Lord Himself commanded him to advance? Was the desire to "look over the land" (Joshua 2:1) a lack of faith on his part? Or perhaps it shows that the assurance of divine assistance and providence does not excuse us from doing our homework.

But why only two spies this time—and not 12, as in Moses' case?

# The Big Event Tomorrow

Two possible reasons: (1) much of the findings of the original mission (see the description of their task in Numbers 13:17-20) would have remained unchanged, and (2) a large group of men entering a small town such as Jericho—even in separate units—obviously would have attracted too much attention. In fact, we may assume that even when the original 12 went out, they probably traveled in pairs, having a much more extensive area to cover. We can be almost certain that they did not go through the towns and countryside of Canaan as a 12-man delegation.

The work of a professional spy is one of the most demanding and dangerous jobs on earth. And the two men who entered Jericho from the Israelite camp at Shittim had that assignment. Most probably soldiers trained in espionage, the men were to "look over the land . . . especially Jericho" (Joshua 2:1). As Israel's first target across the Jordan, Jericho, a well-guarded fortress town, was of critical strategic interest to Joshua and Israel. A failure here would be a terrible psychological disaster for them. "The site [was] strategically located. From Jericho one [had] access to the heartland of Canaan. Any military force attempting to penetrate the central hill country from the east would, by necessity, first have to capture Jericho."[7]

On the other hand, a decisive victory here would send shock waves throughout the entire region, unnerving less-protected rulers in the surrounding countries. "This city was virtually the key to the whole country, and it would present a formidable obstacle to the success of Israel."[8]

No chance was to be taken. Jericho and other cities of western Palestine had had 40 years to beef up their defenses since the news of the Red Sea crossing first arrived. Accordingly, Joshua dispatched the two spies to make a careful on-the-ground assessment.

One can get the impression from reading Joshua 2:1 that the men made a beeline to Rahab's house. That, of course, is not necessarily so. It's probably more in keeping with what actually happened to imagine them entering the town, mixing casually with the people, taking mental notes of items of strategic significance—all the while keeping their eyes open for a place to spend the night. It would be exceedingly perilous for a spy to get caught stranded at nightfall.

# Crossing Jordan

### Night in a Harlot's Boudoir

We don't know the details—Joshua's brevity does not cater to our curiosity at every point. But it's virtually impossible for a stranger to enter a small Middle Eastern city without notice—true then as now. And evidently, sometime toward evening the local inhabitants spotted the strangers (see Joshua 2:2). They observed them entering the house of the town prostitute, which, as a source of lucrative intelligence, was no doubt carefully watched by Jericho's counterintelligence agents. The town leaders, after all, could hardly have been unaware of the Israelite threat just across the Jordan.

How did the spies come to stay at Rahab's house? What led them to her dwelling? Was it chance? Or was it providence? One possibility is that Rahab's was the only open house in town, by reason of her trade. Perhaps she ran a boardinghouse or inn. Or perhaps she thought she had customers. That last reason, however, falls short of explaining the later developments of the story and Rahab's own evaluation of the psychological panic in Jericho and the reason behind it.

It would appear that these two spies—whether by accident or necessity or both—sensed a clear streak of honesty and basic goodness in this otherwise immoral woman and felt safe to trust her with their lives. We do not have all the answers. Whatever the situation, it must go down to the everlasting credit of both her and her visitors that neither side made any attempt to exploit the other.

Whether the men felt any temptation amid the allurements of Rahab's boudoir, Scripture does not say. And whether the possible economic potential of the visit crossed Rahab's mind, we do not know. What we do know from the record is that the encounter was a deeply spiritual one (see verses 8-13).

Word of the strangers' presence quickly reached the king of Jericho, and a royal delegation appeared at Rahab's door with a message from his majesty: "Bring out the men who came to you and entered your house, because they have come to spy out the whole land" (verse 3).

"The men who came to you." The inference was suggestive and negative, but the officials were completely wrong. Yet as regards the wider purpose of the visit, they were dead on target. "They have come to spy out the . . . land."

# The Big Event Tomorrow

With the king's messengers at the door, how would Rahab deal with them? How should she respond? Were you in her place, what would you do?

With a cunning gained from years in her line of business, Rahab emerged with a concocted answer on her lips: "Yes, the men came to me, but I did not know where they had come from. At dusk, when it was time to close the city gate, the men left. I don't know which way they went. Go after them quickly. You may catch up with them" (verses 4, 5).

Much discussion has occurred in Christian circles over the years about the rightness or wrongness of Rahab's response. Unable to dodge the fact that her answer clearly was out of sync with the plain truth of the situation, many Christians have settled the question by suggesting that we should not judge a woman of such questionable morals by our high Christian standards. "To a Christian a lie can never be justified," observes *The Seventh-day Adventist Bible Commentary,* "but to a person like Rahab light comes but gradually. . . . God accepts us where we are, but we must 'grow in grace.'"[9]

The clear implication here is that as enlightened Christians we'd have acted differently. So what, indeed, would we have done under similar circumstances?

Let us make it clear at the outset that truth is and remains the watchword for the Christian. "Each of you," said the apostle Paul, "must put off falsehood and speak truthfully to his neighbor" (Eph. 4:25). And Jesus couldn't have been more emphatic when He described falsehood as the devil's "native language." He is "a liar," Jesus said, "and the father of lies" (John 8:44). As the Revelator, He lists among those outside the Holy City "everyone who loves and practices falsehood" (Rev. 22:15). Lying has no place in the Christian life.

Amazingly, however, even this high principle can get turned on its head. In some quarters one encounters the argument that if a person is not at home, it would be wrong for them to leave the lights or the radio on to scare off a potential thief. To give the impression that you're home when you're not, the argument goes, is deception. I once had an elder in one of my churches who believed that to take your telephone receiver off the hook while you're extremely busy or are praying is tantamount to telling a lie, since it gives the caller the impression that the line is legitimately engaged.

That kind of irrational overzealousness caricatures the ninth commandment and trivializes the whole issue of truth and falsehood. Interestingly, those who hold such extreme positions rarely question the basic idea of spy-sending in the first place. Isn't concealment the spy's fundamental strategy? Almost invariably spies must represent themselves as being who they're not. At the very least, they must disguise and camouflage their intentions, employing half truths (cf. 2 Sam. 15:32-36; 16:15-19). That being the case, was it not already an act of deception for Joshua and Moses to commission spies?

To come to that conclusion, however, is to run up against the fact that the sending of the spies under Moses occurred at God's express command (see Num. 13:1-3; cf. Deut. 1:22, however, which ascribes it to the will of the people, albeit with Moses' concurrence [verse 23]).

And how about Jochebed's strategy to protect the infant Moses? One can argue that every day that she kept the lad concealed, Jochebed lived a lie as she went about her regular duties in the community. In effect she was representing herself as standing in compliance with the Egyptian edict while, in fact, she was not. And after Jochebed finally placed her baby in a basket in the Nile, unable to keep him hidden any longer, didn't little Miriam play her role well? When she offered to find "one of the Hebrew women" (Ex. 2:7) to assist the princess in rearing the child, did she do the right thing? Or should she have said: "Mind if I get *the child's mother* to help you, Your Royal Highness?"

And do you imagine the princess had no idea of the plot? Can't you almost see a wink in her eye at Miriam's suggestion? And would we have applauded the princess if she would have announced throughout the palace that she'd found, as a matter of fact, a Hebrew child in the Nile that morning? Was it not a cover-up *not* to announce it?

So to return to the original question: What would you have done were you in Rahab's place? Would you have said to the agents: "I'm mortified by your question, but as a Christian I have to tell the truth: The men are on the rooftop, under the flax"? Is that what the ninth commandment is all about?

# The Big Event Tomorrow

The excesses of "situation ethics" notwithstanding, Christians (and everyone else, for that matter) sometimes find themselves forced to choose between two or more options, each with fatal consequences for human life. In such cases God does not condemn us for choosing the best of the bad options. Rahab could have remained silent, of course, refusing to utter an untruth. But that would have been deadly for the spies, because it would have triggered an exhaustive search of the premises. On the other hand, to disclose the whereabouts of her visitors would have led to the certain death of God's servants at a most critical time in Israel's history.

Thus she took what she considered the best of the bad options before her: *she prevaricated,* sending the murderous pursuers on a wild-goose chase. We find an almost exact parallel to this story in 2 Samuel 17:15-22, in which the wife of an Israelite farmer protected the lives of David's spies during Absalom's attempted coup d'état. It was a critical decision that saved the day for David and his regime.

The writer of the book of Joshua, says Dale R. Davis, "is not very interested in picky ethical questions . . . endless wranglings . . . about whether it was right for Rahab to lie to the Jericho police and so on. It is tragic when people snag their pants on the nail of Rahab's lie . . . and never get around to hearing Rahab's *truth* (verses 8-13), which the writer has conspired to make the center of the whole narrative."[10] Yet Davis himself felt the need to distance himself from Rahab. Thus he argued in a footnote that "it does not mean that the biblical writer approves of Rahab's lie or that he authorizes us to go and do likewise."[11]

*So the question remains: What should a Christian do under similar circumstances?*

The issue is a universal one: what to do, when telling the naked truth can result in the direct loss of innocent human life. Should we use the ninth commandment to offer simplistic solutions to complex issues involving the loss of innocent human life? A naive understanding of the ninth commandment could have resulted in the slaughter of additional thousands of Jews during the Nazi pogrom in the 1940s. The brave Christians and others who sheltered them from their butchers broke no law—human or divine. Indeed, so far as divine law is concerned, they acted in perfect conformity to its spirit.

Such an admission frightens some modern Christians. They see it as opening the floodgates for liars and cheaters. What such Christians should remember, however, is that we're dealing here with extraordinary events, extreme situations—situations that 99 percent of us will never encounter in an entire lifetime.

Moreover, what we have in mind here should not fall under the common definition of falsehood. If a lie is the simple utterance of an untruth, then the editors of the Chicago *Daily Tribune* were lying when, following the U.S. presidential election of 1948, they trumpeted the headline "Dewey Defeats Truman" when exactly the opposite was the case. Common sense would dictate that *intent* and *motive* must come into the equation. As I see it, to lie (in the classical sense) *is to make a false statement knowingly, with wicked or malicious or selfish intent to deceive or mislead.* Under this definition Pharaoh's midwives were not culpable, even though their report to the monarch did not conform to the facts of the case (see Ex. 1:15-20). Nor should the defenders of the innocent during the Nazi atrocities be faulted in any way. Or Rahab.

The tacit condemnation of this great woman (as she turned out to be) is wholly unwarranted. The very Bible we quoted at the beginning in regard to truth does not condemn her. Declares the author of Hebrews: "By faith the prostitute Rahab, because she welcomed the spies, was not killed with those who were disobedient" (Heb. 11:31). (Had she reported them—thus sentencing them to instant death—would Hebrews have commended her for *welcoming* them? I don't think so.) James went even further: "In the same way, was not even Rahab the prostitute considered righteous for what she did when she gave lodging to the spies and sent them off in a different direction?" (James 2:25). She protected them, Ellen G. White said, "at the peril of her own life." [12] And she ended up becoming an ancestor of Jesus the Messiah (Matt. 1:5).

## A Nation in Panic

Having dispatched the Jericho counterintelligence agents on their fruitless mission, Rahab ascended the roof of her house (a flat area in almost all Middle Eastern dwellings of the period [see Deut. 22:8] and even today) for a nocturnal dialogue with the two Hebrew men. It was perhaps the most critical conversation of her whole life.

The exchange, which took place just before the men went to sleep in their hiding place (Joshua 2:8), showed Rahab's insight into the current political, psychological, and spiritual realities of the region. "I know," she said to the spies, "that the Lord has given this land [perhaps meaning Canaan as a whole, and not just Jericho] to you and that a great fear of you has fallen on us, so that all who live in this country are melting in fear because of you" (verse 9).

Rahab's reference to God in this encounter was not, as it would be in English, a general allusion to a divine being. Rather it was a specific designation pointing, in particular, to Yahweh and giving evidence of a budding faith in the God of Israel. "I know," she said, "that [Yahweh] has given this land to you." In other words, the impending victory would not be because of Israel's own strength, ingenuity, or prowess, but rather would come directly from the Lord. Thus this "lady of the night" showed that she'd already grasped the rudiments of righteousness by faith. For the same is true of salvation: victory comes from the Lord.

Rahab's description of the psychological condition of her country was intelligence of the first order—priceless. And it must have galvanized the courage of Joshua and all Israel to receive it (see verses 23, 24).

The people of Jericho knew "how the Lord dried up the water of the Red Sea" ahead of Israel. They'd learned what Israel did to the Amorite kings, Sihon and Og, east of the Jordan. "When we heard of it," said Rahab, "our hearts melted and everyone's courage failed because of you." Ending her testimony, Rahab confessed her faith in Israel's God: Yahweh "is God in heaven above and on the earth below" (verses 10, 11).[13]

The picture Rahab painted was that of a city in total panic in anticipation of an invasion by the Israelite forces camped only 15 miles (24 kilometers) away. It must have shaken her up to see such individuals—perhaps some of them her regular or former clients—tremble with fear and apprehension at the impending crisis.

## The Scarlet Cord

Rahab's mission to the rooftop that evening was not simply to pass on intelligence on the state of panic in Jericho. It also involved a critical request: "Please swear to me by the Lord," she begged her guests, "that you will show kindness to my family, because I have shown kindness to you. Give me a sure sign that you will spare the lives of my father and mother, my brothers and sisters, and all who belong to them, and that you will save us from death" (verses 12, 13).

Her concern went beyond her own personal safety. Apparently single and probably childless at the time (she would later give birth to Boaz by a Jewish father, presumably her husband, and thus become an ancestor of Jesus—see Matthew 1:5), her plea demonstrates a tender solicitude for her parents and closest relatives.

Most of us think of people of Rahab's profession as criminal, wicked, and absolutely without moral standards or sensitivity. But consider Jesus' reaction to the woman caught in adultery (John 8:1-11) or His response to the former streetwalker who washed His feet with the costly perfume in Simon's house (Matt. 26:6-13). Perhaps one lesson to draw from such stories is that however accurate in certain respects, the usual stereotypes of such people tend to miss a native goodness that often lies buried beneath a sordid exterior.

But God looks at the heart (1 Sam. 16:7)—the reason Jesus could say to some of His superficial, self-righteous contemporaries: "The tax collectors and the prostitutes are entering the kingdom of God ahead of you" (Matt. 21:31).

Was Rahab's family aware of her lifestyle? How could they not be in a town the size of Jericho? It's also possible that by the time of these developments she'd already abandoned the trade, though still found herself stuck with the "title." We do not know. But whatever her present condition, Rahab apparently felt accepted by her family. Notwithstanding her shady occupation or her distasteful past, the bond between her and them had not been severed.

In her time she'd probably seen her fair share of broken promises. And that's probably why she now pressed the two Hebrews for "a sure sign" (Joshua 2:12) that she and her family would be spared during the coming crisis.

"Our lives for your lives!" the men promised on oath (verse 14). But in true covenant fashion, they laid down some conditions of their own:

# The Big Event Tomorrow

1. She was not to disclose the nature of their mission (verse 14).

2. As a signal to the invading forces, she was to tie a scarlet cord in the window through which she'd let them down. No scarlet cord, and the deal was off (verse 18).

3. All members of her family to receive protection should be under her roof—at one location only (verse 19).

4. The agreement would be considered null and void should Rahab compromise their mission in any way (verse 20). (The fact that this last condition is virtually identical to the first emphasized the top-secret nature of the undertaking. The Israelite agents could not tolerate any breach of security.)

However reasonable these conditions, they no doubt presented Rahab with an extremely delicate situation as she tried to assemble her family in her house on the eve of the invasion. What reason would she give for having everyone holed up at her place for seven days or more? Yet it's not too difficult to imagine that, impressed by her extensive street smarts—and given the impending threat—family members would be willing to take her word for it.

Whatever the method Rahab used to pull the family together and keep them quiet, she kept her end of the bargain. And the house of the local prostitute would become their "Noah's ark" in the impending calamity.

Perhaps we should not unduly exaggerate the significance of the scarlet cord, the sign on Rahab's house. Undoubtedly the spies chose red because it could be spotted easily against the drab exterior of Jericho's walls. However, from our perspective, the whole incident is too tempting to pass over without remark.

The incident evokes memories of Israel's final night in Egypt. At God's command each family that, like Rahab's, wanted to be protected from the impending plague was to "take some of the blood [of the Passover animal] and put it on the sides and tops of the doorframes of the houses where they eat the lambs" (Ex. 12:7). And the reason for the sign was explicit: "On that same night," said the Lord, "I will pass through Egypt and strike down every firstborn—both men and animals. . . . The blood will be a sign for you on the houses where you are; and when I see the blood, I will pass over you" (verses 12, 13).

# Crossing Jordan

That crimson mark on Rahab's house also brings to mind one of Ezekiel's graphic visions (see Eze. 8). There, in the face of impending judgment upon Israel, the Lord commissioned a special messenger to "go throughout the city of Jerusalem and put a mark on the foreheads of those who grieve and lament" over the specter of national idolatry (Eze. 9:4). And as the destroying angels went forth on their bloody mission, the rules of engagement were clear: "Slaughter old men, young men and maidens, women and children, but do not touch anyone who has the mark" (verse 6).

The idea of a mark or sign comes to full bloom in the book of Revelation, in which we have not only the mark (or seal) of God, but also the *mark of the beast*. Like the saints in Ezekiel's time, God's last-day remnant receive God's mark, God's seal, on their foreheads (Rev. 7:2, 3); while the devil's followers get his mark in their foreheads and on their hands (see Rev. 13:16). Both signs—the seal of God and the mark of the beast—are fraught with eternal consequences for those who bear them.

Thus the story of Rahab is rich with spiritual and theological lessons for God's people to the end of time.

Their mission being of a highly confidential nature, the spies probably returned to camp in the dead of night, going directly to Joshua's tent to present their report. The tone of that account must have reminded the cautious leader of the one he and the fearless Caleb had presented some 40 years earlier. "The Lord has surely given the whole land into our hands," the men said; "all the people are melting in fear because of us" (Joshua 2:24).

Wasting no time, Joshua and the people headed for the banks of the Jordan, there to encamp for the last time before the actual crossing (see Joshua 3:1).

## Follow the Ark

With the pillar of fire and cloud apparently no longer in evidence, the ark now became the visible symbol of God's leading. The priests bearing it were to be in the vanguard (Joshua 3:3, 4), with the people following—not in random fashion, but according to well-established order and sequence, one tribe at a time (see Num. 10:11-28) and keeping a careful "distance . . . between . . . [them] and the

34

# The Big Event Tomorrow

ark." "Do not go near it," officials told the people (Joshua 3:4).

That "distance" was to remind Israel of God's transcendence, God's unapproachableness, God's awesomeness—what German theologian Rudolf Otto referred to as the *"mysterium tremendum."* [14] It was in keeping with long-established protocols of deference for the sacred symbol of Yahweh's presence (see Num. 1:51; 3:10, 38). In every place where Israel camped, it had "restrictions placed upon freedom of access to the tabernacle area by the 'buffer zone' of Levites and priests," suggesting that "although tabernacled amid His people, God was still the transcendent, unapproachable One of awful holiness and majesty." [15]

The people were to *follow* the ark of the covenant. "Then," the officers said, "you will know which way to go, since you have never been this way before" (Joshua 3:4). What a powerful lesson in this simple directive! With the divine presence leading the way, we cannot go astray, however untried the path, however rugged the way, however dark the night.

Again and again the account of the crossing would make reference to "the ark of the covenant" (see, for example, verses 3, 6, 8). The purpose was to call attention to Yahweh as the God of truth, the one who keeps His promise and is thoroughly dependable. The theme runs through the entire book: Yahweh is the covenant-keeping God. And because He is, His people must be faithful also.

Thus the two and a half tribes would honor the promise made to Moses to stand shoulder to shoulder with the rest of Israel in the conquest; the spies would keep their promise to the prostitute; and the nation would not go back on its promise to the conniving Gibeonites (see Joshua 9).

In what appears to be an intimate, final pep talk with the people before the crossing, Joshua says: "Come here and listen to the words of the Lord your God. This is how you will know that the living God is among you and that He will certainly drive out before you the Canaanites, Hittites, Hivites, Perizzites, Girgashites, Amorites and Jebusites. See, the ark of the covenant of the Lord of all the earth will go into the Jordan ahead of you" (Joshua 3:9-11).

Joshua's purpose was to steel the courage of Israel as they entered the floodwaters of the Jordan. There they would witness a phenomenon not seen since the dividing of the Red Sea: water standing up "in a heap" (verse 13). It would be as if God were saying to them: "I'm the same God who brought you out of the land of bondage, who opened the Red Sea before your ancestors. I'm the Lord, the covenant-keeping God. I never change."

The ark of the covenant at the head of the procession sent the message that "it is Yahweh himself who leads his people into Canaan, who cuts off flooding waters and holds them back as it were with his hand." "The whole affair is Yahweh's feat and the Israelites, though active, are still primarily spectators."[16]

## Consecration

As part of the final preparation to cross over into Canaan, the people were to "consecrate" themselves, for, said Joshua, "tomorrow the Lord will do amazing things among you" (verse 5). Why the need for consecration? Were the "amazing things" God intended to perform dependent upon the people's spiritual condition? What relationship is there between our inward preparation and the actual events of sacred history?

Answers to such questions don't come easy. But we find in Scripture numerous examples in which personal and corporate consecration on the part of God's people preceded God's miraculous intervention in their behalf. It was so on the eve of the departure from Egypt (Ex. 12); at Sinai (Ex. 19:10, 11, 14); in the time of Esther (Esther 4:15, 16); on the eve of Israel's departure from Persia (Ezra 8:21-23); and before the outpouring of the Holy Spirit at Pentecost (Acts 1:12-14).

Such special preparations were stipulated "whenever Yahweh was to reveal Himself in a special way." It was "crucial that Israel recognize that what happens is indeed Yahweh's work; and unless they have proper insight, expectancy, and preparation, they could see Yahweh's work and yet not understand its true value and significance."[17]

Like ancient Israel, we stand today on the verge of the Promised Land. Should our preparation for that event be any less intense? The times demand the most thorough consecration on the part of God's people as we see the day approaching.

# The Big Event Tomorrow

## Questions for Reflection
### Joshua 1:1-3:13

1. How might God's message to Joshua following the death of Moses help you cope with the tragedy of death, whether in the family or in the church?

2. Have you ever had to trail an outstanding "performance"— one that left you thinking: *What an act to follow!* What did you find in the Joshua story to encourage you?

3. Reread Joshua 1:8. Is meditation a lost art for you? If it is, what steps can you take to recapture it?

4. God told Joshua that "no one will be able to stand up against [him] all the days of [his] life" (verse 5). What does this promise mean for you personally? Do you think it implies that you will never know defeat?

5. What does the reference to the two and a half tribes (verses 12-18) teach about interpersonal/intergroup relationships?

6. How has the story of Rahab helped you to modify your perspective on people and their behavior? What prejudices or stereotypes did you have to abandon in the light of her story?

7. We're often called upon to decide between two or more bad options. How does the story of Rahab help us face such situations? What principles should come into play?

8. The spies who brought back an unfavorable report to Moses were punished, while Caleb and Joshua, with a positive minority report, were commended by Moses and rewarded by God. In Joshua 2 the spies also returned with a positive report and (we may assume) were commended. So what's the message of these accounts? Do they indicate that every report we give today on the challenges facing the church should be "positive"?

---

[1] Thomas Gray, "Elegy Written in a Country Churchyard."

[2] See Ellen G. White, *The Desire of Ages* (Mountain View, Calif.: Pacific Press Pub. Assn., 1898), pp. 36, 37.

[3] For a more detailed treatment of these various groups, see J. Maxwell Miller and Gene M. Tucker, *The Book of Joshua* (London: Cambridge University Press, 1974), pp. 37, 38; *Seventh-day Adventist Bible Dictionary* (Washington, D.C.: Review and Herald Pub. Assn., 1960, 1978) under the various terms.

[4] R. K. Harrison, *Introduction to the Old Testament* (Grand Rapids: William B. Eerdmans

Pub. Co., 1969), p. 678.

[5] Alexander Solzhenitsyn, in *Time,* June 19, 1978, p. 33.

[6] Ellen G. White, *Testimonies for the Church* (Mountain View, Calif.: Pacific Press Pub. Assn., 1948), vol. 9, p. 221.

[7] Bryant G. Wood, "Did the Israelites Conquer Jericho?" *Biblical Archeology Review,* March/April 1990, p. 45.

[8] Ellen G. White, *Patriarchs and Prophets* (Mountain View, Calif.: Pacific Press Pub. Assn., 1890), p. 482.

[9] *The Seventh-day Adventist Bible Commentary,* vol. 2, p. 183.

[10] D. R. Davis, *No Falling Words,* p. 26.

[11] *Ibid.*

[12] White, *Patriarchs and Prophets,* p. 483.

[13] Strictly according to law, Rahab had committed treason against her country and had betrayed all her neighbors. Yet I've not met a single Christian who has called that aspect of her behavior into question. But we go berserk over the fact that she misled the Jericho police! Neither do those Christians who get hung up on Rahab's conversation with the Jericho authorities ever raise any questions about the fact that Joshua and his forces were about to destroy thousands of people, in apparent violation of the sixth commandment. I find that very instructive.

[14] Rudolf Otto, *The Idea of the Holy* (New York: Oxford University Press, 1923), pp. 12-30.

[15] Roy Adams, *The Sanctuary: Understanding the Heart of Adventist Theology* (Hagerstown, Md.: Review and Herald Pub. Assn., 1993), p. 24.

[16] Davis, p. 33.

[17] *Ibid.,* p. 34.

# Chapter 2

# Miracle at the Jordan

## Joshua 3:14-4:24

*The section now before us constitutes the heart of the book of Joshua. Everything before it pointed forward to it. And everything after it will look back to it. In it we have the culmination of the Exodus story, the sequel to God's great redemption act, and the fulfillment of His ancient promise to Abraham.*

*In this portion we'll see the decisiveness of Joshua's leadership, the indispensability of the priesthood, and the enthusiastic cooperation of an entire nation. The most spectacular miracle since the crossing of the Red Sea will capture the attention of a new generation of Israelites, only teenagers or younger at the time of the Exodus. The long-awaited entry into the Promised Land will take place, and Joshua will experience a quantum leap in stature in the eyes of the people.*

*The end result of all this, in keeping with the basic purpose of the book itself, is that "all the peoples of the earth might know that the hand of the Lord is powerful," and that Israel "might always fear the Lord" (Joshua 4:24).*

### At Last, Zero Hour

It must have been an electrifying moment. The exact hour for the crossing had finally arrived—zero hour. "The people broke camp" for the last time before the historic entry into the land across the river (Joshua 3:14).

The Israelite camp was a thoroughly organized entity. Numbers 2 describes its careful arrangement, with the sanctuary—the depository of the sacred ark—at its center and the tribal units in prescribed locations all around it. And although by definition an encampment is a temporary setup, one as elaborately structured as that of Israel created the idea of permanence, tempting its dwellers to become smug, to settle down, to forget their pilgrim status. But suddenly the time had come to pull up stakes. This they must do if they would follow the ark, the symbol of divine presence.

That presence, made visible through the pillar of cloud by day and fire by night, had led them throughout the period of the Exodus and their time in the desert. Their safety and success depended on their willingness to recognize that guidance and to follow it. "Whenever the cloud lifted from above the Tent," as Moses vividly described it, "the Israelites set out; whenever the cloud settled, the Israelites encamped" (Num. 9:17). Repeated some seven times in the passage (see verses 15-23), this detail emphasizes the fundamental point that Yahweh was Israel's supreme leader.

The cloud and the fire, according to Ellen White, still appeared after Moses' death (some 70 days or so before the crossing).[1] But we find no mention of them as Israel started on its final trek. Instead the ark comes into focus, providing the people a continuing sense of confidence, safety, and assurance. In succeeding centuries they would seek to exploit and manipulate the sacred object, trying to benefit from its power while living in rebellious violation of the principles it symbolized (see 1 Sam. 4). But such an approach never worked—and never will.

Today, as well, our safety lies in following where God leads, for none of us has been this way before, and perils lurk along the way. Our prayer, individually and corporately, should parallel that of the nineteenth-century Christian John H. Newman:

> "Lead, kindly Light, amid the encircling gloom,
> Lead Thou me on;
> The night is dark, and I am far from home;
> Lead Thou me on.
> Keep Thou my feet; I do not ask to see
> The distant scene; one step's enough for me."[2]

Sometimes in our weakness and discouragement we may follow—as did Peter—only "at a distance" (Matt. 26:58). But we must follow. And when nothing but fog and darkness lie ahead, let's move forward in the trusting faith represented in the words of Minnie Louise Haskins:

> "And I said to the man who stood at the gate of the year:
> 'Give me a light that I may tread safely into the unknown.'
> And he replied: 'Go out into the darkness and put your
> hand into the hand of God.
> That shall be to you better than light and safer than a
> known way.'"[3]

The ark meant all that for Israel.

## The River Divides

The crossing occurred at harvesttime (Joshua 3:15)—thus the flax bundles (and also barley, no doubt) drying on Rahab's rooftop (Joshua 2:6; cf. Ruth 1:22; 2 Sam. 21:9). Most areas of the world are dry at harvesttime, and ancient Palestine was no different (see 1 Sam. 12:16-18). "The 'latter rains' of April and May [some would say March and April] brought an end to the rainy season and indicated the beginning of the harvest."[4]

Accordingly, the level of the Jordan River at harvesttime resulted not from rain but rather from the melting snow on Mount Hermon to the north. It was thus the warming temperature that brought the Jordan to "flood stage" (Joshua 3:15) at harvesttime.

Like many other rivers and streams in Palestine, the Jordan could easily be forded most of the year. "The Old Testament frequently reports how individuals and even large groups crossed the Jordan without difficulty (cp. Judges 3:28; 8:4; 1 Sam. 13:7; 2 Sam. 17:[22], 24)."[5]

This explains why the writer of Joshua took time to mention the season of the crossing. It prepared the reader for the extraordinary event about to occur. For the Jordan—normally a wadable stream for much of the typical year—was now at flood level.

Not that it was impossible to cross it even then—the spies, after all, had done it only a few days earlier (Joshua 2:23). But from a human standpoint, getting an entire nation across at harvesttime— with women, children, small livestock, and household goods and equipment—would be a virtual impossibility. We know this from the fact that fording the river under those conditions ranked as an act of valor even for trained warriors. Thus the chronicler listed among the exploits of the Gadites that they "crossed the Jordan in the first month when it was overflowing all its banks" (1 Chron. 12:15).

Yet God chose that particular time for Israel to cross for at least four reasons:

1. To reassure the people of His mighty power, as if to say: *Remember that the God of the Exodus is still with you. He has not forsaken or abandoned you. Nor has His awesome power abated with the passage of time.* The crossing of the Jordan, then, would form in the mind of Israel a psychological link to the crossing of the Red Sea. It showed that the people required the same divine power to enter freedom as to exit bondage.

2. To unnerve the surrounding nations and nullify the effect of their 40-year military buildup. As we might expect, these nations, emboldened by Israel's wilderness paralysis, had seized the opportunity to strengthen their defenses. By having Israel cross at such an impossible time, God wanted to send a clear message that He was still ruler of nature, was still present amid His people, and was still powerful to execute His purpose.

3. For surprise. "The Israelites had camped east of Jordan for months without making any attempt to cross over, with the result that the Amorites felt secure, especially now that the river was in flood stage."[6] Surely a group as large and unwieldy as the approaching Israelites could never ford the river during harvesttime. But the Canaanite military strategists had obviously failed to reckon with the resourcefulness of Israel's God.

4. To facilitate the transition between Israel's dependence on manna and its reliance on the produce of the land. God does not engage in gratuitous miracles. He does not work wonders when the natural order of things would suffice. Thus He led His people into the Promised Land at harvesttime, when much of the food needed for their sustenance would be out in the open fields, rather than locked up in storage facilities within fortified towns and cities. Harvesttime meant a ready source of food supply for the invading forces and the people. Not surprisingly, the manna stopped as soon as Israel ate the food of Canaan (Joshua 5:12).

# Miracle at the Jordan

But let's return now to the event itself. What exactly happened at the Jordan? The biblical account says that "as soon as the priests who carried the ark reached the Jordan and their feet touched the water's edge, the water from upstream stopped flowing. It piled up in a heap a great distance away, at a town called Adam in the vicinity of Zarethan, while the water flowing down to the Sea of the Arabah (the Salt Sea) was completely cut off" (Joshua 3:15, 16). The Hebrew word translated "heap" in verse 15 may also be rendered "mound" or "wall," giving the incredible picture of a water buildup. The passage leaves us in no doubt that the river did, indeed, divide. But many have speculated through the years as to how such a phenomenon could actually take place.

One explanation that has commanded a large following is that the splitting of the river might have resulted from damming brought about by, say, a landslide or an earthquake. According to John Gray, many commentators refer to the Arab historian en-Nuwairi, "who attests the damming of the Jordan about ed-Damiyeh for some ten hours on the night of December 7, 1267, through the undermining of the high marl [clay] banks by flood and by natural collapse or local earthquake." It has also been reported that "a similar phenomenon, also about ed-Damiyeh, for twenty-one and a half hours occurred in 1927."[7] Gray believes this to be entirely possible—that "the high, dry marl banks, unprotected by turf, in the exceptionally tortuous course of the swift Jordan might easily collapse with this effect, especially in flood time."[8]

If the implication is that this damming was simply a natural occurrence, then "such explanations fail to account for the very convenient timing of this blockage, or—more important—for the character of the story itself, in which the miraculous nature of the event is emphasized."[9]

But the major problem of using examples of natural damming as models for what might have happened during the crossing is that the stoppages mentioned by en-Nuwairi and others "did not occur during the flood season. It would have been impossible to dam the Jordan during that time"—"certainly not long enough for such a large contingent of people to cross."[10]

If the argument is that what happened when Israel crossed the

# Crossing Jordan

Jordan was simply a natural damming of the river, then the observations just cited (about its impossibility at flood stage) are irrefutable. But if the case being made is that the damming, both in terms of timing and duration, was a supernatural event, then it would be irrelevant to argue that harvesttime would have been impossible for it to occur, since divine power, by definition, can block the river at any season.

But the concept of supernatural damming also has its problems. Look carefully at the text again. It says that "as soon as the priests who carried the ark reached the Jordan and their feet touched the water's edge, the water from upstream stopped flowing. It piled up in a heap a great distance away, at a town called Adam . . . while the water flowing down to the Sea of the Arabah . . . was completely cut off" (verses 15, 16).

Those who argue for a supernatural damming locate the occurrence (based on verse 16) *at* the town of Adam, some 20 miles upstream from the crossing site. This is permissible since the Hebrew word translated "from" (KJV) may also be rendered "at" (NIV). In the first instance (though the KJV translation "from" is very unclear) one would picture the buildup of the water as extending from the point of crossing all the way back to the town of Adam. In the second scenario ("at," NIV), the buildup (or damming) takes place at Adam itself, 20 miles upstream.

Let's focus on the second scenario (with the first receiving indirect mention as we proceed), and let's assume that the floodwaters of the river moved at the rate of, say, 20 miles (32 kilometers) per hour. This is half the rate of the swift currents in mountainous regions that produce deep gorges like the Grand Canyon in Colorado.[11] (Although the figure may still be high, let's use it for purposes of illustration.)

According to the passage before us, the bare ground of the river bed appeared only when the priests' feet touched the water's edge (verse 15). At that precise moment "the water from upstream stopped flowing" (verse 16). If this describes a damming situation *at* Adam—(20 miles away), then that damming would have had to take place some one hour earlier, to allow time for the back end of the advancing floodwater (the downstream side of the damming) to pass the point of crossing precisely at the moment the priests' feet touched the water's edge.

# Miracle at the Jordan

But if that's how it happened, we find ourselves left in a quandary to explain why the Israelites themselves would have been impressed, let alone astonished, by the phenomenon. For unless we envision the people crossing the riverbed in single file, or something close to it, we'd have to assume, based on the scenario just described, that those members of that vast procession who were north of (or upriver from) the priests would actually have been able to cross ahead of the ark, since the riverbed would have become empty where they stood before the same thing happened where the priests were preparing to enter farther down. That, of course, would be completely incompatible with the basic thrust of the account before us.

It seems crystal clear that what the narrator wants us to visualize is a scenario in which the people, coming up against the threatening floodwaters of a raging Jordan, immediately sense their utter helplessness. And it's against this background that they witness the awesome power of God manifested through the dividing of the river before their very eyes.

For them, in other words, the dividing of the river was not something distant, not an event occurring 20 miles upriver from them. When we rob the event of its proximity and immediacy, we also steal its eye-bulging characteristics. In a damming scenario, then, there would have been no reason that both Israel and its enemies would not have considered the development simply an accident of nature.

And why do we think that a damming of the river far away is somehow more plausible or acceptable than the miraculous restraint of the water *at the point of crossing,* with its effect extending clear back to the town of Adam? While we may readily concede that God sometimes (and perhaps even often) uses natural means to execute His will, we need to question whether we should feel obliged to force a natural explanation for every event regardless of its obvious supernatural context. Did not Elijah, centuries later, strike the waters of the same river with his mantle (at approximately the same spot) and divide it (2 Kings 2:8)? And did not Elisha repeat the same feat shortly thereafter (verses 11-14)? I suspect the company of prophets watching from a distance (see verse 15) noticed no landslide or felt any earthquake.

I feel satisfied that what we have described in the narrative of the crossing is a gravity-defying phenomenon. The writer wants us to visualize a wall of water that was clearly visible to the Israelite multitude, reports of which struck terror throughout the surrounding nations. Had Israel's enemies considered the stoppage of the river as simply a natural phenomenon, regardless of its timing, the psychological effect would not have been what the Bible clearly implies it was (Joshua 4:23-5:1). The Canaanites might reasonably have argued that the desperate hordes across the Jordan simply took advantage of a natural fluke and made a run for it.

Ellen G. White's vivid description of the scene captures the biblical depiction exactly: "All [Israel] watched with deep interest as the priests advanced down the bank of the Jordan. They saw them with the sacred ark move steadily forward toward the angry, surging stream, till the feet of the bearers were dipped into the waters. Then suddenly the tide above was swept back, while the current below flowed on, and the bed of the river was laid bare."[12]

Whatever theory or conclusion we adopt, it is misguided if it detracts in any way from the fact that an event approaching the magnitude of the Red Sea miracle took place at the Jordan.

## The Role of the Priests

The role of the priests in the crossing of the Jordan invites our interest. They were the ones who led the way. And it was they who stood in the middle of the riverbed while the people crossed over (Joshua 3:13, 15-17).

What lessons can we learn from this? Who in Israel was God's representative? Was it the "political" leader Joshua? Or was it the priests, the spiritual leaders? And how did these leadership roles interface with each other? Joshua was commander in chief, but he was not to lead the way into the Jordan. On the other hand, the priests (who led the way) were not the ones to decide the time or give the order to cross.

Then there is the role of the ark, the symbol of divine presence. Without it the priests would have no power. And without the priests, the ark could not perform its function, since no one else— not even Joshua—had authority to carry it or even to touch it (see 1 Chron. 15:2, 13).

# Miracle at the Jordan

I suspect there are lessons in here somewhere, not easy to draw out—important truths in all of this, but difficult to articulate. Was this simply a way to maintain checks and balances of power within the nation? Or, considering the smoothness and efficiency of the operation—at least at this juncture in the nation's history—does it point, however imperfectly, to something beyond itself? Perhaps to the functioning of the Trinity?

That could be a stretch, and it all borders too closely on the speculative for our comfort. Perhaps any lesson we might gain from this phenomenon might better remain personal and unspoken.

On a related point, though, I find it significant that the priests bearing the sacred ark were necessary not only for the splitting of the Jordan, but for the *continuation* of the miracle while the people crossed over. It was as if the Lord wanted the entire nation, as it passed the spot where the priests stood, to reflect on the cause of the extraordinary event transpiring before their very eyes. As if God wanted those in succeeding generations to realize as they would read the story that the destructive forces of the world are not held at bay by some distant (deistic) fiat, but rather by God's active, immediate power.

The phenomenon shows, moreover, the impregnability of the divine presence. Standing in the midst of the riverbed with the ark—the supreme earthly symbol of God's presence and authority—on their shoulders, the priests, in actual fact, were indestructible. The same God who'd set boundaries for the waters of the sea (Jer. 5:22) had now hedged up the river's flow. And not all the water in the universe could overwhelm that sacred symbol of divinity, that shining token of God's ancient covenant.

The lesson is for us today, as well. If God's presence is with us, nothing whatsoever can overwhelm us.

## Climax of a Drama

As Joshua 3 ends, one is conscious of at least two things: (1) the story of the crossing has essentially been told and (2) there's still much more to tell.

There's more to tell, one senses, because the story is too big to end as abruptly as it does in chapter 3. The priests, after all, cannot be left standing in the middle of the Jordan (as they are at the conclusion of the chapter). And verse 12 has left one curious thread dangling—something about choosing 12 men. What was that about? The author has not told us yet. It is tantalizing, unfinished business, heightening our expectation for the rest of the story in chapter 4.

It's a literary approach that has sent many critical students of Joshua on a speculative field day, some charging "inconsistencies and repetitions" that came about, they claim, because of "the combination of several traditions and the work of more than one writer."[13] "Where, for example, were the 12 stones set up?" ask Miller and Tucker. "According to verse 9 [of Joshua 4] they were erected *in the middle of the Jordan,* but according to verses 8 and 19-20 they were set up in Gilgal."[14]

But is confusion really what we see in the story? Or is it the report of someone (an Eastern someone, to boot) bubbling over with the absolutely mind-boggling account of a raging river brought to halt during flood stage? If you were an eyewitness to such an extraordinary event, how do you hold yourself together as you tell about it? Sitting at our rationalistic desks—having never experienced any phenomenon more hair-raising than a fierce thunderstorm—we often err when passing judgment on those who had the privilege to witness the eye-bulging wonder of some of the most extraordinary events in human history, and whose hands trembled with excitement at the telling.

In the glow of the remembered miracle the eyewitness storyteller gives us (in typical Eastern style) layer upon layer of interlocking narrative. The author mentions details at one point, then follows it several verses later by repetition, elaboration, and expansion. It's an interweaving of themes and memories that can easily frustrate the impatient Western reader. Things don't run in strict chronological sequence. Instead, in typical Eastern style, retrospective and prolepsis, backtracking and anticipation, all seamlessly interweave.

I believe it's this style that's led, quite understandably, to the conclusion (based on Joshua 4:9) that Israel also erected a monument in the middle of the Jordan. Admittedly, the Hebrew text, on the face of it, suggests that such a conclusion is plausible, and perhaps there's really no watertight argument against it. The approach I take, however, is that it doesn't make sense. In the first place, 12 stones (each light enough to be carried by an ordinary Israelite on the shoulder) would hardly be seen above water, even if (impossibly) placed on top of each other. Second, it's hard to envision the construction of a monument that, in the time (we imagine) available, would be strong enough to withstand the force of the raging flood when the water returned.

Undoubtedly, then, the eyewitness narrator meant to refer to just one memorial event, transpiring on the other side of the river—a view that the NIV translation, using the pluperfect tense, captures well: "Joshua set up [at Gilgal] the twelve stones *that had been* in the middle of the Jordan at the spot where the priests . . . had stood" (verse 9). When thus considered, the entire account hangs together perfectly.

Here's what I see happening, all the way back to the early part of chapter 3. God tells Joshua what to do and what will happen (Joshua 3:7, 8). Israel's leader then explains to the people what will take place and what they should do (verses 9-13). Next he describes what actually occurred (verses 14-17), going over the ground later, after the fact, to fill in gaps (Joshua 4:1-9). Finally he returns to the main story, with details of its dramatic end (verses 10-18).

This typically Eastern brand of circumlocution, sometimes confusing to the Western reader, kept the interest of the Eastern audience.

So as the author returns to the story of the crossing in chapter 4, he begins precisely at the point where he'd left it back in chapter 3, making Joshua 4:10 almost a carbon copy of Joshua 3:17. But though it parallels it at many points, Joshua 4:10 does not simply repeat the information in Joshua 3:17. The emphasis in verse 17 is on the fact that the priests stood their ground *"until the whole nation"* had crossed over. Joshua 4:10 adds that they held their place *"until everything the Lord had commanded"* had been done by the people. So while the emphasis in chapter 3 falls on the people as such, that in chapter 4, in keeping with the other major concern of that chapter (the memorial stones), falls on God's special assignment for His people, a mission whose purpose was to keep alive the memory of that climactic day.

The people as such are not forgotten, however, and the author gives an added detail about them. He says that they "hurried over."

# Crossing Jordan

Why did they do that? The sacred writer does not say. Probably it was a question of not taking the miracle for granted. God's hand was over the river, to be sure. But it was no time to picnic or go rock hunting on its empty bed. And just as the exit from Egypt took place *in haste* (see Ex. 12), so the actual entrance into Canaan, notwithstanding 40 years of delay, occurred *in a hurry*. The people did not presume on God's power or patience. They could not know how long the water would remain at bay. Thus they moved quickly.

Moreover, the ark was not a light object. Neither could the priests set it down on the riverbed so that they might rest their shoulders. Thus the need for haste. It would take time for thousands of ordinary people to cross, even if they went 1,000 abreast. There was need for hurry. Would that all God's people today had that same sense of urgency to leave sin's stultifying wilderness for the promised rest across the river!

With the crossing narrative nearing its dramatic climax, the author struggles between sequence and suspense. It's almost as though the writer has lost all sense of order while recalling the exciting day. So here, in the middle of the account of the emergence of the priests, the narrator drops in the story of the men of Reuben, Gad, and the half tribe of Manasseh. They crossed over, he said, "armed, in front of the Israelites, as Moses had directed them" (Joshua 4:12).

These men, 40,000 strong, had left their families on the other side of Jordan in order to keep faith with the rest of Israel. Judging from the census taken a few months earlier (Num. 26), as many as 96,000 able-bodied men from these tribes remained on the eastern side to guard their loved ones and their property. But the rest crossed the Jordan with the other tribes of Israel, armed for combat.

Finally, after many detours, the author gets to the climax. The same One who'd ordered the priests into the Jordan—on His own timetable—now directed them, through Joshua, to emerge (Joshua 4:15-17). There they come now, "carrying the ark of the covenant of the Lord" (verse 18), with the whole nation gazing at the hair-raising scene in astonished wonder (verse 11). *What will happen now?* must have been the unspoken question on every mind.

And they didn't have long to wait. The moment the priests set foot upon the other side, "the waters of the Jordan returned to their place and ran at flood stage as before" (verse 18).

What do you imagine was the reaction of the people at this moment? Thunderous applause in recognition of Yahweh's awesome power? Shouts of praise in thanksgiving to the God of heaven for the exciting deliverance? Stunned silence in contemplation of the astounding miracle that had just transpired before their very eyes? We do not know. But whatever it was, God's concern was that they would never forget what had happened that fateful day, the fortieth anniversary of their departure from Egyptian bondage and the moment they first set foot in the Promised Land.

### So They'd Remember

In a sense God's concern to keep the memory of that historic day alive in the national consciousness forms the overriding burden of Joshua 4: "Each of you [speaking to the 12 selected men] is to take up a stone on his shoulder, according to the number of the tribes of the Israelites, to serve as a sign among you. In the future, when your children ask you, 'What do these stones mean?' tell them that the flow of the Jordan was cut off before the ark of the covenant of the Lord. When it crossed the Jordan, the waters of the Jordan were cut off. These stones are to be a memorial to the people of Israel forever" (verses 5-7).

These sentiments, solemnly repeated at the actual inauguration of the memorial (verses 20-23), form the central focus of the chapter, suggesting the importance of memory in human experience. The God who created us knows the power of ritual in the human psyche, the importance of symbolism for national stability. Thus the directives of Joshua 4:1-7. God intended the 12-stone monument to recall that historic moment in the life of Israel.

Every nation in the history of the world has learned the importance of preserving a memory of the past. Thus we find, scattered across the globe, memorials to the great events and people of yesteryear. As we contemplate these monuments in cities, towns, and villages all around the world, they speak to us. *Don't ever forget,* they tell us, *what happened here, the great events that transpired in this place. Remember the toil of those who preceded you—the hardship, the sweat, the misery, the agony, the sacrifice, the brilliance, the glory, the vision. Remember how the hand of Providence has led us.*

That was Moses' great concern as he prepared to lay down the mantle of leadership (Deut. 6:10-12; 8:7-14). And as the people finally crossed the Jordan, that too was the burden of Israel's new leader: "When your children ask you in years to come: What do these stones mean? tell them the Lord rolled back the Jordan, until you had crossed over" (Joshua 4:21-23, paraphrase). It's an overriding theme of the entire Old Testament. "One generation will commend your works to another," the psalmist declares. "They will tell of your mighty acts. They will speak of the glorious splendor of your majesty, and I will meditate on your wonderful works" (Ps. 145:4, 5; cf. Ex. 24:4).

God's concern that we remember rests on the soundest psychological principles. History has shown that as a movement matures and gains respectability and legal standing, as it enters the third and fourth generations, it has a tendency to forget its reason for existence, a tendency to lose its soul. Apathy develops. And cynicism. A kind of third-generation syndrome.

One of the saddest and most frightening health conditions to afflict the human race during the past 50 years or so is that of Alzheimer's disease—a malady that in its advanced stages causes the brain to degenerate and malfunction. Its victims become disconnected from the past, forgetting vital personal and family particulars, including their own identity and the names of children and other close family members.

This frightening nightmare shows the fundamental importance of memory in human experience. Who we are is inextricably intertwined with what we remember. If we lose our memory, our personal identity vanishes. Indeed, in a manner of speaking, we lose everything. And when a religious movement forgets its identity, then it has succumbed to spiritual Alzheimer's.

My point here is that movements—whether political, social, or religious—often develop this disease by the third or fourth generation. The children, grandchildren, and great-grandchildren of the founders—and let's focus exclusively now on religious entities—come to the place where they lose the zeal, the fervor, the enthusiasm, the drive, the preoccupation of their pioneers. With a shrug of the shoulder, they question whether they'd not been tomfooled, after all, into believing a mirage.

It's a gradual process—brought on, to a large extent, by social and intellectual absorption into the larger society. As we succumb to the mood and spirit of a secular, pagan culture, we lose our sense of having something vital, something urgent, to say to it. We become defanged by it, domesticated by it, spiritually and emotionally confused by it—virtual zombies, not knowing quite who we really are or what we're supposed to *do* or to *be*.

The stone monument at Gilgal was to: (1) stand as "a witness of God's faithfulness in bringing the nation into the land of Canaan"; (2) serve as "a sign to future generations" of what God had done; (3) remind Israel of God's awesome power; and (4) "teach the nations of the earth that the Lord alone is God."[15]

The Gilgal monument is no more. But God's faithfulness still continues. Today the Lord's Supper stands as God's contemporary "monument" to the supreme act of divine deliverance, symbolizing realities whose memory must never fade from human consciousness as long as time shall last. "For whenever you eat this bread and drink this cup, you proclaim the Lord's death until he comes" (1 Cor. 11:26).

Amid the rat race of the modern world we each must take time to erect personal memorials of God's mercy and faithfulness. Not necessarily monuments of stone, but monuments just the same. Perhaps a simple diary in which we record the tears shed in the midnight hour—in times of joy or in deep sorrow. Memorials of the way the Lord has led us—of trials overcome, victories experienced. Our monument might be an object holding special meaning for us, the name of a child, or just a special hiding place where we've had precious moments with our God. "We have nothing to fear for the future, except as we shall forget the way the Lord has led us, and His teaching in our past history."[16]

And so the story of the crossing ends. Presented somewhat as a parallel to its Red Sea counterpart, it reminded Israel that "the entrance into the Promised Land is, in a sense, the conclusion of the Lord's great act of deliverance that began with the Exodus."[17]

The Jordan crossing did for Joshua what its Red Sea counterpart did for Moses: "That day the Lord exalted Joshua in the sight of all Israel; and they revered him all the days of his life, just as they had revered Moses" (Joshua 4:14; cf. Ex. 14:31).

But however great these two leaders, they were still limited in what they accomplished. Moses led the nation out, but could not lead it in. Joshua led it in, but did not lead it out. Jesus does both. And thus He surpasses both Moses and Joshua (Heb. 3:3-6; 4:8). It's Jesus who, having delivered us from sin's oppressive bondage, stands ready to take us over Jordan into the heavenly Canaan.

The spiritual lessons permeating this whole narrative are numerous. But we will consider just three:

1. It is by the power of God that we're released from the bondage of sin.

2. It is by the power of God that we're kept and guided while passing through this earthly wilderness.

3. It is by the sheer power and grace of God that we at last enter God's eternal rest.

In all this, we're not passive—not at all. We cooperate with God, making "every effort to enter that [heavenly] rest" that He has promised (Heb. 4:11). But throughout the journey, clear to its very end, the victory is the Lord's.

## Jericho Ahead

The surprise crossing took place "opposite Jericho" (Joshua 3:16). Or we might say, in the vicinity of Jericho—some five miles (eight kilometers) away from the city. This point is significant for several reasons.

1. Jericho lay on "the main east-west highway, [and] was the first obstacle to [Israel's] invasion of western Palestine."[18]

2. Not only did Jericho loom in the way of the advancing forces; it also happened to be a well-guarded fortress town—almost impregnable in the context of the time. An Israelite victory here would send shock waves throughout the entire region.

3. The miraculous events needed to topple Jericho would strengthen Israel's resolve as it pressed the conquest of the rest of western Palestine.

# Miracle at the Jordan

## Questions for Reflection
### Joshua 3:14-4:24

1. The time eventually came for Israel, after 40 years of wandering in the wilderness, to cross over into the Promised Land. How is our situation like theirs? How is it different? And how eagerly do you look forward to the exciting moment when, with them, it will be our turn to enter the heavenly Canaan?

2. Note the role the ark of the covenant played in the crossing. What significance does that hold for you? What practical lessons might you draw from it?

3. Israel might have crossed the Jordan when the water level was low enough for children to wade safely. Why did the Lord choose the time He did? What message did that send to the surrounding nations? And what lesson does it have for us today?

4. God wanted Israel to remember the miracle of the crossing. Why?

5. What practical steps do you take to create memorials of God's providences in your life and that of your family?

---

[1] See E. G. White, *Patriarchs and Prophets,* p. 481; cf. Num. 34 and Joshua 1.

[2] *The [Seventh-day Adventist] Church Hymnal* (1941), no. 403.

[3] In John Bartlett, *Familiar Quotations,* 12th ed. (Boston: Little, Brown and Co., 1951), p. 869.

[4] Madeleine S. Miller and J. Lane Miller, *Harper's Encyclopedia of Bible Life,* rev. ed. (San Francisco: Harper and Row, 1978), p. 154.

[5] J. M. Miller and G. M. Tucker, *The Book of Joshua,* p. 38.

[6] *The Seventh-day Adventist Bible Commentary,* vol. 2, p. 193.

[7] John Gray, ed., *Joshua, Judges and Ruth* (Greenwood, S.C.: Attic Press, 1977), p. 58.

[8] *Ibid.;* cf. John A. Grindel, *Joshua, Judges, Collegeville Bible Commentary* (Collegeville, Minn.: Liturgical Press, 1970), pp. 14, 15.

[9] Miller and Tucker, p. 38; cf. D. R. Davis, *No Falling Words,* p. 40.

[10] Paul P. Enns, *Joshua* (Grand Rapids: Zondervan Pub. House, 1981), pp. 41, 42.

[11] See *World Book Encyclopedia* (1981), vol. 16, p. 326.

[12] White, *Patriarchs and Prophets,* p. 484.

[13] Miller and Tucker, p. 41.

[14] *Ibid.,* p. 42.

[15] Enns, pp. 43, 44; cf. Joshua 4:6, 21-24.

[16] Ellen G. White, *Life Sketches* (Mountain View, Calif.: Pacific Press Pub. Assn., 1915), p. 196.

[17] Grindel, p. 14.

[18] *The Seventh-day Adventist Bible Dictionary,* p. 550.

# Chapter 3

# A Covenant
# People Once Again

## Joshua 5:1-12

*It was a dark day for Israel. The 12 spies sent out by Moses had returned to base in the Desert of Paran. "The mission is impossible," said 10 of their members. "The situation is hopeless" (see Num. 14).*

*In the ensuing crisis the people, in their minds, had turned back to Egypt. Only divine intervention prevented them from assassinating their leaders (see Num. 14:10) as the first step of their retreat.*

*The situation was ugly. By their attitude and reaction they'd rejected and repudiated their great Deliverer and chosen in His place the helpless gods of their former masters.*

*It's against this background that we should understand the developments at Gilgal, Israel's first encampment in Canaan. What we see here is the radical reversal of the spirit of insubordination and rebellion that had thrown the nation off course and sentenced it to 40 years of misery in the desert. Here on the plains of Jericho Israel is about to be reinstated, to formally become God's covenant people once again.*

### Stricken With Terror

As it stands, Joshua 5:1 seems displaced and disconnected. Some would see it as belonging more properly at the end of chapter 4. Placed there, it would serve as a sort of sequel to verse 24, providing a broad-brush summary of the effect of Israel's miraculous river crossing on the surrounding nations. The verse says that when the Amorites and Canaanites heard what God had done for Israel, "how [He] had dried up the Jordan before [them] . . . , their hearts melted and they no longer had the courage to face the Israelites."

56

# A Covenant People Once Again

But whether at the end of chapter 4 or here at the head of chapter 5, the text provides additional evidence of how the surrounding nations perceived the Jordan crossing—as a totally unnatural event.

Had the stoppage of the river resulted from an upstream damming, that fact, as we suggested in the previous chapter, would not have gone unreported. And were this the case, it would be difficult to understand how the event could have caused such deep and widespread consternation among Israel's enemies and not, rather, be shrugged off as simply a freak of nature.

You will recall that when Moses and Aaron performed their signs and wonders in the Egyptian court, Pharaoh's immediate counteraction sought to blunt the psychological impact of the Hebrew miracles by duplicating (and thereby neutralizing) them (Ex. 7:10-8:6). Only when the Hebrew signs exceeded the ability of the Egyptian magicians to reproduce them did the latter concede that "this is the finger of God" (Ex. 8:19).

There is no reason not to believe that this was the prevailing attitude in Canaan as well. In fact, if we stop to think about it, it is the normal mind-set even today. We give no concession to claims of miracle until we have exhausted all efforts to explain or duplicate the particular occurrence.

Altogether too dramatic to stifle, reports of the miraculous Israelite crossing spread rapidly across the region—all the way to "the Canaanite kings along the coast" (Joshua 5:1). It would be fascinating if we could know how news traveled in those days. How, for example, did word of the spectacular crossing reach the coast as rapidly as the text implies it did, without any of the means of communication we have today? The impression we get from the account is that the immediate area of the crossing, on either side of the river, was unoccupied territory with no existing communities or settlements. So who told the story? How did word about the incident circulate?

We do not know. But might there have been representatives of other nations who witnessed the crossing from a distance? Jericho was only five miles or so away, and the city might have deployed military scouts in the area. Another possibility is that ordinary shepherds and farmers from the Jericho area might have seen something.

After all, it was harvesttime, with (watchful) reapers out in the fields around the district.

However it happened, word spread quickly—as far as the Mediterranean Sea some 45 miles (73 kilometers) away (as the crow flies) and still farther to cities and towns up and down the coast. That distance, only a trifle to modern travelers, represented a considerable journey in those days.

But the terror generated by the crossing had yet another purpose: to provide "cover" while the fighting men of the new nation participated in the circumcision ceremony (see Joshua 5:2, 7, 8).

As far as strenuous physical activity was concerned, this painful rite typically incapacitated its participants for several days. Consequently, the large number of those involved could seriously jeopardize the security of a nation in time of war, making it vulnerable to enemy attack. When Jacob's sons wanted to wreak vengeance on the Shechemites for violating their sister Dinah, that was the strategy they adopted. If you want to marry Dinah, they deceitfully bargained with Shechem, we will give her "on one condition only: that you become like us by circumcising all your males" (Gen. 34:15). "Three days later, while all [the Shechemites] were still in pain, two of Jacob's sons, Simeon and Levi, Dinah's brothers . . . attacked the unsuspecting [and defenseless] city, killing every male" (verse 25).

Against that background, try to picture the situation. Israel has just crossed the Jordan with all the hassles of baggage and livestock and equipment of every kind. The entire nation, notwithstanding the emotional glow from the miraculous crossing, is completely exhausted. Still, they had to set up tents for the night, organize the camp, and provide for the children and livestock.

Then, on top of all this—circumcision! And on a battlefield in enemy territory—for that's what the plains of Jericho essentially were.

Given the almost mysterious way news traveled in those days, we may readily assume that reports of the mass performance of the rite would have spread throughout the surrounding region. And when we consider that the procedure probably involved a sizable portion of the fighting men, then we can understand something of the peril the nation faced at this particular time.

# A Covenant People Once Again

That's why Joshua 5:1 belongs where it is. With perhaps more than half of the military force and thousands of younger males in pain, the nation would have presented a most tempting target to its enemies. Verse 1 explains the reason they did not take advantage of Israel's vulnerability at that critical moment.

### Why Circumcision Now?

If we can judge by the sequence of the narrative in Joshua 5, circumcision stood at the very top of Israel's agenda upon their arrival in Canaan. "Make flint knives," the Lord said to Joshua, "and circumcise the Israelites again" (verse 2).

The Exodus movement involved four groups of males:

1. Those of military age—20 years old and up (Num. 1:3, 18; 14:29)—at the time of the Exodus. Except for Caleb and Joshua, all of them were now dead.

2. Priests and Levites. They were not counted with the rest of the males of Israel. "It seems that the priests, possibly all the Levites, were exempted from the death sentence at Kadesh and that some of them survived. Eleazar, the son of Aaron, is specifically named as entering the Promised Land (see Ex. 6:25; 28:1; Joshua 24:33). There was no representative of the Levites among the 12 spies (Num. 13:3-16), nor among the 'men of war.'"[1]

3. Those not yet of military age at the time of the Exodus—teenagers and younger. They were among the children for whose life and safety those now dead had feared (see Ex. 17:3; Num. 14:3). But they were the very ones who lived to see the Promised Land. Having already been circumcised as infants in Egypt (the clear implication of Joshua 5:5), they, of course, did not participate in the present rite.

4. Males born during the 40-year desert wanderings—those, in particular, born since the crisis at Kadesh-barnea, alluded to by Joshua in Joshua 5:6, 7 (cf. Num. 14). These post-Kadesh-barnea males were the ones now circumcised at Gilgal (Joshua 5:5). They could not participate in the upcoming celebration of Passover without the rite (see Ex. 12:43, 44, 48, 49).

A confusion in the text at Joshua 5:2 seems to give the impression that the rite at this point was a repeat of something that had already happened. The RSV, for example, reads: "At that time the Lord said to Joshua, 'Make flint knives and circumcise the people of Israel again the second time'" (cf. parallel translations in KJV, NASB, etc.). However one translates the text, no one to my knowledge has yet suggested that there could possibly be a physical recircumcision. Thus the straightforward translation of the NIV seems preferable: "At that time the Lord said to Joshua, 'Make flint knives and circumcise the Israelites again.'" This would suggest a reinstatement of the rite after a period of disuse.

However, if the translation in the RSV, KJV, etc., is correct, then it may point to a service of solemn spiritual recommitment on the part of those already circumcised. In fact, nothing would have been more appropriate at this time, and we may reasonably assume that such a recommitment, at any rate, did take place.

But why were these males not circumcised in the wilderness? Surely it couldn't simply be attributed to the unsettledness of the journey. For however bad their situation in the wilderness, there had to have been days that were much less hectic than the period immediately following the crossing of the Red Sea. So why now?

The question brings us to the heart of the message of the chapter.

Circumcision was a divinely established institution, signifying the sanctity of the Jewish nation and its dedication to the exclusive service of Yahweh. Performed on Jewish males (and males of other nations seeking spiritual integration into Israel), it was the outward sign of commitment to the sacred covenant between God and their fathers (see Gen. 17:10, 11).

Pursuant to the fulfillment of that solemn agreement, God had rescued Israel from the clutches of Egyptian slavery to take them to a land of their own, as He had under oath promised to Abraham (Gen. 15). At Kadesh-barnea, however, the people, poisoned by the evil report of the spies, rebelled against their divinely chosen leaders and threatened to return to Egypt.

It was a nasty development. The nation was in rebellion. Thousands lost their lives as God threatened to wipe out the entire pack and, from Moses, raise up an entirely new people. But in one of the most eloquent illustrations of intercession in the entire Bible, Moses successfully pleaded with God for the rest of

# A Covenant People Once Again

Israel (see Num. 14:10-19). "I have forgiven them, as you asked," the Lord responded (verse 20). But this I vow: Not one of the rebels will enter the Promised Land. "Your children will be shepherds here for forty years, suffering for your unfaithfulness, until the last of your bodies lies in the desert" (verse 33).

In rejecting the divine leadership and—in their hearts—turning back to Egypt, the people had thereby committed the most grievous treason imaginable against heaven. They had broken the covenant and, technically, had ceased to be God's people. That fateful day, as the Lord ordered them to head back into the desert, the rite of circumcision was suspended as "a constant witness to Israel that their covenant with God, of which [circumcision] was the appointed symbol, had been broken."[2]

But here at Gilgal all that was behind them. The nation had set foot in Canaan. And the sign of the covenant was reestablished to mark a clear psychological break with the past and signal a new national beginning.

It is significant that the rite of circumcision—the sign of the covenant—came *after* God had delivered the people. No salvation by works here. It's as though the Lord was saying: You have been redeemed; therefore now, enter into the privileges and responsibilities of the people of God.

The large number of males being circumcised together resulted, as we might imagine, in a pile of severed flesh. Covered with earth, it was enough to form a small mound or hill. They dubbed it "Gibeath Haaraloth," meaning "hill of foreskins" (Joshua 5:3), a deft suggestion, I believe, that that mound or hill was to serve as a (delicate) memorial of the historic event.

Though painful, it must have been a joyous ceremony nonetheless. For whereas previous rites *looked forward* to a future time when God would fulfill His long-awaited promise to their ancient forebear, the present ceremony could actually look back upon a fait accompli. They had actually set foot in the Promised Land.

We today may draw hope from this development. Like ancient Israel, we too have been insubordinate and rebellious. How often have we turned back to Egypt in our minds! Much too long we have languished in this modern wilderness. But God yearns to renew the covenant with each new generation—and with each of us as individuals. The commitment of a previous generation will not suffice. Each new generation—and each new believer—must again reestablish the covenant relationship.

The rite completed, God Himself pronounced its theological significance: "Today I have rolled away the reproach of Egypt from you" (Joshua 5:9).

"The reproach of Egypt." What did that mean? Did it refer to the shame of Egyptian slavery? The stigma of foreign servitude? Did it include the fact that, with the renewal of the covenant, Israel had become a new nation?

The answer is: all of the above—and more.

God's purpose in the Exodus was to rescue Israel from Egyptian bondage and plant them in the land of Canaan, the place of His choosing. However, in two major incidents not long after leaving Egypt—that of the golden calf (Ex. 32:1-12) and the rebellion at Kadesh-barnea (mentioned above)—God had come close to destroying the entire nation. Significantly, on both occasions, as Moses pleaded for mercy in behalf of Israel, he pointed to the reproachful sentiments that would fill the headlines of the Egyptian "press." "Why should the Egyptians say," he reasoned with the Lord during the golden calf incident, "'It was with evil intent that he brought them out, to kill them in the mountains and to wipe them off the face of the earth'?" (verse 12). It seemed an argument God Himself could not dismiss. The Majesty of heaven relented, as He did also at Kadesh (Num. 14:10-20).

Nevertheless, the Kadesh crisis, as we have seen, led to Israel's prolonged paralysis in the desert, constituting a terrible reflection on God—on His ability to complete the task He had begun. "Heathen nations . . . reproached the Lord and His people because the Hebrews had failed to take possession of Canaan, as they expected, soon after leaving Egypt."[3] It was as if the terrible blight of slavery still rested on the people. For, notwithstanding the signal evidences of divine protection and providence along the way, they were still wanderers, still refugees, still not yet home, still stymied in the wilderness—as if by some dreadful curse.

"Their enemies . . . mockingly declared that the God of the

# A Covenant People Once Again

Hebrews was not able to bring them into the Promised Land."[4] It was a stalemate that bred reproach, derision, and scorn on the part of Israel's adversaries, especially Egypt. But now that "the Lord had . . . signally manifested His power and favor in opening the Jordan before His people, . . . their enemies could no longer reproach them."[5]

With this sacred rite, the whole nation—not only those physically being circumcised—renewed its covenant with Yahweh, becoming, so to speak, His covenant people once again, *in their own land*. In the accomplishment of this mission, in fulfillment of the ancient covenant, the reproach of Egypt "rolled away" from Israel. And in memory of the historic transaction, the place of its occurrence forever changed its name. Henceforth it would be known as "Gilgal." Almost identical in sound to another Hebrew word, *galgal* (meaning "a rolling thing"), Gilgal would ever bear witness to the place where God rolled away the stigma of failure, defeat, and bondage from His people.

## Passover Returns

One of the strong undergirding motifs of the entire episode of the crossing and its aftermath is the importance of remembering. Whether implicit or explicit, memorials appear everywhere. The dividing of the Jordan, itself not to be forgotten, was to remind the people of the dividing of the Red Sea at the time of the Exodus (Joshua 4:23; cf. Ex. 14:21, 22). The 12 stones would ever recall the miraculous crossing, while harking back to the 12 stone pillars earlier erected by Moses at the foot of Mount Sinai (Ex. 24:4). Joshua himself would serve as a living reminder of the hero of the Exodus (Joshua 4:14), and the date of Israel's emergence from the river (the tenth day of the first month [verse 19]) would recall the preparation for that first Passover down in Egypt (Ex. 12:3). And, as we have argued, even the spot where the men discarded their foreskins became a place to be remembered every time they said the name Gilgal.

Thus the whole account forms a grid, depicting the interconnectedness of God's action and activity in behalf of His people and showing how the whole complex of events hangs together. The intent is to present the picture of a single people with an integrated history and a common destiny.

# Crossing Jordan

Pursuant to this purpose, the writer now comes to Israel's most important national memorial, the Passover. "On the evening of the fourteenth day of the month, while camped at Gilgal on the plains of Jericho, the Israelites celebrated the Passover" (Joshua 5:10).

God had so timed the crossing that its future commemoration would also coincide with that of the great deliverance from Egypt—a deliberate attempt on His part to make it an anniversary of double significance for future generations.

This was only the third Passover observed in the nation's history. Originally intended as an annual observance (Lev. 23:5), the people celebrated the event just prior to the Exodus and on the first anniversary following their departure from Egypt (Num. 9:1-14). But after the rebellion at Kadesh, in which they vowed to return to the land of their captivity, the ceremony, together with the rite of circumcision (as we have seen), was suspended. How could it continue in the wake of such open revolt? How could its celebration by the Kadesh-barnea generation be anything short of mockery, given the fact that its purpose was to honor deliverance from a condition to which they now desired to return?

Thus for some 38 years the important memorial remained unobserved as "an evidence of the Lord's displeasure at [the people's] desire to return to the land of bondage."[6] "Now, however, the years of rejection were ended," and God once more "acknowledged Israel as His people."[7]

It was the first Passover in the Promised Land; and one wonders what kind of mood prevailed among the people as families solemnly gathered round flickering lights in newly reerected tents? What thoughts occupied their minds?

For some—perhaps for most—this was their first Passover. For others it was their second. For still others, it became their third. No one had known more than that number. But whether from their own experience or through countless stories heard on the knees of parents and grandparents, they probably all went back in thoughts to that first dramatic observance down in Egypt that fateful night 40 years earlier.

"When you enter the land that the Lord will give you as he promised, observe this ceremony," the Lord had said. "And when

# A Covenant People Once Again

your children ask you, 'What does this ceremony mean to you?' then tell them, 'It is the Passover sacrifice to the Lord, who passed over the houses of the Israelites in Egypt and spared our homes when he struck down the Egyptians'" (Ex. 12:25-27).

It was the final night in Egypt. At midnight all across the country the firstborn of every household would perish—from Pharaoh's palace to the hovel of the humblest citizen (Ex. 11:5). There would be only one protection from the dreadful curse: blood—of lamb or kid—upon the doorpost. "When I see the blood," God said, "I will pass over you" (Ex. 12:13). What a solemn moment for every Hebrew family that tense evening! How they must have checked and double-checked that the blood had been applied!

As the destroying angels struck at midnight (verse 29), the dreadful cry from numerous homes in Egypt broke the eerie silence and echoed as far as Goshen, where the Hebrews lived. But among the Israelites "not a dog . . . [barked] at any man or animal" (see Ex. 11:7).

Long before daybreak they were on their way, heading out of that oppressive land—driven out in haste, in fact, by petrified Egyptian officials and people worried that even more deadly pestilences were on their way (Ex. 12:31-33). Thus, after hundreds of years in Egypt (verse 40), Israel suddenly left, loaded down with the country's goods (verses 35, 36)—and with dough, unleavened and unbaked (verse 34). Backs long bent straightened now with pride and hope. Excited little children clapped and skipped and shouted. From Goshen and all across the country the Hebrew people were on the move, the wind of freedom blowing in their face.

That night, across the camp at Gilgal, they remembered. It was probably the youngest group who would ever keep the Passover. Apart from Caleb, Joshua, and perhaps a few priests and Levites (see Joshua 24:33), no one in the camp was older than 59. That would never happen again!

The first Passover transpired in the midst of crisis; this one in the wake of a most spectacular deliverance—the crossing of the Jordan. In the first, however, the struggle, so to speak, lay behind them. Now it lay ahead. The first took place in alien territory; they celebrated this one on the soil of their new homeland.

Both ceremonies, however, focused attention on the same

event—the time the Lord placed His seal upon His people for their protection, salvation, and deliverance. And notwithstanding the pain of the recent rite and the apprehension about what lay ahead, joy must have filled the camp.

How should Christians relate to this today? Positively, I would say. We cannot be unmindful of the spiritual implications and power of Passover even now. But we recognize that in its historical context, its focus, as such, was the nation of Israel. To the extent that the Jewish people today sense a solidarity with their ancient ancestors, they quite properly may observe the feast as a national or religious memorial. But for the Christian—whether Jew or Gentile—the coming of Jesus changed the entire landscape.

It was no accident that God timed the entrance into Canaan to coincide with the Passover, thereby merging—and thus enhancing—the great celebration of national emancipation. Similarly, it was not chance that Christ arranged the ceremony of the Last Supper to coincide with Passover, for this service was to replace it. For the new memorial of emancipation must find resonance with all people—those of Israel and those of Egypt, Jews and Gentiles. Completely unidentified with any particular culture, it must appeal to every nation, kindred, tongue, and people.

That's why the apostle Paul, zeroing in on the spiritual application for Christians today, referred to Christ as "our Passover lamb." He "has been sacrificed" for us, Paul says; "therefore let us keep the Festival, not with the old yeast . . . , but with . . . the bread of sincerity and truth" (1 Cor. 5:7, 8).

It's Jesus' blood—not that of lambs or kids—that we need to have applied to the doorframes of our hearts if we are to escape the destroying angels in the final judgment hour (see Rev. 9:4; 16:1, 2).

## The Manna Stops

*"The day after the Passover, that very day, they ate some of the produce of the land. . . . The manna stopped the day after they ate this food from the land; there was no longer any manna for the Israelites, but that year they ate of the produce of Canaan"* (Joshua 5:11, 12).

As suddenly and miraculously as it had started 40 years before, the manna now ceased. It had been Israel's food for four decades.

# A Covenant People Once Again

Almost nothing is known about it, and one wonders how such an (apparently) simple product (as we assume it was, from Exodus 16:31 and Numbers 11:7) could have provided either sustenance or variety for a whole nation for so long.

But we needn't be embarrassed by our ignorance, however; for the very name "manna" was a question in the Hebrew, meaning: "What is this?" From this we may assume that those who actually saw the substance had their questions too.

It being harvesttime when they entered Canaan (Joshua 3:15), Israel no longer needed food direct from heaven. As we have already observed, God performs the miraculous only when regular means will not suffice. The manna fed a hungry people, helpless in a dry and barren desert. But now that they could eat the produce of the land, the miracle stopped.

The disappearance of the manna signaled the passing of an era. The people had reached the end of their journey. They'd arrived at their destination. Their wanderings were over. God had kept His word.

## Questions for Reflection
### Joshua 5:1-12

1. What do you see as the deeper meaning of circumcision? How does it apply to us today, regardless of gender?
2. Israel's rebellion and insubordination made necessary a new beginning. In what areas do you need a new beginning in your life? Because of disobedience, thousands who began the journey from Egypt fell along the way, short of Canaan. What lessons might we learn from their experience?
3. After crossing over into Canaan, Israel took time to celebrate (Joshua 5:10). How often do we remember to honor God's goodness and providence in our lives?
4. "Today I have rolled away the reproach of Egypt from you" (verse 9). What does that statement say about grace?
5. The ceremony of the Lord's Supper has supplanted the ancient Passover observance in the Christian church. How do you understand its deeper meaning? And how joyously do you participate in this Christian service in your local congregation?

Do you understand its deeper meaning?

6. The experience of the manna was long ago and far away. And though it continued for some 40 years, it was essentially a one-time experience. What lessons, nevertheless, might you learn from this episode in the history of Israel? How can it strengthen confidence in God's providence and watch care?

---

[1] *The Seventh-day Adventist Bible Commentary,* vol. 2, p. 194.
[2] E. G. White, *Patriarchs and Prophets,* p. 485.
[3] *Ibid.,* p. 486.
[4] *Ibid.*
[5] *Ibid.*
[6] *Ibid.,* p. 485.
[7] *Ibid.*

Chapter 4

# The Walls Come Down

## Joshua 5:13-6:27

God had made clear His will to Joshua and to Israel. It was His intention, on the strength of covenant oath, to give them the land of Canaan. Now, after 40 years, He had miraculously brought them across the swollen river. Jericho, their first challenge in the Promised Land, stood before them—a sturdy bulwark, locked up tight and in a state of siege.

What should they do now? If you'd been in Joshua's sandals, what would have been your next move?

We miss the full impact of these biblical stories unless we pause long enough to live through each episode in its original setting. Hampered, for example, by our prior knowledge of how the Jericho story ends, we do not often capture the sense of total helplessness that must have gripped the Israelites—Joshua, in particular—at the sight of that well-defended fortress. Is this really where it all begins? Joshua must have wondered. What weapons do we bring to match these walls? He felt his need of God, his need for a power beyond himself.

Thus our section opens with the soldier-prophet lying prostrate outside the impregnable fortification and ends with him standing tall amid the ruins of the flattened city.

### Joshua's "Burning Bush" Experience

"Now when Joshua was near Jericho, he looked up and saw a man standing in front of him with a drawn sword in his hand" (Joshua 5:13).

With these arresting words the author abruptly launches us into the story of the fall of Jericho. The impression given is that Joshua was alone. But if he was, then what was he doing there? What was his mission? How likely is it that the commander in chief of Israel's army would undertake a solo mission in that dangerous area at such a critical time? And what might have been his reaction upon seeing a combat-ready warrior standing before him? Was he afraid, apprehensive? It was a most perilous hour for Israel, and any mishap now could leave the nation leaderless.

I believe that what we're watching here is a prayer warrior in full "combat" mode—on his knees, on his face. And the burden of his supplications would be obvious. "Lord," Joshua must have prayed out loud, being alone, "You've promised to give me every place on which I set my foot [Joshua 1:3]; that my territory will extend from the Euphrates to the Mediterranean [verse 4]; and that 'no one will be able to stand' before me throughout my days [verse 5]. You promised all that, Lord. But here's Jericho, where it all must start. The place is shut down tight, in a heightened state of siege. How do I get this mission off the ground?"

From Joshua's place of solitude he could probably see the walls of Jericho. *How could his army with its meager resources ever break through that impregnable bulwark?* We often forget that at this point in the story Joshua has no sense what direction events would take, no idea how they might come to pass. *We* know now—after the fact. But he didn't. Put yourself in Joshua's place. What thoughts would fill your mind as you stand outside that fortress town with just a bunch of desert-weary foot soldiers?

If any mission ever seemed impossible, the one now facing Joshua did. Jericho's "massive walls of solid stones seemed to defy the siege of men."[1] But as these frightening thoughts made his head hurt, Joshua "looked up and saw a man" standing before him, fully armed.

In the confidence drawn from communion with the throne of infinite power, Joshua approached the unexpected warrior and demanded that he declare himself: "Are you for us or for our enemies?" (Joshua 5:13). The question was genuine. And it was urgent.

The stranger obviously did not belong to the Israelite army, or Joshua would have recognized him. Nor could he, given his look of confidence, have come from Jericho (cf. Joshua 2:9; 5:1). With sword drawn, the visitor obviously posed a threat. Yet there was something about him—something about his attitude, perhaps—that left the Israelite commander puzzled as to where the man stood in respect to the impending struggle. "Are you for us or for our enemies?" Joshua asked.

Not being aware of the person's identity, he framed the question in human terms. But the heavenly intruder, for His part, responded from the divine perspective, indicating that Deity stands above the human fray, above partisan human categories or distinctions.

Was He for Israel or for Jericho? "Neither," said the combat-ready warrior, "but as commander of the army of the Lord I have now come" (Joshua 5:14).

What did He mean? The issue is significant.

The word translated "neither" is the Hebrew particle "lo," variously rendered as "nay" (KJV), "no" (RSV), and "neither" (NIV). It can also mean "of a truth," or "verily," or "indeed." Based on that last meaning ("indeed"), J. A. Soggin interprets the visitor's reply as "affirmative with regard to the first half of the question, and consequently implicitly negative with regard to the second half." In other words, Soggin said, "the commander of the army of Yahweh can only declare himself to be favorable to the people of the promise."[2] This interpretation, though plausible, seems forced.

So what does *lo* mean in this context? Notice that the author uses the word in response to an either/or inquiry on the part of Joshua. Therefore, the translation "of a truth" would not fit—especially not when followed by the strong adversative "but." For the same reason, the word "verily" would not do. "No" and "nay" will fit, but only if used in the sense of "neither." Thus, I would consider the NIV translation to be correct, and we may render the visitor's response: "As such, I'm neither for you nor for your adversaries; but I've come as commander of the army of the Lord."

Might this (unexpectedly) noncommittal response be a deliberate attempt to teach a deeper lesson, a timeless truth? Is it not a universal human tendency to try to co-opt the Lord into the service of our own particular team or clique or party? Are we not more concerned to claim Him for our own side than we are about being on *His?*

If ever there was an appropriate occasion for an unequivocal answer to a question like Joshua's, now was the time. The people, only a few days earlier, had consecrated themselves in preparation for the crossing (Joshua 3:5), and their hearts were still aglow at its miraculous outcome. Still in pain from the recent circumcision, the sign of the covenant between Yahweh and the Hebrew people (Joshua 5:2-9), the new generation had joined the entire nation in celebrating the Passover, the great memorial of Yahweh's deliverance of the nation from Egyptian bondage. In what better spiritual state could Israel be?

Yet it was precisely at this high spiritual juncture in Israel's experience that God revealed Himself as standing eternally above every human alliance or confederation. The Supreme Majesty, He takes no sides. He had come, rather, "as commander of the army of the Lord."

The incident is instructive for the way we talk about war and peace in a complex world. One cannot discuss the Second World War, for example, in the same way in the United States as in Japan. Nor would people see eye to eye on that issue in the Philippines and Germany or in the United Kingdom and Russia. No, in almost any audience there would be descendants of the "victors" and of the "vanquished."

It's not easy to nuance the stories of victory and providence in time of war without leaving the impression that God was somehow "on our side." But the reply of the divine messenger here gives us, indirectly, a way to proceed. For in the light of that response to Joshua, the question then becomes, not whether God is on *my* side, but whether I'm on *His*. Am I or my country fighting on the side of justice, equality, morality, and respect for human dignity?

Though a cursory reading of the Old Testament tends to give the impression that God unconditionally takes the part of Israel, much evidence reveals that His support of that people has always been *on condition of their faithfulness to the covenant,* a covenant whose benefits embrace the entire world. You cannot read Deuteronomy 27 and 28 and miss that point. Hundreds of years later it was also the burden of Azariah's message to King Asa and the people: "The Lord is with you when you are with him" (2 Chron. 15:2; cf. 2 Chron. 12:5).

So here God came to Joshua on the eve of the Jericho offensive. And though the Israelite leader does not yet know it, a serious breach of the covenant would occur during it, forcing the Lord to withdraw His protection from His people. God's response to Joshua was meant, among other things, to draw attention to the conditional nature of divine support, a recognition that would, in the wake of the Ai fiasco, send Joshua and all of Israel heading to Mount Ebal to renew the covenant (see Joshua 8:30-34). They were to learn the significance of God's words through Moses at the foot of Sinai: "If you listen carefully . . . and do all that I say, I will be an enemy to your enemies and will oppose those who oppose you" (Ex. 23:22).

"As commander of the army of the Lord I have now come." Without question the expression "army [Heb. *tsaba*] of the Lord" can refer to Israel. In fact, Scripture used it in that sense in the context of the Exodus movement itself, to which the conquest of Canaan is theologically linked. Moses wrote: "And it came to pass at the end of four hundred and thirty years . . . that all the hosts *[tsaba]* of the Lord went out from the land of Egypt" (Ex. 12:41, KJV). But since Israel was the "us" in Joshua's question ("Are you for us. . .?"), then we'd have to assume that the divine negation of Joshua's two alternatives (us or them) ruled out any easy identification of the "army of the Lord" with Israel in this context.

And if we rule out Israel in this context, then to what does "army of the Lord" refer?

To the angels, it would seem—and for that we have ample scriptural evidence. In a vision received just before the battle in which Ahab, king of Israel, would meet his death, Micaiah saw "the Lord sitting on his throne with all the host *[tsaba]* of heaven standing around him on his right and on his left" (1 Kings 22:19). At another time of crisis, following King Uzziah's death, Isaiah had a similar vision, in which he heard voices singing, "Holy, holy, holy, is the Lord of hosts *[tsaba]*" (Isa. 6:3, KJV). Another clear identification of "the army [host] of the Lord" with the angels appears in the literary parallelism of Psalm 148:2: "Praise him, all his angels, praise him, all his heavenly hosts *[tsaba]*" (cf. Ps. 103:21). (In this construct "heavenly hosts" clearly parallels "angels.")

It was this invisible host that gathered to defend Elisha when the Arameans surrounded him. In response to Elisha's prayer, "the Lord opened . . . [his] servant's eyes, and he looked and saw the hills full of horses and chariots of fire all around Elisha" (2 Kings 6:17).

The common thread running through all the examples just given is *crisis*. In every case, God's people found themselves facing the enemy with their backs to the wall. That was Israel's condition now, and heaven had deployed its invisible army in their behalf. It was Jesus Christ Himself, the commander of that heavenly host,[3] who now made Himself visible to the apprehensive soldier-prophet at this critical hour.

His cryptic response to Joshua's question was not a denial that He had come in behalf of Israel. Indeed, that was precisely the purpose of the theophany. But the words suggest that God stands completely above the human fray (cf. Acts. 10:34).

After 40 years of insubordination Israel had just renewed its covenant with the Lord, fully committing itself to fight *on His side*. And Joshua's reaction to the Stranger's words suggests that, however cryptic they might be, he understood them. And he was now utterly relieved to know that a stronger hand than his guided the human army he commanded. In fact, angels, the best "fighters" in the universe, had just reinforced it.

In solemn reverence "Joshua fell facedown to the ground" (Joshua 5:14), recognizing the presence of the Almighty. "What message does my Lord have for his servant?" he asked anxiously (verse 14). What up-to-the-minute directives do You hold? What critical course correction do You prescribe? What final assurance do You bring?

"Take off your sandals," said the Lord, "for the place where you are standing is holy" (verse 15).

The episode evokes memories of Moses' experience at the burning bush (Ex. 3:1-10). The Horeb theophany came at the beginning, and that at Jericho at the end, of the same mission. The first theophany explained the entire purpose of the mission: "I have come down," said the Lord, "to rescue [My people] . . . and to bring them . . . into a good and spacious land" (Ex. 3:8). Here, on the eve of the first campaign, on the soil of the very land promised in the Exodus theophany, Joshua receives assurance that the same one who had appeared to Moses in the burning bush will be with him. And thus we find a powerful theological linkage of the two events.

Prostrate before the mighty Visitor, Joshua was still puzzled. How would he, with his ragtag army, take a fortress city, completely battened down with no one entering or leaving it (Joshua 6:1)—no room, in other words, even to sneak a single agent in? If Israel should fail here, all was lost. Hence the timeliness of the divine assurance: "I have delivered Jericho into your hands, along with its king and its fighting men" (verse 2).

It reminds one of God's assurance to Zerubbabel at another critical period in the life of Israel: "Not by might, nor by power, but by my spirit, saith the Lord of hosts [tsaba]" (Zech. 4:6, KJV). Jericho will be taken, not by the skill and prowess of Joshua's army, but by the power of God, whose invisible heavenly army had arrived upon the scene.

Sometimes in our weakness and shortsightedness we can see only walls ahead of us—unscalable and impregnable. The mission seems impossible. But if, like Joshua, we'd "look up" with the eyes of faith, we'd catch a vision of the Lord of hosts standing by our side, armed for combat.

Still prostrate, Joshua receives a final briefing from the divine Commander in Chief on the exact operational tactics for the defeat of Jericho. The plan was at once simple and unconventional: The army of Israel—not the entire nation, as we sometimes think—was to "march around the city once" each day for six days (Joshua 6:3), accompanied by ram horn-tooting priests and preceded by the ark of the covenant (verses 3, 4).

The seventh was the crucial day. They would encircle the city seven times, then at a prearranged signal from the priestly trumpets, shout in unison (verses 4, 5). When that happens, the divine Messenger explained, "the wall of the city will collapse" and the surrounding army could then attack from all directions (verse 5).

## The March for Jericho

Buoyed up by his encounter with the heavenly warrior, Joshua wasted no time putting the divine plan into action. Within hours, it would appear, the march was on: armed guards at the very front, then seven priests blowing trumpets—perhaps in solemn, dirgelike tones. Next came Levites with the sacred ark, and finally, troops armed for battle (verses 7-9).

Except for the trumpet-blowing priests, the entire group

marched in total silence. "Do not give a war cry," Joshua had commanded. "Do not raise your voices, do not say a word until the day I tell you to shout. Then shout!" (verse 10). One can almost hear the emphasis in the general's voice as he pepped up the army for the assault on Jericho. One can almost see him thrust his fist into the air as he said those last two words: "Then shout!"

The Hebrew word for "shout" is *rua*. The word reminds us of the English "hurrah" or "hurray" used to express exuberant joy, excitement, exultation—as in the vigorous, festive shout: "Hip, hip, hurray!"

What a sight they must have made! What consternation as the sages of the nervous town puzzled to give meaning to the bizarre activities outside the walls! What on earth are these eccentrics after? What exotic madness, marching round a city once a day, then going home again!

But no one would dismiss as mindless folly such daily events— not when they remembered what had happened at the Red Sea and at the Jordan. Unnerved by the memory of such mighty acts of Israel's God, the Jericho authorities came nowhere close to laughing. What are those Hebrews up to now? What dark mischief lies in store for Jericho? "The mystery of the scene struck terror to the hearts of priest and people."[4]

And they could do only one thing about it: wait. It was psychological warfare of the highest order.

According to the account, Joshua did not brief the army on the outcome of the unconventional tactic. The marchers had no idea what would happen next. But they trusted Joshua and his God. Thus the book of Hebrews could make the statement that it was "by faith [that] the walls of Jericho fell, after the people had marched around them for seven days" (Heb. 11:30).

How did the Sabbath feature in the seven-day march around the city? It's quite possible that they skipped the Sabbath. But if the seven days were consecutive, then one of them had to have been a Sabbath. We need not conclude, at any rate, that "the seventh day" on which the city fell was, necessarily, the Sabbath. The expression in this context simply describes the seventh day of the march and could have been any day of the week. And while it's doubtful Joshua would have timed the undertaking to have its violent climax coincide with the weekly Sabbath, we must keep in mind that the mission, though fatal for the inhabitants of Jericho, was (from the divine perspective) a sacred one and thus in keeping with the spirit of the Sabbath day.

One of the elements in the divine instructions to take the city that catches our attention is the dominance of the number 7. We find "seven priests carrying trumpets" (Joshua 6:4). The people were to march around the city seven days (verses 3, 4). On the seventh day they were to encircle the city seven times (verses 4, 15). One gets the sense that the pattern is not simply accidental—that there exists a deeper significance here.

We know from the rest of Scripture that the number 7 in certain contexts does have theological meaning—denoting *perfection* or *completeness*. Balaam seemed to understand this when he called upon the king of Moab to provide him seven oxen and seven rams to sacrifice on seven altars before he could proceed to pronounce the perfect curse on Israel (Num. 23:1, 29; cf. 1 Chron. 15:26).

If you are faithful, God had promised Israel, your enemies "will come at you from one direction but flee from you in seven" (Deut. 28:7)—meaning, obviously, that Israel's enemies will flee in *all* directions. When Delilah enticed Samson to reveal the secret of his strength, he well understood what words to use to dupe his vengeful hosts: If you bind me "with *seven* fresh thongs" (Judges 16:7), he said; or "weave the *seven* braids of my head" (verse 13). "She who was barren has borne *seven* children," Hannah sang in her joy (1 Sam. 2:5), meaning that the formerly barren woman was now completely fertile. "The words of the Lord," says the psalmist, are "like silver refined in a furnace of clay, purified *seven* times"—which is to say, they're "flawless" (Ps. 12:6).

It's a feature that runs through the entire Bible all the way to Revelation. Here we find *seven* churches (Rev. 1:4, 11); *seven* golden candlesticks (verse 12); *seven* stars (verse 20); *seven* horns (Rev. 5:6); *seven* spirits (verse 6); *seven* thunders (Rev. 10:4); and *seven* plagues (Rev. 15:1). Most arresting of all (for linguistic parallel with the passage before us) are the *seven* angels with trumpets, like the priests outside the walls of Jericho (Rev. 8:2, 6; cf. 15:1).

It would seem that the use of "seven" in the Jericho story was deliberate and had theological significance—at least for Israel. A significance they probably understood in the context of Moses' last message to them on the plains of Moab, east of Jordan: The Lord will lead you into the Promised Land, Moses had said, and will drive out before you "many nations—the Hittites, Girgashites, Amorites, Canaanites, Perizzites, Hivites and Jebusites, *seven* nations larger and stronger than you" (Deut. 7:1).

Yes, *seven* nations, indeed!

God probably intended the seven-day encirclement of the city to indicate that the people should regard the conquest of Jericho as a sign, a token—the firstfruit—of what God meant to happen throughout Palestine. It was as if each day's encirclement symbolized the fall of yet one more nation before Israel, with the sevenfold encompassment on the seventh day serving to reemphasize God's intention to bring about the complete destruction of the targeted nations, of which the Jericho victory was the perfect starting point. And perhaps that is why He designated the spoils of Jericho as absolutely sacred (completely "devoted") to the Lord (Joshua 6:17).

An intriguing element of the Jericho story was the blowing of the trumpets. In the Old Testament such activity formed a part of worship (Num. 10:10; Ps. 47:5), but it also had a widespread association with times of war (see, for example, 2 Chron. 13:12-15; Num. 10:9) and in heralding the start of something new and momentous—a year of jubilee, for instance (see Lev. 25:9, 10).

The motif, as manifested especially in the Joshua story, comes to full flowering in the book of Revelation, particularly with the trumpet symbolism beginning in Revelation 8. Like its ancient counterpart, the references in the Revelation passages seek to convey the sense of imminent judgment, of impending doom. Just as Joshua's trumpets signaled the overthrow of the kingdom of Jericho, the trumpets of the seven angels of Revelation announce the overthrow of the entire earthly political establishment. Thus as the seventh angel sounds his trumpet, the prophet hears loud voices in heaven saying: "The kingdom of the world has become the kingdom of our Lord and of his Christ, and he will reign for ever and ever" (Rev. 11:15).

# The Walls Come Down

## On the Verge of Collapse

Joshua carried out the directives of the divine Warrior to the letter and records it all for us. Here again one encounters the same kind of repetition as that in the narrative of the Jordan crossing. But that does not mean that "the narrative . . . has passed through many different hands before reaching its present form."[5] As for the suggestion that the repetitions in the story show the existence of two accounts of Jericho's fall, R. K. Harrison's reaction is on the button: a "figment of literary-hypercritical imagination."[6]

What we have here is, quite simply, another example of dramatic Near Eastern storytelling that treats the listener to layer upon layer of story, organized for effect rather than in strict chronological sequence.

In the case before us, we know (from Joshua 6:2-5) the basic outline of the plan for Jericho's capture. Accordingly, the narrator could have—in Western style—dispensed with most of what follows in the chapter in one sentence: "And Joshua carried out the command of the Lord."

But that simply would not do—not in the Eastern context. We must hear it again as Joshua instructs the priest and leaders, using just about the exact words in which he himself first received the directive (verses 2-7)—and which the reader, of course, already knows. Then, to add repetition upon repetition, the text goes on to detail how Israel actually carried out Joshua's orders, giving the listener one more dose of it (verses 8-11).

And as if all that were still not enough, the narrator finds it necessary to describe the process one more time as it played out every day (see verses 12-14), ending with the statement that "they did this for six days," words that might well have come way back at the end of verse 11 to shorten the whole account. But brevity was not part of the plan. The story is too big to hurry.

Eventually, however, every narrative comes into its final stretch. For this one, it centers on the events of the seventh day, happenings with which the reader, however, is already acquainted from the telling and retelling of the story: After the seventh encirclement, "when the priests sounded the trumpet blast, Joshua commanded the people, 'Shout! For the Lord has given you the city!'" (verse 16).

And then, unbelievably, the narrative gets interrupted one

more time—just as we're sitting at the edges of our seats to know the outcome. An extremely important detail, omitted up to now, must come first. It's about the ban—the special prohibitions the people were to observe in the conquest of Jericho.

Awkwardly, it might seem, the author puts it at this critical point, interjecting it into the dramatic war cry: "The city and all that is in it are to be devoted to the Lord" (verse 17). Everything and everyone in it must be completely liquidated with just two exceptions: first, the prostitute Rahab and all members of her extended family physically present in her house on the day of battle (verses 17–19). Second, Israel was to preserve certain precious metals as sacred to the Lord (verse 19). With this detail behind him, the author now concludes the narrative: "When the trumpets sounded, the people shouted, and . . . the wall [of Jericho] collapsed" (verse 20).

Earlier we referred to speculation as to what caused the Jordan River to divide. Uncannily, however, scholarly speculation is usually silent about what made the walls of Jericho fall. It seems that most either accept the phenomenon as pure miracle or they reject it.

If you've grown up in the Judeo-Christian tradition, then you've probably heard the Jericho story told, in word or song, a thousand times or more. I would imagine, however, that not all our songs and stories put together come close to capturing the eye-bulging excitement of that extraordinary day. For six days the pressure on the city had been building. And by the seventh day you could have cut the apprehension within Jericho with a knife. Hearts atremble and knees as soft as jelly, Jericho's military establishment probably gathered about the walls, hoping to detect some hidden signal from the strange procession on the plains below. In their gut they felt a climax approaching.

Suddenly, as I imagine it, the procession stops. The dirgelike trumpet blasts pause. Total silence.[7] The marchers on all four sides face the city. Joshua gives the signal. A thunderous shout explodes. The walls of Jericho, loaded with dispirited soldiers and a frightened populace, begin to shake. The people panic. They scramble helter-skelter. The walls collapse. Total chaos.

In their wildest dreams the inhabitants of Jericho could never have imagined the magnitude of the nightmare. As the Israelite army charges forward, only token resistance confronts them. How can the Jericho military put up a fight in the wake of such earthshaking phenomena? "How easily the armies of heaven brought down the walls of Jericho, that proud city whose bulwarks, forty years before, had struck terror to the unbelieving spies!"[8]

No need to build siege ramps—the walls are down!

No need to storm the city gates—the walls are down!

No need to starve the city out—the walls are down!

The Captain of the heavenly hosts has brought them down.

Joshua and his army have won the day.

## Tagged for Destruction

"They devoted the city to the Lord and destroyed with the sword every living thing in it—men and women, young and old, cattle, sheep and donkeys" (verse 21).

These words introduce us to a most difficult issue—the role of violence in God's plan in Old Testament times. At first sight it outrages our contemporary sensibilities. Miller and Tucker speak about *"the brutal practice* of slaughtering all the enemy."[9]

How should we relate to such apparent atrocities? The killing of women, children, even animals! And in the name of God! How could this be?

The issue, one of immense theological concern, will occupy our attention in chapter 8. There we shall have opportunity to grapple with it more fully against the larger context of the conquest. But for the moment we may note that, however strange to us today, the Lord had targeted Jericho as a symbol of the "firstfruit" of the conquest of Canaan. The city represented "all that was vilest and most degrading in the religion of the Canaanites."[10] And just as the firstfruit of the land in Israel was sacred to God, just so Israel was to devote the firstfruit of victory to the Lord.

This was similar to the concept of the firstborn (Ex. 13:11–16). Jericho was, so to speak, the "firstborn" of the conquest of Canaan and, as such, to be offered totally in sacrifice to the Lord (cf. Joshua 6:26). The big difference here, of course, was that human beings would comprise part of this "offering," even though humans were always exempted from destruction in the ordinary law of the firstborn (see Ex. 13:12, 13). For the moment, however, it's helpful not to cloud the issue by throwing into it the divine prohibition against human sacrifices. The situation is complex and runs on an altogether different track, as we'll see when we take up the question of violence and holy war in chapter 8.

The concept broached in Joshua 6 is that of the "devoted things"—"the ban," as otherwise described by Scripture. It helps explain the seriousness of Achan's sin (Joshua 7) and why (as discussed in the following section) it was a matter of such enormous significance that there was just one exception to the terrible curse—an exception made to honor the promise of the spies to a certain lady of the night in Jericho.

## Keeping Promises

The directive was clear: "The city and all that is in it are to be devoted to the Lord" (Joshua 6:17). This meant that "every living thing in it—men and women, young and old, cattle, sheep and donkeys" must be eliminated (verse 21). And they were (verse 24).

It's against this background that we can fully understand the extraordinary exception made for the prostitute Rahab and her family. "Only Rahab the prostitute and all who are with her in her house shall be spared" (verse 17).

As the first march around the city commenced, Rahab probably took that as a sign that the time had come to call her family to her residence. Amid the chaos and confusion in the city, their gathering probably attracted no attention. Rahab's house being part of the city wall (Joshua 2:15), she and her family probably watched with anxiety and hope every move of the Israelite army. Everyone knew the critical stipulation: No one must leave the premises (see verses 18, 19).

Of the soldiers marching round the walls, two had been assigned a special search-and-rescue mission—the two who'd stayed at Rahab's house. We do not know how far the military procession kept their distance from the walls, but it was perhaps close enough for all to see the secret signal (verse 18). All eyes kept alert for it. That brave deed of Rahab's, her act of kindness and courage, must never be forgotten.

# The Walls Come Down

And as the walls of Jericho fell, Joshua commanded the two agents who'd encountered the brave woman: "Go into the prostitute's house and bring her out and all who belong to her, in accordance with your oath to her" (Joshua 6:22).

"Go into the prostitute's house . . ." How could this be? Was not her home part of the now-collapsing walls of the ill-fated city (Joshua 2:15; 6:20)? "This is further proof that . . . [chapters] 2 and 6 are independent [of each other],"[11] Soggin claims. Or, to cite Miller and Tucker, "the basic account of the destruction of the walls does not remember that the prostitute's house was built against the wall."[12]

Such observations are shortsighted—almost ludicrous. Once we concede that God could bring down the massive walls of Jericho, then we do not cavil about His ability to preserve the house of Rahab. In the words of Paul P. Enns: "The Lord may have preserved Rahab's house by performing a miracle similar to the one he performed in sparing Israel in Goshen" during the plagues on Egypt.[13]

The preserving of Rahab's house is an indictment on our better-than-thou mentality. The premises of all the respectable people of Jericho, from the king on down, had been flattened. Only one structure still stood—a house of disrepute that belonged to Rahab. Her immoral past notwithstanding, she'd now responded to the gentle wooing of the Spirit and, in her heart, had surrendered to the God of Israel. The visit of the spies, sealing her commitment, had changed her life forever. Her den of sin, transformed into a citadel of righteousness, had now withstood the fury of the storm. Is there a more powerful lesson on grace anywhere in Scripture?

What a meeting it must have been as the two soldiers, fully armed—and perhaps backed up by a specially trained detachment—arrived at Rahab's house! What tears of joy flowed down to moisten sharpened swords! Rahab and her family—safe!

Taken to "a place outside the camp of Israel" (Joshua 6:23), the group would undergo rites of purification, especially needed in this case, since their "uncleanness" would have been "aggravated . . . by the curse [on Jericho] to which they ordinarily would have been subject."[14]

How long did they have to remain outside the camp? Perhaps seven days, perhaps even longer—we do not know. But we can imagine that for Rahab no time was too long, once it meant eventual integration with the people of God. One wonders, however, about the mood of her family at this point. What was their conception of Israel and of Israel's God? What might have been their motive for joining Rahab? Was it simply to save their own skins? Or had they become convicted by the strength of her faith and the stupendous acts of divine providence they'd just witnessed? We do not know. And we hear nothing more about them.

As for Rahab, she became, in due course, fully integrated into the family of Israel (verse 25). Scripture lists her name as one of the ancestors of David—and of Jesus Christ Himself (Matt. 1:5, 6, 16).

All this because Israel kept its promise in accordance with their oath to her (Joshua 6:22). Nobody had signed any papers, and no independent witnesses to the agreement existed. Only a verbal promise, the swearing of an oath by word of mouth. But it was done before the One who is invisible—and it carried weight.

The whole incident is completely in line with one of the basic themes of Joshua: *keeping promises.* Even one made to a prostitute, under oath, is binding. Binding to the extent that the Lord honors it, notwithstanding the most solemn curse imposed on her town.

Our generation needs to learn lessons about promise keeping, about standing by our word. So far have we drifted from such values that today we must by all means "have it in writing." And not merely in the simple vernacular, either. No, we need professionals to prepare the document, to ensure that every loophole has been plugged, to tighten the language till it becomes virtually incomprehensible to the ordinary person. Even then, the promise is no good unless properly notarized. And after all this we still can find legal experts to absolve us of the pledge we made.

The spirit of the times has infected all of us to some extent. Fewer and fewer are the people of whom we can say: "His word is his bond/her word is her bond." The typical "politician" only represents the tendency in the heart of all of us—to flow with the tide, to bend under pressure, to break our "campaign promises."

Aren't our homes in shambles and our marriages on the rocks because of it? Do we really mean it when we pledge our troth—"for better or for worse, for richer or for poorer, in sickness and in health, till death do us part"? Do we not find, in spite of those noble words, "irreconcilable differences" behind every burnt casserole? And aren't we ready to let go our spouse at the drop of a dirty sock? Is that part of the promise we made at the marriage altar?

What a different world it would be if individuals, institutions, and nations would return to the ancient value of keeping promises!

### Extending the Ban

The curse pronounced on Jericho extended even into the future. The city must remain desolate (verse 26), a symbol of the fate of evil. Anyone undertaking to rebuild it in contravention of the ban would come under a deadly curse. "At the cost of his firstborn son will he lay its foundations; at the cost of his youngest will he set up its gates" (verse 26).

The pronouncement that Jericho would remain in perpetual desolation seems, on the face of it, to run up against the facts of subsequent history. We see in the book of Joshua itself the mention of Jericho as one of the cities given to the tribe of Benjamin (Joshua 18:21) and later (under its name "City of Palms") its capture by Eglon the Moabite during the time of the Judges (Judges 3:13). When Hanun the Amorite had humiliated David's emissaries, David told them to "stay at Jericho till your beards have grown" (2 Sam. 10:5; cf. 1 Chron. 19:5). And Jericho was one of the places Elijah visited before his translation (2 Kings 2:4).

How are we to explain the apparent discrepancy? Woudstra is correct, I think, when he argues that the curse was not pronounced on him who merely built the city, but rather on him who "fortifies" it, who "renders [it] strong."[15] "The underlying Hebrew term [for "rebuild"] is . . . used [in the sense of military fortification] in 1 Kings 15:17 and 2 Chronicles 11:5."[16] It would also seem reasonable to imagine that the area where the city of Jericho once stood would retain the name long after the city itself had disappeared.

God's intention, however, was that the very name "Jericho" would become a byword in Israel and among the nations, a perpetual example to future generations of the wages of sin. And the prohibition indicated remained in place for 500 years—until the lawless reign of Ahab. In those wicked times Hiel from the neighboring city of Bethel rebuilt Jericho, incurring the curse pronounced by Joshua: "He laid its foundations at the cost of his firstborn son Abiram, and he set up its gates at the cost of his youngest son Segub" (1 Kings 16:34).

With the fall of Jericho the fame of Joshua "spread throughout the land" (Joshua 6:27). That a mysterious hand guided Israel was clear to every nation west of Jordan. But not one would condescend to bow in submission to Israel's God. Instead, goaded by a veritable death wish, they would bind themselves together to confront His chosen people, an alliance that would begin in earnest in Joshua 10.

Meanwhile, difficult days lay ahead for Israel, and hard lessons to learn.

## Questions for Reflection
### Joshua 5:13-6:27

1. As the challenge of Jericho loomed, Joshua sought a quiet place near Jericho apparently to commune with God alone. What does that say to you as you confront the big issues before you?

2. In an age of vulgarity and irreverence, what lesson can you learn from the Lord's command to Joshua to take his sandals off (Joshua 5:15)?

3. When the difficulties before you seem overwhelming and insurmountable, how can the story of the battle of Jericho give you hope?

4. What can the experience of Rahab teach you about your own salvation? What does it say about the concern you should have about the salvation of your own family? about the salvation of those you consider hopelessly lost in sin?

5. How do you see the need for keeping promises in today's world? What experiences have you had with broken promises? And what strategies to face them have you adopted?

[1] E. G. White, *Patriarchs and Prophets,* p. 491.
[2] J. Alberto Soggin, *Joshua: A Commentary* (Philadelphia: Westminster Press, 1972), p. 78.
[3] See White, *Patriarchs and Prophets,* p. 488.
[4] *Ibid.*
[5] J. M. Miller and G. M. Tucker, *The Book of Joshua,* p. 53.
[6] R. K. Harrison, *Introduction to the Old Testament,* p. 675.
[7] See Marten H. Woudstra, *The Book of Joshua* (Grand Rapids: William. B. Eerdmans, 1981), p. 110; White, *Patriarchs and Prophets,* p. 491.

[8] White, *Patriarchs and Prophets,* pp. 492, 493.
[9] Miller and Tucker, p. 57. (Italics supplied.)
[10] White, *Patriarchs and Prophets,* p. 487.
[11] Soggin, p. 83.
[12] Miller and Tucker, p. 54.
[13] P. P. Enns, Joshua, p. 62.
[14] Woudstra, p. 115.
[15] *Ibid.,* p. 116.
[16] Enns, p. 63.

# Chapter 5

# Painful Lesson Learned

## Joshua 7; 8

The children of Israel are now in the land, and the major task before them is to conquer and subdue it. Upbeat over the smashing victory at Jericho, they set their sights on Ai, a smaller city some 12 miles or so northwest and, from the perspective of the soldiers sent ahead to assess the military situation in the place, far less protected than Jericho. Only a fraction of the army would be necessary to ensure victory, they advised Joshua.

However, unknown to them and the rest of Israel was the fact that a most grievous breach of the covenant had occurred during the capture of Jericho. That violation would spell disaster for the Ai mission and throw the nation and its leaders into panic.

As they worked their way through the terrible crisis they would learn again that the "commander of the army of the Lord" (Joshua 5:14) would stand by them only as they submitted to Him in covenant loyalty. They would discover that disobedience and rebellion would prove every bit a menace to Israel as to its wicked neighbors.

But the lesson learned, Israel captured Ai, then headed north to renew the covenant in the place prescribed by Moses. The extraordinary ceremony would make clear to every man, woman, and child in Israel that the very existence of the nation—as well as its stability and prosperity—depended upon its continuing faithfulness to the terms of the solemn agreement between Yahweh and their ancestors.

### Israel Defeated

In the detailed briefing of the troops preceding the battle of Jericho Joshua had taken pains to make one thing crystal clear: "The city and all that is in it are to be devoted to the Lord" (Joshua 6:17). Everyone must "keep away from the devoted things, so that you will not bring about your own destruction" (verse 18).

The concept of the "devoted thing" (Heb. *herem*) is foreign to the Western frame of reference. Such categories of thought never enter our everyday life experience. But for ancient Near Easterners, *herem* (or its equivalent in the respective languages) would have been as familiar and as real as the air they breathed.

For Westerners, the concept becomes even more confusing, because, in practical terms, it could have meanings completely opposite to each other. On the one hand, for example, it could refer to something dedicated to the Lord, in the sense of being sacred to His worship—thus to be *preserved, respected, held inviolate*. On the other hand, it could mean that the object or person in question was cursed and, as a consequence, marked for complete destruction. Complicating the whole idea even further was the fact that between these two poles there existed intermediate degrees that mitigated or only partially executed the prescribed penalties (see Deut. 13:16; 20:10-18; 1 Sam. 15:3).

But while the idea is unfamiliar—even confusing—to us, not so to the members of Israel's armed forces who listened to Joshua's briefing on the plains of Jericho. That's why it must have come as an overwhelming surprise to the nation to learn, as it did later, that in the midst of the spectacular supernatural power displayed during the overthrow of Jericho any Israelite would have had the gall to violate such a sacred prohibition.

But Achan's greed was greater than his judgment. Somehow, amid the chaos of Jericho's fall, he'd surreptitiously managed to purloin certain valuables for future personal use (Joshua 7:1). For a while Achan thought he had gotten away with it. No one had spotted him.

The opening words of chapter 7 ("But the Israelites acted unfaithfully . . .") provide the reader insight to understand the following narrative. They reveal the subject of the chapter: *the consequence of disobedience*. The reader knows what Joshua and the other participants in the story do not yet realize—that something has gone dreadfully wrong.

In his ignorance, then—and before the dust of Jericho had even settled—Joshua proceeded with immediate plans for the capture of

Ai. Ever cautious, he dispatched a reconnaissance team to assess the military situation in the area and to determine the kind of force needed to take the town. Time was of the essence, the reason he sent the men "from Jericho" (verse 2). (While it's possible the expression could describe the Israelite camp at Gilgal (see Joshua 5:10), it would seem unlikely that the author would use such a terminology for the camp, given what had just happened at Jericho.)

If my reasoning is correct, the sending of the spy team from the crumbled city would indicate the urgency Joshua attached to the mission. Perhaps he wanted to ensure that news of Jericho's fall would not reach Ai before the spies had had time to survey the area. Therefore, it must have been a rapidly moving reconnaissance team that made its way to Ai, perhaps setting out even before the final Jericho mop-up was complete.

A number of interesting questions remain unanswered about the incident. How, for example, did the espionage group make its assessment? Did it simply observe from a distance? Or did it penetrate the town? We should note that the city of Ai lay in the path of a major north-south trading route, with merchants and other travelers going back and forth, a condition that probably gave the spies the kind of cover they needed for their mission. Besides, the rocky and rugged terrain of the area surrounding the town would have provided ample places for concealment.

Whatever their strategy, the spies returned to Gilgal upbeat. It would, they reported, require only a fraction of the army to take the town—"two or three thousand" at the most (Joshua 7:3). Furthermore, they said, "do not weary all the people" (verse 3), a commendable concern indeed, given the fact that the army had just completed the Jericho siege on foot—covering in the process a distance of some 75 miles (when we compute all the daily round trips from Gilgal, plus the encirclements of the city). And although the march from Gilgal to Ai would be only about 15 miles or less, it was a difficult one. "Gilgal was 900 feet below sea level, while Ai was about 2,600 feet above, making the march a tedious uphill trek."[1]

The team's report was in stark contrast to that of their counterparts at Kadesh-barnea 40 years before (see Num. 13:26-33). But they could not predict the disaster that awaited the ill-fated mission.

# Painful Lesson Learned

One gets the impression of purely human planning here, without the usual seeking for divine direction and guidance on the part of Joshua and the people. Had Joshua and his advisers not been so cocksure—had they taken time to consult the Lord—would He not have revealed to them that something very seriously was amiss?

Under ordinary circumstances the spies' assessment would have been correct. But they did not know that someone had committed a terrible sin in the camp of Israel. Achan's action had invited God's wrath, and the entire nation, as a corporate unit, was in peril. As a consequence the 3,000 troops dispatched to Ai were routed, leaving about 36 dead (Joshua 7:4, 5).

However small the number of casualties, the incident sent the nation into shock. "The hearts of the people melted and became like water" (verse 5). Under God, Israel had come to forget the word "defeat" (see Num. 31:48, 49). Failure was simply not in the cards. How could this happen in the very wake of the spectacular victory at Jericho? They had nightmares about the psychological boost the Ai fiasco would give to the surrounding nations. "Defeat at this juncture was symbolically as significant as had been the miraculous capture of Jericho."[2]

In the agonizing prayer that followed, Joshua vividly expressed the national mood in the wake of the terrible development: "O Lord, what can I say, now that Israel has been routed by its enemies? The Canaanites and the other people of the country will hear about this and they will surround us and wipe out our name from the earth" (Joshua 7:8, 9).

Joshua's fears were not unfounded. The surrounding nations, though paralyzed with fear, were yet in a state of high alert. Propelled by that very terror, they could quickly seize the initiative and capitalize upon the slightest sign of weakness to make their move against the upstart nation.

In a state of deep crisis, "Joshua tore his clothes and fell facedown to the ground before the ark of the Lord" (verse 6). Here was help, he knew, stronger than human arms or armament. For no human ally, however powerful, could match the awesome force symbolized by that sacred ark in the sanctuary at Gilgal.

It was before that very symbol of Yahweh's presence, you will

recall, that Hezekiah, king of Judah, found assurance when a bloodthirsty Assyrian army approached Jerusalem in the seventh century
B.C. Upon hearing the deadly threats from the Rabshakeh, he, like
Joshua, "tore his clothes and put on sackcloth and went into the
temple of the Lord" (2 Kings 19:1; cf. 18:32-35). With the threatening ultimatum from the Assyrian king clutched tightly in his nervous hands, Hezekiah approached the "God of Israel, enthroned
between the cherubim" (2 Kings 19:15). Hezekiah and Joshua knew
from hard experience what Hugh Stowell, thousands of years later,
would set to poetry:

> "From every stormy wind that blows,
> From every swelling tide of woes,
> There is a calm, a sure retreat;
> 'Tis found beneath the mercy seat."[3]

The comparison between the way Joshua and Hezekiah faced
their respective crisis is instructive. But we should not miss the contrast. For however vulnerable Hezekiah must have felt, he at least
had city walls to protect him. But Joshua had no physical barriers
between himself and the enemy. With the rest of Israel he was
camped out in open country with no defensive fortifications. Yet
Joshua had something Hezekiah did not have. Hezekiah could not
look back, as could Joshua, on evidences of God's mysterious providence so fresh and so spectacular.

Yet Hezekiah's was a prayer brimming with confidence in the
power of God. Extolling God as the great Creator and the ruler
"over all the kingdoms of the earth," he deplored Sennacherib's
threats as an "insult [to] the living God" and begged the Lord to take
action "so that all kingdoms on earth may know that you alone, O
Lord, are God" (verses 15-19). The tone was that of a suppliant desperate for help—help undeserved.

By contrast, Joshua's prayer seems, on the face of it, self-serving:
"Ah, Sovereign Lord, why did you ever bring this people across the
Jordan to deliver us into the hands of the Amorites to destroy us?"
(Joshua 7:7).

Is this the great Joshua that we hear? Hadn't the Lord just
opened the Jordan before him and his people? Hadn't the Sovereign

of the universe, only days before, flattened the city of Jericho in their behalf, without the loss of one? Yet, with just 36 Israelite soldiers dead, Joshua panics!

The general did well, of course, to express indignation at the loss, however small. For all we know, those killed might have been some of his best soldiers—brave men, fighting at the rear of the fleeing army, providing cover. Still, we find it difficult to understand how Joshua, in the wake of the extraordinary providences he'd just witnessed, could seem to echo the rebellious murmurings of the wilderness crowd who, in their criminal shortsightedness, often brought down God's judgment upon the people. "If only we had been content to stay on the other side of the Jordan!" Joshua lamented (verse 7).

Were these sentiments much different from that of the rebels at Kadesh when they received the spies' report? "If only we had died in Egypt!" they had grumbled. "Why is the Lord bringing us to this land only to let us fall by the sword? . . . Wouldn't it be better for us to go back to Egypt?" (Num. 14:2, 3).

Was the prayer of Joshua cut from that same cloth?

We cannot judge from the words alone. It could well be that if we went back to the actual situation as Joshua was able to see it at the point of his prayer, we might make a different judgment. For one thing, at the time of his petition Joshua is unaware of what the reader already knows. So far as he could see, Israel, having kept its end of the covenant bargain, nevertheless had just experienced crushing defeat at the very start of its Canaan operation. What could this possibly mean for the future of the mission?

Sentiments, though similar on the surface, may flow from vastly different motives. As Joshua ends his prayer, for example, it becomes clear that his primary concern, unlike that of the desert rebels (see Num. 14:4), was for Yahweh's "great name" (Joshua 7:9). So that what we're seeing here is not rebellious murmuring on Joshua's part, but intercessory complaint, in line with the prayers of a burdened Moses, for example, in times of crisis. (See Ex. 32:11-13; Num. 14:13-19; Deut. 9:25-29). And God was not offended: "Stand up!" was His mild response to Joshua. "What are you doing down on your face? Israel has sinned" (Joshua 7:10).

### The Sin of Achan

However sad and unfortunate, it must have come as a huge relief to Joshua to discover the reason for Israel's crushing humiliation at Ai. God was not abandoning His people, nor was He being unfaithful to the covenant. The problem, rather, was with Israel. The people had violated the ban, the Lord said, speaking as if the entire nation had pilfered the offending objects with one huge corporate hand. The indictment was clear and devastating: "They have taken some of the devoted things; they have stolen, they have lied, they have put them with their own possessions" (verse 11). The covenant had been broken (verse 11).

The words were strong and candid. "Israel's historiography is not aimed at celebrating the great accomplishments of a superpeople, even though Israel could rightly claim to be God's elect." Rather, its "failures and frustrations are frankly set forth in the sacred record."[4]

So long as the issue remained unresolved, Israel could not advance. The infraction had effectively identified it with the "devoted" objects, thereby contaminating the entire nation and legally putting it in line for destruction. The critical divine communiqué on the Ai disaster even contains a subtle hint that things could have been worse—that the entire contingent sent to that city might have been wiped out, had it not been for the restraining hand of God. According to the text, "they [had] [all] been made liable to destruction" (verse 12).

The divine solution was to "destroy whatever among you is devoted to destruction" (verse 12). A harsh sentence indeed! But we find mercy even here. For although the entire nation, in the corporate sense, had become tainted, only the actual culprit(s) would face destruction.

It was evening after an all-day prayer vigil with the other leaders of Israel (verse 6) when God revealed Himself to Joshua. Yet Israel's leader had much to do before his head could hit the pillow, if it ever did that night. One can imagine that messengers went throughout the camp, waking many from an early slumber: "Consecrate yourselves in preparation for tomorrow; for this is what the Lord, the God of Israel, says: That which is devoted is among you, O Israel. You cannot stand against your enemies until you remove it" (verse 13).

# Painful Lesson Learned

The entire encampment understood the seriousness of the crisis, the gravity of the offense. And as the solemn trial commenced the following morning, tribe after tribe appeared before Joshua, lots being cast to nail the culprit. Finally the ever-tightening noose held Achan in its grip (verses 16-18). Exposed at last, he was now ready to confess. After a period of total silence, it was remarkable how candid he became, disclosing even the psychological process that led up to the fatal yielding. In his own words: "I saw . . . I coveted . . . and [I] took . . ." (verse 21). With a truthfulness that came too late, he listed the items stolen: a beautiful robe (imported from Babylonia, no less—expensive stuff!); 200 shekels (about 5 pounds [2.3 kilograms]) of silver; and a wedge of gold weighing 50 shekels (about 1.3 pounds [.6 kilograms]) (verses 20, 21).

It's virtually impossible to assess the value of these commodities in today's economy. But whatever their worth to Achan, how could they ever compare to the value of his life? Even if we should gain the whole world, Jesus said, it is absolute folly if by so doing we lose our own souls (Mark 8:36; Luke 9:25). But aren't we doing the same today? Selling our souls for a pound of gold, a few days "in the sun," a few moments of pleasure?

What makes the Achan story so frightening is that, notwithstanding the clear prohibition enunciated by Joshua before the capture of the city, the deed he committed seemed to him (and probably to many of us) so harmless—a "victimless crime," if a crime at all. It was valuable stuff going to waste, Achan must have reasoned—items that he and his family could use or trade. Here's a guy who probably would never rob a bank or snatch a purse filled with jewelry. And had he seen the Babylonian garment hanging in a storefront window, no way in the world would have ever thought of lifting it.

But in the chaos of Jericho's fall the valuable objects are about to be trampled by human feet in the confusion of a devastated city. Why not take them? Their owners were dead or soon would be, so why not grab them? No one would ever know the difference. And no one would mourn their loss.

Ah, but God had proscribed it, a point that Joshua had taken pains to make crystal clear. Moreover, the Lord had earmarked the precious metals among the loot for the sacred treasury (Joshua 6:19). Stealing that was like putting the tithe to personal use, like appropriating the sacred hours of the Sabbath for one's own gain or pleasure. In fact, in a sense, it was even worse. Because Jericho had been made a sacred, national firstfruit by means of the ban, Achan's act represented an attitude of criminal contempt for the Lord and for the symbolic significance of the victory God had so signally accomplished for the nation. The episode suggests the importance of obedience in those areas where purely rational explanations are not obvious.

A final observation about the Achan incident seems in order here. As already noted, his crime had compromised the Israelite mission and put the entire nation in peril. Until it was expunged, they would remain paralyzed.

Over the years people have drawn parallels with other incidents and experiences. And there has been the tendency to make the Achan incident a model for explaining what some see as spiritual paralysis in the church today. "There are Achans in the camp," some say.

While in a sense Achan's sin does shed light upon our current spiritual plight, it could be misleading to draw the parallels too closely or too hastily. In the first place, his sin was specific for that special, first engagement in Canaan. In other words, what Achan did at Jericho was not intrinsically evil, since Israel (on the surface) would do the same openly and at God's express command in subsequent battles. When Israel eventually conquered Ai, for example, the Lord told the soldiers that they "may carry off . . . plunder and livestock for [themselves]" (Joshua 8:2).

What made Achan's behavior so reprehensible was the fact that Jericho, as we've seen, *was a special case*. It had become a sacred symbol *(herem)* of the divine judgment that had begun to fall on all of Canaan. In the words of Ellen White, "Achan's sin was committed in defiance of the most direct and solemn warnings and the most mighty manifestations of God's power."[5]

So the empirical evidence will not sustain the view that "a single sin in the camp," as some contend, can indefinitely hold up the entire work of God. If that were so, Israel could never have won a single battle or advanced an inch. Nor could the church today. For the wheat and the tares will grow together *in the church* until the harvest. Only at the end of the age will the church be rid of tares. And angels—not humans—will be the ones to do that delicate work (Matt. 13:39).

It's interesting—and instructive—that Joshua did not use Achan's own confession as sufficient evidence to convict him, a principle of jurisprudence still respected and practiced in many countries around the world today. Thus, following Achan's confession, Joshua immediately dispatched officers to the man's tent to unearth and confiscate the incriminating proof.

The terrible sentence pronounced on Achan fell on his family as well. And the question is Why? Didn't Moses write that "fathers shall not be put to death for their children, nor children . . . for their fathers"? But that, rather, "each is to die for his own sin"? (Deut. 24:16; cf. 2 Kings 14:6; Eze. 18:20).

Perhaps what we have here is a case of contamination by association, the same phenomenon that had put the entire encampment in danger. It's as though the closer one gets to the center of the contamination, the greater the peril—and Achan's immediate family were at ground zero. Beyond that, they were probably accessories to the crime, by their silence and collusion becoming coconspirators with him.

In Achan the penalty of *herem* was fully executed. Before the day was over, "Achan . . . the silver, the robe, the gold wedge," together with his "sons and daughters, his cattle, donkeys and sheep, [and even] his tent and all that he had" had been destroyed (Joshua 7:24-26). You have brought trouble on Israel, Joshua said, and so God has brought trouble on you today (verse 25).

In this judgment we hear echoes of God's response to Joshua's question: "Are you for us or for our enemies?" (Joshua 5:13). "Neither," God had said. He is no respecter of nations or persons. "If the account [of Achan's treatment] is related to the wider context of the conquest of the nations, then Achan's family receives exactly the same treatment as the doomed cities of the land. . . . The similarity between the treatment consigned to apostate Israelites and the nations is focused in the contrast between the treatment given to Rahab the Canaanite and Achan the Israelite."[6]

# Crossing Jordan

## Victory the Second Time Around

The words of Joshua 8:1 do for chapter 8 what Joshua 7:1 did for chapter 7. They set the tone, giving us background that helps put the ensuing narrative in perspective: "Then the Lord said to Joshua, 'Do not be afraid; do not be discouraged" (Joshua 8:1). The words say something about Joshua's mental state following the messy affair of Achan. How could all that blood and gore and hysterical shrieking in the Valley of Achor not have affected him? Every leader knows something about the psychological toll they suffer when they must perform unpleasant duty. And every seasoned leader remembers that however extraordinary their experience—however miraculous or spectacular or recent—they're always potential candidates for discouragement or crippling fear. Thus at every juncture of our lives we need to hear again the voice of God speaking hope, and courage. "Don't be afraid."

The words came as a reaffirmation of God's promise to Joshua at the commencement of his mission—the promise to be with him, never to leave him or forsake him (see Joshua 1:9).

The command of the Lord to Joshua in regard to Ai is remarkable. In sharp contrast to the earlier advice of the spies (Joshua 7:3), God now directed him to engage the whole army in the attack, "for I have delivered into your hands the king of Ai, his people, his city and his land" (Joshua 8:1). This is covenant language at its best, and it assures the one who receives it that all is right with God. And it shows a God who will never leave His servant in uncertainty and limbo. Sin emerges; we confess it; we get back to God; we're restored; we move on. That's what God wants!

As in the case of Jericho, God called the shots at Ai. He prescribed the strategy Joshua was to follow: "Set an ambush behind the city," the Lord told the Israelite leader (verse 2). The ambush strategy, recommended here by the Lord Himself, has relevance to Rahab's act in misleading the Jericho authorities. Those who are ready to fault the shady woman of Jericho for what she did must reckon with what happens here at Ai. Clearly the idea was to trick the Ai army into thinking that the Israelites were taking to their heels again, as in the previous skirmish (verse 6). They'd give chase, leaving the city open and unguarded. It was a ruse, all right, but it bore the divine sanction. In fact, it came from God Himself.

And it worked. Israel defeated and destroyed Ai and its people (verses 9-29). After surrounding, scattering, and finally wiping out the Ai army, the Israelite forces doubled back to the city and obliterated everything that moved—"twelve thousand men and women" (verse 25).

The initial failure at Ai had called God's faithfulness into question in the minds of Joshua and the people—and *faithfulness,* you recall, is one of the themes of the book. It was a serious crisis, as we may see in the way Joshua ended his heartrending intercessory: "The Canaanites," he said, reflecting on the Ai defeat, "and the other people of the country will hear about this and they will surround us and wipe out our name from the earth." Not a big deal, given the fact that other names were being wiped out and denigrated left and right. But, Joshua added, "what then will you do for your own great name?" (Joshua 7:9).

With his question Joshua touched a divine nerve. It was in that great name—the name of Yahweh—that Moses had approached the suffering slaves in Egypt. When they would ask, "Who sent you to us?" he was to reply, "The God of your fathers sent me." And what was he to say if they asked about His name? "His name is the Great I AM—Yahweh, the covenant-keeping God, the one who ever lives to keep His word, and who amid all earthly change remains the same—strong, true, constant."

The defeat of Ai constituted a huge reassurance to Israel of Yahweh's continuing faithfulness.

### A Historic Renewal

On the plains of Moab east of the Jordan, after they'd wandered 40 years in the desert, Moses had gathered all Israel together in solemn convocation. In a final, comprehensive address, he recounted Israel's history, recalled God's providences, and recited and reemphasized the stipulations of the covenant. The book of Deuteronomy constitutes a record of Moses' historic speech.

In the very heart of the document Moses pleaded with Israel to "carefully observe" the commandments they'd received. They were to "love the Lord," to "walk in all His ways," and "hold fast to him"

(Deut. 11:22). If they would remain faithful to God, He would look out for them. They would dispossess powerful nations, and no one would be able to stand up to them (verses 23-25). The alternatives were clear and unambiguous: blessings if they obeyed, curses if they didn't (verses 26-28).

Here was the heart of the covenant, to be rehearsed again and again before the nation. And Moses specifically stipulated that when Israel arrived in Canaan, they were to "proclaim on Mount Gerizim the blessings, and on Mount Ebal the curses" of the covenant (verse 29). This solemn recital was to emphasize, among other things, the central place of obedience and loyalty for the well-being of the nation.

The disaster at Ai had come as a stark reminder of the Mosaic warnings on the plains of Moab. It was a tough and frightening lesson, one that neither Joshua nor Israel wanted to repeat. So now, fittingly, Joshua gathered the entire nation, as Moses had directed, for a recital of the law and a solemn renewal of the covenant.

Moses had been quite specific as to the place of the solemn gathering: Mount Gerizim and Mount Ebal, "across the Jordan, west of the road . . . near the great trees of Moreh . . . in the vicinity of Gilgal" (verses 29, 30). Separated by a narrow valley, the two mountains stood at the very center of Palestine. To execute the renewal at that location would symbolize the fact that that covenant was to become normative and binding throughout the land, governing the conduct and allegiance of all its inhabitants.

But when, exactly, the ceremony of renewal took place has always been a question with students of Joshua. And one would have to concede that the account does appear rather abruptly in the text, with no apparent contextual connection with the materials before or after it. In fact, you can remove Joshua 8:30-35 completely and the remaining text would connect without the slightest difficulty—which naturally leads to the question as to whether the passage belongs where it now stands in the book.

Moreover, as several students of Joshua have pointed out, it would have been a major undertaking to move the entire nation from Gilgal to the Shechem area, some 20 miles (32 kilometers) away, the location of the two mountains. Miller and Tucker offer additional observations: 1. The Israelites had just come into the land,

and Scripture offers no report of their having secured the Mount Ebal area. 2. As Joshua 9 begins, it finds the people back in the camp at Gilgal, where we would expect them to have gone immediately following the Ai battle. 3. The events described in Joshua 8:30-35 resemble those recounted in Joshua 24, thus favoring the view that it belongs with that chapter.[7]

Such arguments are persuasive but not conclusive. One major difficulty would be to explain how the passage found its way into Joshua 8 if it didn't belong there in the first place. I think the only way to appreciate the placement of Joshua 8:30-35 is to understand the profound trauma of the Ai defeat, a defeat linked directly to a breach of the covenant.

Thus it is no accident that we find the covenant-renewal passage immediately following the successful resolution of that conflict. It was designed to forestall any repetition of a similar crisis. The leaders of Israel, determined to put first things first, headed north for the renewal of the covenant, possibly leaving the camp at Gilgal guarded only by a skeleton staff.

Arriving at the appointed place, Joshua followed the stipulations laid down by Moses exactly, building an altar of natural materials and offering sacrifices (verses 30, 31; cf. Deut. 27:5-7). In what must have been a most dramatic demonstration he set up large stones, coated them with plaster, and began copying the law of Moses upon them.

The entire nation, including "aliens and citizens alike, with their elders, officials and judges" (Joshua 8:33; cf. Deut. 27:2-4), viewed the solemn scene. Moses, when he had issued the directive, declared: "And you shall write very clearly all the words of this law on these stones you have set up" (Deut. 27:8). Everyone must be able to decipher and understand them.

As the ceremony proceeded, the people stood on both sides of the ark, half of the tribes on Mount Gerizim "to proclaim . . . the blessings," while the other half took a position on Mount Ebal to pronounce "the curses," with the priests and Levites leading out from the valley between (see Deut. 11:29; 27:12-26). Moses had described the entire covenant renewal ceremonies, complete with even the litany of service—or, as we might say in this context, the covenant formula.

# Crossing Jordan

Conceivably, the major elements of both the blessings and the curses had been written in large letters on the stones that Joshua had erected (Joshua 8:32)—"very clearly," as Moses had directed (Deut. 27:8). The acoustical qualities of the site, reportedly, would have been ideal for such a reading.

What a solemn ceremony that must have been! What deep impressions it must have made on the entire congregation! What inspiration must have come to the "aliens" among them! What excitement must have welled up in the minds of youth and children! Coming on the heels of an historic Passover, and in the wake of the spectacular capture of Jericho and Ai, the memory of that remarkable day would live in the people's hearts forever. Theirs was a heritage worth preserving, a dream worth dying for.

It thus comes as no surprise that "Israel served the Lord throughout the lifetime of Joshua and of the elders who outlived him and who had experienced everything the Lord had done for Israel" (Joshua 24:31).

O that that history would repeat itself today!

## Questions for Reflection
### Joshua 7; 8

1. Without succumbing to legalism or paranoia, how concerned are you about becoming another Achan in the modern camp of Israel? And what is your responsibility if you think that someone else is "an Achan in the camp"? (See Matt. 18:15-20; Gal. 6:1, 2.)

2. Evidently the overwhelming victory at Jericho made Joshua and the people less vigilant about the need for divine guidance. How do you handle success? To what extent are you in danger of resting on your spiritual laurels, neglecting to seek the Lord for every new endeavor?

3. Why do many tend to panic in the face of defeat—even in the wake of previous spectacular victory?

4. How vital is prayer in your life? How strong is the tendency for gadgets and technology to crowd out your need to depend on God?

5. If you break your personal covenant with God, how can you renew it? What is the role of obedience in your covenant walk with God? What is the place of trust?

---

[1] P. P. Enns, *Joshua,* p. 65.

[2] M. H. Woudstra, *The Book of Joshua,* p. 123.

[3] *The Seventh-day Adventist Hymnal* (1985), no. 527.

[4] Woudstra, pp. 124, 125.

[5] E. G. White, *Patriarchs and Prophets,* p. 495.

[6] Gordon Mitchell, *Together in the Land: A Reading of the Book of Joshua* (Sheffield, Eng.: JSOT, 1993), p. 74.

[7] J. M. Miller and G. M. Tucker, *The Book of Joshua,* pp. 71, 72.

Chapter 6

# The Sun Stops Dead

## Joshua 9; 10

We've seen repeatedly now that the stories in the book of Joshua display a pattern of repetition. This phenomenon notwithstanding, the narrative of the book, considered as a whole, wastes no time. And as we near the midpoint of the document, we can look back with genuine astonishment at the swift pace of Israel's perilous mission: Jericho has been liquidated. Ai overrun. And, by the end of Joshua 10, Israel has brought the entire southern region of Palestine under virtual submission. In fact, the speed of the mission is such that it's impossible for Israel to establish a presence in much of the captured territory.

In the segment now under consideration we examine the story of how Israel, sucked in by an elaborate hoax, enters into treaty with its Gibeonite neighbors, a development that would change the entire strategy of the battle for Canaan. Up to now, Israel, directed by the Lord, had itself instigated the military action it encountered. Now we would see it responding to hostilities initiated by the surrounding enemy nations.

After receiving word of Israel's initial conquest in the land, all the western kings joined forces "to make war against Joshua and Israel" (Joshua 9:1, 2). That decision would set in motion a chain of events that begin in chapter 10 with the virtually complete subjugation of the southern section of Palestine, and end in chapter 12 with the defeat of some 15 kings in the northern half of the region. By the time it's all over, 31 Canaanite kings west of the Jordan will have been conquered (Joshua 12:24).

### Taken by a Hoax
One of the things the serious reader notices about Joshua 9 is that

the first two verses seem utterly disconnected from what follows them in the rest of the section. It's as though the author, becoming distracted after writing the opening lines, suddenly changes the subject to take up the seemingly unconnected episode of the Gibeonites. In fact, however, that is not the case, as we shall see.

But first, let's give attention to the Gibeonites, the main subject of the chapter.

We notice striking similarities here to the Rahab story (compare Joshua 9:9-11 with 2:8-13). Like Rahab, the Gibeonites had heard about the mighty acts of God in connection with the Exodus and were well aware of Israel's military intentions in Canaan. Like Rahab and her family, the Gibeonites wanted to live, and, like Rahab, they struck an agreement with the invaders. But while Rahab's deal with the Israelites was strictly on the level, that of the Gibeonites involved subterfuge and cunning.

How should we evaluate their action? It's easy to brand their approach as naked fraud. And, indeed, it was (Joshua 9:4). But when you stop to think about it, is that not what espionage, in the wider sense, is all about? It's possible to make the point that the Gibeonites approached Israel with the same cunning by which the latter had dealt with Jericho. A reconnaissance team cannot penetrate the security of a hostile nation without resorting to ruse. So we ought not to think of the Gibeonites as doing something completely out of the ordinary for operations of that kind. In the case of the Israelite spies, they probably wanted to look like the typical Jericho resident, or like ordinary merchants or wayfarers. The Gibeonites, for their part, sought to appear as emissaries from a distant country. The basic approach, though different in detail and motive, is fundamentally the same.

And the Gibeonites' fear, after all, was not unfounded. They probably were familiar with the stipulations as to how Israel should deal with nearby cities: in those cities, they were "[not to] leave alive anything that breathes" (Deut. 20:16). Only a stone's throw from Shechem, where the Israelites had recently renewed the covenant, the Gibeonites perhaps had witnessed the solemn ceremony from a distance, or perhaps had read the messages on the stones they left behind. Can we fault them for doing the best they knew to preserve their own lives?

# Crossing Jordan

At first the Israelite officials react with deep skepticism as they hear the Gibeonite story (Joshua 9:7). Could they trust these strangers? What if it was a trick? What if, instead of being "from a distant country," as they claimed, they were actually next-door neighbors? That was perhaps the concern behind a new line of questioning pursued by Joshua himself, following an initial round of interrogation by his subordinates: "Who are you?" Joshua asked them, "and where do you come from?" (verse 8).

The response (verse 9) was vague. "Your servants," they said, "have come from a very distant country" (adding, we may observe, the word "very" to their earlier testimony in verse 6). One almost feels like urging Joshua to demand: *What's the name of your country? If it's as distant as you say, why then this urgent interest in a treaty with us?* Yet, sadly, he does not raise such vital queries.

Meanwhile, the Gibeonite emissaries, evidently well aware of the vagueness of their answers, launched into a mouthful of flattering platitudes. They'd come the long distance, they said, "because of the fame of the Lord your God," based on the reports that had reached them (verses 9, 10). Joshua and his advisers, apparently entranced to learn that the reputation of Yahweh had reached such distant lands, drank in the tale without further questions. *How much easier that would make my work!* Joshua must have thought.

As many Bible scholars have observed, the Gibeonite delegation carefully avoided reference to recent events such as the conquest of Jericho and Ai, the mention of which might have given them away. They'd come too far, you see, to be aware of such current local developments.

Joshua listened on as they spelled out, one more time, the purpose of their mission: having heard such wonderful things about your God, "our elders and all those living in our country" had commissioned us, they said, to seek a treaty with your nation (verses 9-11).

Experts in body language, the Gibeonites sensed their message getting through and moved in for the final spiel. Although they had left with fresh bread, they said (with all the poignancy they could muster), now all they had was moldy food. New wineskins taken for the expedition had dried out and cracked. And the lengthy journey had tattered and torn their clothing (see verses 12, 13).

# The Sun Stops Dead

The clincher came when skeptical individuals among the Israelite inquisitors sampled the delegation's provisions (verse 14). That did it. The men are genuine, they concluded. Bring in the treaty documents! Thus "Joshua made a treaty of peace with them to let them live, and the leaders of the assembly ratified it by oath" (verse 15).

Three days after ratifying the agreement, however, the Israelites "heard" (perhaps from traders traveling in those parts or even from their own reconnaissance agents in the area) that their visitors were next-door neighbors (verse 16).

Like a thunderbolt, it suddenly hit them. Once again they'd failed to seek specific direction from the Lord. The passage says they "sampled [the Gibeonites'] provisions but did not inquire of the Lord" (verse 14).

Who'd have thought that after the Ai debacle Joshua and the rest of Israel's leaders would ever fail again to consult the Lord on any major enterprise? Yet that's precisely what happened in the Gibeonite episode. The Bible's candor in recounting this and other unflattering incidents speaks volumes about its bedrock honesty and authenticity. No flowery tales of shining heroes who did no wrong, but earthy accounts of men and women with passions such as ours.

For Joshua and Israel the incident could hardly have been more embarrassing. They'd been "outmaneuvered—not on the battlefield but in negotiations."[1] They felt betrayed—duped, in fact. In modern times this sort of thing could bring down governments and send powerful leaders packing.

Mortified, Joshua dispatched a military investigation team to Gibeon (verse 17). Arriving upon the scene, they discovered that Gibeon was, in fact, a tetrapolis (a four-city confederation—the other members being Kephirah, Beeroth, and Kiriath-jearim). The Israelite army, poised to teach the impostors an ugly lesson, needed strong words to restrain them. But they had made a promise. "The leaders of the assembly had sworn an oath to [Gibeon] by [in the name of] the Lord, the God of Israel," and they must honor it (verse 18).

As the grumbling spread through the ranks over the decision not to attack (see verse 18), Joshua and the other leaders, however humiliated, held their ground: "We have given them our oath by the Lord, the God of Israel, and we cannot touch them now" (verse 19). Covenant obligations must be honored.

We see this fundamental respect for covenant in Joshua's treatment of the Gibeonites. After a severe reprimand he sentenced them, in accord with the covenant (see Deut. 20:10, 11, 15), to perpetual servitude to the nation (Joshua 9:20-23), a fate they readily accepted, reasoning perhaps that the most menial service was better than death, the only fate they could envision for those who dared oppose the sweep of Israel across the land. It was "a striking evidence of the terror with which the Israelites had inspired the inhabitants of Canaan, that the people of such a city [as Gibeon] should have resorted to so humiliating an expedient to save their lives."[2]

## Why the Gibeonite Story?

The story of the Gibeonites is one of those accounts whose telling, on the face of it, does not seem particularly critical to the development of the narrative in the book of Joshua. On the surface, it would seem that the book could well have made its point without it, that the narrator might have omitted the story without damage to either the literary or thematic coherence of the document.

It's not the first time that this phenomenon has occurred in Joshua. Israel's renewal of the covenant at Shechem (Joshua 8:30-35), as pointed out earlier, falls in the same category. Arising as if from nowhere, the story simply sits there at the end of Joshua 8. We hear nothing about Israel's journey to Mount Ebal or about its return from there. The narrative that preceded the Ebal story (verses 1-29) was all about the Ai conquest, the repercussions of which form the subject of Joshua 9—namely, the reaction of the surrounding nations (the Gibeonites, in particular) to those developments. In other words, Joshua 9 connects smoothly and logically to 8:1-29; and 8:30-35 might vanish without notice.

The Gibeonite account, as we said, falls into the same category. Besides, it would have been in Israel's political interest simply to kill the embarrassing tale. Yet the narrator presents it in all its discomforting detail.

Why does Joshua devote so much space to the accounts of Ebal and Gibeon—accounts that on their face seem disconnected and expendable? Perhaps it has something to do with the relationship of these two stories to the basic theme and purpose of the book. In both stories, if we read between the lines, we see three things:

1. The importance of covenant faithfulness.
2. The constant need for divine direction.
3. The tenderness of God to His repentant people.

Seen in this light, the placement of the Ebal story is far from accidental. It acknowledges that the Ai fiasco resulted from a serious covenant breach. And it impressed upon the entire nation that the success of its mission was inextricably tied to covenant faithfulness. The story also showed that Israel's national leaders recognized their need for divine direction in the mission ahead, and the danger of precipitous action, as in the quick attack on Ai with its disastrous consequences. The Ebal convocation signaled their return to God following a particularly egregious breach of the covenant (see Deut. 30:1-3; cf. Joshua 7:10-12).

The Gibeonite incident runs in the same vein—but with a twist. When it turns out that the nation has been duped, Israel must yet honor its promise made on oath. To attack the Gibeonites or, on the other hand, to refuse to defend them would constitute a violation of Israel's treaty obligations and bring down the wrath of God on Israel's head (see Joshua 9:16-20).

Thus God would teach His people to be faithful to their promise, just as He is faithful. And it's significant that one of the most spectacular battles in the whole conquest of Canaan—the day the sun stood still—began as a defense of Gibeon in compliance with Israel's treaty agreement, regardless of the deception that had given birth to it (Joshua 10:6-14).

Thus we might conclude that the story of Mount Ebal and that of Gibeon, far from being incidental to the book of Joshua, lie at the very heart of its theme: *faithfulness to covenant, seeking the Lord for guidance, and returning to Him in confession when we stray.*

### Fluke or Providence?

A certain dimension to the Gibeonite story running beneath its surface especially intrigues me. As one studies the interrogation of the Gibeonite delegation at Gilgal, one is struck by the shocking oversight on the part of Israel's leaders in general, and Joshua in particular. Earlier we noted that they did not ask obvious questions, follow up obvious hints, or come to obvious conclusions. This situation, completely uncharacteristic of the savvy soldier-prophet, leads me to the conclusion that, regardless of the unsavory circumstances that precipitated it, the resulting treaty was actually an act of providence.

Why do I think so?

By the time we come to Joshua 10:5 we will have noticed three major passages that hint at one identical threat, namely, the formation—or potential formation—of a massive military coalition against the budding Israelite nation.

The *first* such hint comes in Joshua 5:1, just after the report of the miraculous crossing of the Jordan. It tells about the reaction of "all" the Amorite kings west of the Jordan to the recent extraordinary developments on behalf of Israel: "Their hearts melted and they no longer had the courage to face the Israelites."

The *second* hint, representing a significant change of psychological mood, occurs at the beginning of chapter 9 (verses 1, 2). From the state of nearly total paralysis we noticed in Joshua 5:1, Canaan's leaders—regardless of any lingering fear—had become energized, perhaps on account of Israel's failure at Ai, a fiasco that in their view exposed the upstart nation's vulnerability. Emboldened by that development, "they came together to make war against Joshua and Israel" (verse 2), seeking to wipe out the nuisance that had emerged to unbalance the military equation in the region.

These two passages (Joshua 5:1 and 9:1, 2), both seemingly unconnected with their respective contexts, hint at a development that, had it been put in operation as originally intended, would have posed a most dangerous threat to the security and the very existence of Israel. We see this indicated by the extensive geographical area from which the threat emerged, as M. H. Woudstra observes, commenting on Joshua 9:1, 2:

"The *hill country* . . . stands for the central mountain region of Palestine, so named in contrast to the lowland (cf. [Joshua] 10:40, 11:2, 16; Num. 13:17; Deut. 1:7). The *lowland* . . . [or *shephelah*] refers always to the region between the Palestine plain and the mountains in the center. . . . *The coast of the great sea* is the Mediterranean seacoast (cf. [Joshua] 1:4; 15:12, 47; 23:4). This plain is said to reach *to over against Lebanon.* Apparently the author intends to draw the circle of Israel's opponents as wide as possible."[3]

What we are watching here, then, is nothing less than the attempted formation of a pan-Canaanite military coalition, involving *all* the kings of western Palestine, north and south, to face a common threat. From a human standpoint, had these forces managed to converge on Israel (camped, as it was, in the center of the region), it could have spelled disaster for the new nation.

We should not discount the significance of this reality by suggesting that God could still have given Israel the victory. That consideration is not in dispute here. What we must note, however, is that through the entire account thus far, we have observed clear evidence that God, in spite of His awesome power, always takes the human factor into consideration. That's why, for the second Ai offensive, he directed that Joshua "take the whole army" (Joshua 8:1). Though the ultimate victory was still God's to give, the particular strategy to be employed at Ai called for the deployment of thousands of soldiers in the field.

With such considerations in mind, we can sense the danger of a pan-Canaanite military confederation formed against Israel, notwithstanding God's presence with His people. Any development of that kind would put enormous strains on the fragile faith of the new nation. You might recall that God had avoided the most direct route when He led Israel out of Egypt, concerned that "if they face war, they might change their minds and return to Egypt" (Ex. 13:17).

Against this background the Gibeonite episode takes on new significance. For by jumping ship, the Gibeonites (part of the Hivites mentioned in Joshua 9:1; cf. verse 7) threw a monkey wrench into the plans of the coalition, precipitating a chain of events that threw the emerging strategy into disarray.

By the time we come to Joshua 10:1-5, the *third* reference to a military confederation, the possibility of a pan-Canaanite alliance has dissipated. And all because of the unexpected action of Gibeon.

This leads to the following four points:

1. The Gibeonite decision to submit to Israel, notwithstanding its

questionable elements, in the providence of God blocked a massive pan-Canaanite military coalition then in the process of forming against Israel.

2. Because of the pivotal role the treaty with Gibeon would play in the overall mission of the conquest, God (I would suggest) governed the encounter between Israel's leaders and the Gibeonite delegation. Hence the glaring oversights in the interrogation process, oversights that allowed the treaty to come to birth. (The divine respect for the agreement appears hundreds of years later when a three-year famine descended on Israel because of Saul's precipitous attempt to eliminate the Gibeonites [see 2 Sam. 21:1-6].)

3. While it's impossible to know all the factors that motivated the Gibeonites, we must admire them for their courage and initiative. Also for their cunning. And it would not be inappropriate to take the statement in Joshua 11:19, 20 as a backhanded commendation of their action here. The passage observes that "except for the Hivites living in Gibeon, not one city made a treaty of peace with the Israelites." It's as if it means to say that what happened in the case of Gibeon (not, of course, in regard to the specific strategy) would have been desirable on the part of other cities as well.

4. Recognizing the awesome power of Israel's God, Gibeon made a calculated and voluntary decision to submit to His people, refusing to join its neighbors in suicidal resistance. Pledging themselves "to renounce idolatry," they accepted the worship of Yahweh. [4]

Today, with purer motives, we each have the privilege of submitting to God and joining the ranks of Israel—not as slaves, but as "fellow citizens with God's people and members of God's household" (Eph. 2:19).

## The Battle of Gibeon

Joshua 10 makes three salient points:

1. When God's people remain faithful to Him, every confederacy formed against them will collapse.

2. When God's people make a valid promise—to God or to their neighbor—they must keep it.

3. When God's people seek His counsel before engaging the obstacles in their way, He will release even the forces of nature in their behalf.

# The Sun Stops Dead

These three points form the outline for what follows.

1. *Every confederacy formed against God's people will collapse.*

The text does not explain why Adoni-Zedek, king of Jerusalem (Joshua 10:1-4), was the one to summon the other powers together against Gibeon. But a quick look at the geography of the area shows the strategic importance of Gibeon. Because of its location it would be the frontline state in any struggle with a powerful enemy based at Gilgal. With Gibeon's defection, the only significant buffer between Jerusalem and Gilgal had now disappeared, making Jerusalem the frontline state overnight—not a development that city welcomed. "Although Jerusalem was a major stronghold, having valleys to the south, east and west, it was vulnerable from the north, where Gibeon was located."[5]

But perhaps a more important reason that Jerusalem was the leader of the southern flank of the emerging pan-Canaanite coalition was the fact that it was the most powerful state in the south (and, incidentally, one that would successfully resist Israel for centuries, as we will have occasion to note below.) Thus it fell to Adoni-Zedek to hold the southern flank together.

The southern alliance, psychologically solidified by Israel's defeat at Ai, had experienced a weakening of its resolve following Israel's comeback victory. And that victory, just 6.5 miles (10.5 kilometers) away from Gibeon—much too close for any comfort the coalition could provide—led Gibeon to defect. In an independent initiative to protect its own security, Gideon forged an alliance with Israel to the consternation of the other powers in the southern flank. That's what I believe is happening in the first verses of chapter 10.

But we cannot fully understand the developments in that chapter unless we see their connection to Joshua 9:1, 2 and the Gibeonite saga that followed. The description of the emerging coalition in verses 1 and 2 clearly suggests that it was to include the entire region, north and south. Yet the passage seems just to stand there, as we said, unconnected to anything else. That, of course, is because we do not often see its vital link with the Gibeonite story that follows it.

Notice now how verse 2 connects with verse 3. Verse 2 reports the Canaanite powers as coming "together to make war against

Joshua and Israel," giving rise to the logical question: "So then, what happened? Why did they *not* attack?"

The answer comes in verse 3: "However, when the people of Gibeon heard what Joshua had done to Jericho and Ai, they resorted to a ruse." The author here seeks to show that the Gibeonite action constituted the fly in the coalition's ointment, the monkey wrench in the emerging military confederation.

Gibeon's action "much alarmed" Adoni-Zedek and his people. And we see the reason for their concern spelled out in the rest of the verse: "Gibeon was an important city" (Joshua 10:2). It had served as a buffer between Joshua's forces and the rest of the coalition. Its defection was, therefore, a major setback for the group.

But Gibeon was important for another reason as well. Though it apparently had no king (we hear of the "elders" of Gibeon—not about its monarch—making the important decisions [Joshua 9:11]), it was, nevertheless, "like one of the royal cities" (Joshua 10:2). Royal cities were larger and more elaborate than most, as befitting the residence of a king. Gibeon was "larger than Ai," the text goes on to say, "and all its men were good fighters" (verse 2). It means that not only was Gibeon a frontline state, but its warriors were renowned for their military skills. With its default, then, the confederation, apart from losing a powerful ally, now faced the specter of confronting a formidable new enemy.

It explains the anger of the other southern powers against Gibeon, leading them to implement drastic and immediate hostile action (verses 3-5). They sought to accomplish two things: (a) take revenge on Gibeon for what they considered a cowardly betrayal and (b) remove a powerful ally of Israel, thus restoring the integrity of the pan-Canaanite coalition.

However, this gallant attempt to salvage the crumbling southern wing of the alliance would collapse. For by the Gibeonite action God had set in motion a series of events that could not be turned back.

2. *God's people keep their promise.*

For Israel the battles of Jericho and Ai were now behind them. They'd journeyed to Shechem for the renewal of the covenant and had returned to Gilgal. Now where on earth do they go from there? What's to be their strategy for the rest of Canaan? Though we seldom think about it, such questions must have weighed heavily on the mind of Joshua and the rest of Israel's leaders. *What to do next?*

Enter now the Gibeonites spinning their elaborate tale. A treaty forms. And the entire picture immediately changes. For that treaty would be the catalyst for the all-out offensive on the region.

The story is familiar. Adoni-Zedek, hearing about Gibeon's pact with Israel, hits the ceiling. Marshaling the leaders of the southern city-states, he marches north to Gibeon's southern border (verse 5), an action that sends troubled Gibeonite emissaries scrambling farther north to Gilgal to seek the aid of Joshua (verse 6).

Should Israel respond to the self-inflicted plight of these impostors? Might this be yet another scheme to entrap them? This time Joshua and the rest of Israel did not forget to seek the Lord. They'd finally realized how swiftly disaster could come when, cocksure and overconfident, they failed to talk with God. As they prayed, the green light flashed. "Do not be afraid of them," God said to Joshua, "I have given them into your hand" (verse 8), the same assurance He had provided before the battle of Jericho (Joshua 6:2) and before the second attack on Ai (Joshua 8:1). Completely unexpected and unplanned, the needed opening into the rest of Canaan had emerged.

But notice that it came as Israel moved to honor the solemn agreement they'd made. Thus, in the decision by Joshua and the rest of the Israelite leaders to honor the agreement with their unscrupulous neighbors, we see a powerful restatement of the major theme of the book. The faithfulness of Joshua and the people reflects the faithfulness of God (see Joshua 21:45; 23:14; cf. Joshua 9:16-20; 2:12-14, 17-20).

3. *When we seek the Lord, He works for us.*

As indicated earlier, Israel had learned well the lesson that failure to consult the Lord could spell disaster—not only when the course is difficult, but especially when it seems most clear. Thus they earnestly sought the Lord before embarking upon the battle of Gibeon, and God responded (see Joshua 10:8).

The magnitude of the undertaking was clear to Joshua, and he committed the "entire army, including all the best fighting men" (verse 7) to the campaign, perhaps leaving only a skeleton contingent to guard the Gilgal camp. Scripture does not provide details, but it's probably appropriate to assume that, as at Jericho and Ai,

God might also have outlined to Joshua the strategy for the battle of Gibeon. Therefore, it was not simply coincidental that the strenuous 25-mile (40-kilometer) "all-night march from Gilgal"—from lower to higher terrain—put the Israelite army on the battlefield in the early hours of the following day, with the enemy forces at their most vulnerable (verse 9). The arrival of Israel was totally unexpected. It "took them by surprise," the record says (verse 9).

The Canaanite confederation was startled because most military movements and activity in those days ended with the disappearance of daylight. That's why Joshua would later pray that the sun would stop. Moreover, probably well knowing that the Gibeonites—in spite of their military strength—would never initiate an attack on the combined forces of five nations, the allied armies no doubt spent a good part of the night in revelry and dissipation, totally unprepared for the rude awakening the next morning.

The divine role in the whole event is crystal clear: 1. God had timed the arrival of the Israelite army for maximum impact. They took the enemy "by surprise" (verse 9)—an exceedingly important advantage in time of war. 2. God "threw [the enemy] into confusion before Israel" (verse 10)—"divinely inspired panic," Gordon Mitchell calls it.[6] 3. As the enemy fled before Israel, incurring in the process a multitude of casualties, God exacerbated their difficulty by hurling "large hailstones down on them from the sky," killing more of them that way than would die from Israel's sword (verse 11).

And God did one more thing for Israel—something absolutely spectacular and unique in the history of warfare. Evidently, as the battle waged throughout that fateful day from the early hours of the morning when Israel arrived upon the scene, Joshua sensed the need for additional daylight to pursue the enemy and complete the mission. As he "stood at the summit of the pass at Beth-horon and looked down upon the vast multitudes of the enemy fleeing to the southwest toward their strongholds, he feared that the day would prove too short to bring complete victory. He knew the opportune time to strike was while the enemy was disorganized. Delay would give them time for reorganization."[7]

And so, in an act of extraordinary faith, and in the presence of the entire army, Joshua uttered a most unusual prayer, ending with a call to inanimate nature to carry out the mandate of his petition:

> "'O sun, stand still over Gibeon,
> O moon, over the Valley of Aijalon.'
> So the sun stood still, and the moon stopped,
> till the nation avenged itself on its enemies"
> (verses 12, 13).

How should we understand what happened that day? Are we dealing here with mere poetry and figures of speech?

The passage does not seem to permit that conclusion. Moving from poetry to prose, the author returns to the event for a final summary, giving that summary in the factual, objective language of common speech. In everyday parlance—as popular then as now—he says: "The sun stopped in the middle of the sky and delayed to go down about a full day" (verse 13). And to leave us in no doubt about the uniqueness of the phenomenon, he adds: "There has never been a day like it before or since" (verse 14).

The passage indicates that the sun was already "in the middle of the sky" when Joshua uttered his astonishing prayer. And that it "delayed going down about a full day." I understand the phrasing to mean that that particular day lengthened by some six hours, so that instead of the sun setting in six hours from the point of Joshua's prayer, as it normally would on any other day, it went down instead in 12 hours.

How did this happen?

As some suggest, God may have used the phenomenon of reflected light or some other special pyrotechnics to produce the effects our author describes as the stopping of the sun. We cannot rule out such a conclusion. But we do well to question the need to always resort to such naturalistic explanations. Why this deep reluctance to accept the reality of raw miracle? We seem afflicted by a latent rationalism that sees reality within a closed, naturalistic continuum, with no possibility of any influence from outside that narrow sphere.

Though it reached full bloom in the rationalism of the eighteenth century, this tendency is much older, going way back into hoary antiquity. It was this attitude that led to Sarah's memorable laugh at the thought of getting pregnant in old age (Gen. 18:10-12).

And it was that same latent rationalism God addressed when He put the penetrating question to her husband: "Is anything too hard for the Lord?" (Gen. 18:14; cf. Jer. 32:17).

Indeed, there is nothing. "His wisdom is profound," as Job affirms, "his power is vast" (Job 9:4). "He performs wonders that cannot be fathomed, miracles that cannot be counted" (verse 10). Ask the kings of Judah and Israel, gathered with their soldiers before Elisha, to explain how the prophet was able to fill the ditches in a dry valley with water in the absence of wind or rain. ("This is an easy thing in the eyes of the Lord," Elisha explained [see 2 Kings 3:15-18].) And ask that Israelite widow and her son if they'd ever doubt that the power of God can bring oil out of nowhere (see 2 Kings 4:1-7).

Martin Noth is correct to note that "at the very center of the history of 'Israel' we encounter phenomena for which there is no parallel at all elsewhere, not because the material for comparison has not yet come to light but because, so far as we know, such things have simply never happened elsewhere."[8]

### Other Items of Interest

Three additional points are relevant at this juncture:

1. As we indicated in the introduction, the incident with the sun forms a vital part of the underlying structural development of the book—namely, the distinguishing of Joshua, the enhancement of his stature to fill the shoes of Moses. That's why the command to the heavenly bodies took place "in the presence of Israel" (Joshua 10:12). Especially was this reaffirmation of Joshua necessary in the wake of the humiliating incident with the Gibeonites.

2. Joshua, we should note, did not utter this address to inanimate nature on his own account or in his own power. The peculiar construction we have in Joshua 10:12 ("Joshua said to the Lord in the presence of Israel: O sun . . .") means to suggest that his command to the sun and moon had divine approval. If the enemies of Israel worshipped the sun and moon (as many Bible scholars suggest), then the form of Joshua's prayer showed that their *gods* were subject even to the *servant* of Yahweh; and that far from defending their devotees, they were obliged, upon command, even to aid their enemies. And if such command could come from a servant of Yahweh, what hope

was there of their gods ever standing up to Yahweh Himself?

3. We cannot know exactly how the lengthening of that special day occurred. But we can be sure that the surrounding nations would have noted the phenomenon, bringing added terror to their forces.

Some have also wondered why Joshua needed to address the moon as well. Although the inclusion of the moon might simply be a poetic complement, it may also suggest the reality of the situation. If, as I indicate above, the time of Joshua's prayer was about midday, then we can imagine that in his westward push in pursuit of the enemy he had come to a point where he could look back (eastward) toward Gibeon with the sun hanging almost directly over it and westward over Aijalon where the fading moon still stood. And it would be logical for him to reason that if the sun were to stand still, then the moon would naturally have to do the same.

Another possibility might be that the two sections of the prayer, combined as we read them in our Bibles, might have been uttered at different times of that same day. It could be that when the sun finally set, Joshua still needed just a little extra time that the light of a full moon might have provided. It was in the glow of that same moon that he and his forces had made the treacherous journey from Gilgal to Gibeon the night before.

## Finishing the Job

The rest of Joshua 10 explains what happened in the wake of the extraordinary miracle. Verse 15, which suggests that Joshua and the army returned to Gilgal at this point, seems misplaced, probably confused in the copying process with verse 43 (where it belongs). Or perhaps it is a part of the quotation from the book of Jashar referred to in the text (see verse 13).

Now that it had obtained additional light, the Israelite army pressed the battle with relentless vigor. Determined to utilize every minute of the extended day, Joshua did not even pause upon hearing that the five culprit kings had holed up in a cave at Makkedah. Block it with large rocks, he barked, and post a guard in front of it. "But don't stop! Pursue your enemies, attack them from the rear and don't let them reach their cities" (verse 19). It's not by your own power that you prevail, he reminded the army, but "the Lord your

God has given them into your hand" (verse 19).

Meanwhile, Joshua himself remained at Makkedah to lead the attack against that city. Totally destroying it and its inhabitants, he put its king to death (verse 28). The text does not indicate how Makkedah came to be included in the struggle, but we may assume that it was also hostile to Israel and thus represented a threat to Israel's rear flank as it pursued the fleeing allied forces. The rest of the Israelite army overtook the bulk of the remaining enemy forces, destroying them almost completely. A "few" escaped, however, and "reached their fortified cities" (verse 20).

The last item of business of that long day (the execution of the five culprit kings) came when the army returned to Joshua at Makkedah, where he'd set up temporary headquarters. In a symbolic gesture of triumph, a reminder that the entire region would become subject to the Israelite forces, Joshua's commanders put their feet on the necks of the defeated monarchs and slew them. It was a sign, Joshua said, of what the Lord will do all over Canaan (verses 22-26).

That long day was the commencement of what Bible scholars have called the southern campaign. During the ensuing weeks the Israelite forces would move with lightning speed to complete the conquest of the allied cities and other towns in their way. By the time the mission ended, they had eliminated seven cities with their inhabitants: Makkedah, Libnah, Lachish, Eglon, Hebron, Debir, and Gezer (verses 29-39).

We might note that this list of conquered cities does not synchronize with the primary listing given in verses 3-5. At the same time, it includes other cities that Adoni-Zedek did not enlist in the coalition. Here's how it all breaks down:

    1. Cities mentioned in the primary list (Joshua 10:3-5):

        Jerusalem

        Hebron

        Jarmuth

        Lachish

        Eglon

    2. Cities in the primary listing not mentioned among the defeated entities in verses 28-42:

Jerusalem

Jarmuth

3. Cities not included in the original five, but mentioned in verses 28-42:

Makeddah (verse 28)

Libnah (verses 29, 30)

Gezer (verse 33)

Debir (verse 38)

Clearly, most of the additional cities lay in Joshua's way and were, indeed, part of his military agenda from the start. (See the map entitled Israel's First Campaigns West of the Jordan [*The Seventh-day Adventist Bible Commentary*, vol. 2, p. 206] for the possible movements of Joshua's army during the southern campaign.) Their inclusion in the list of defeated territories should not surprise us. Gezer, which was clearly off Joshua's path, probably became involved by voluntarily sending soldiers to fight Israel. But it's strange to find that Jerusalem, whose king had instigated the conflict in the first place, does not appear among the defeated cities. And that's because Joshua's forces never completely captured it. Even with the entire region subdivided and the area of Jerusalem allotted to the tribe of Judah, they "could not dislodge the Jebusites, who were living in Jerusalem" (Joshua 15:63). The Jebusites, in fact, held their ground (perhaps, however, with significant setbacks—see Judges 1:8) all through the period of the Judges and beyond—until David finally defeated them four centuries later, about 1000 B.C. (see 2 Sam. 5:6-9).

The summary passage at the end of Joshua 10, however, seems to include the entire southern area in its sweep: "So Joshua subdued the whole region," it says, "including all the hill country, the Negev, the western foothills and the mountain slopes, together with all their kings" (verse 40). In other words, the southern threat had been eliminated.

## Echoes of Armageddon

I close this chapter by returning to the phenomenon of a halted sun.

For quite some time now I have wondered why such a spectacular phenomenon had to occur in connection with a battle seemingly of such little consequence as that of Gibeon. Why such a dramatic demonstration relative to such a puny conflict—in fact, one precipitated by impostors?

I know now that that line of reasoning is incorrect. For as we have seen, this was no ordinary battle. The Israelite-Gibeonite alliance and the conflict it engendered held immense strategic importance for the whole mission of Israel in Canaan, thwarting, as it did, the emerging pan-Canaanite coalition. The military engagement triggered by the treaty with Gibeon wrecked the southern alliance and resulted in Israel's securing the southern half of the country. With the south subdued, and Jericho and Ai in the middle eliminated, Israel could now concentrate its attention on the next major segment of the region: the north.

Thus the battle of Gibeon was a pivotal one. Victory here must be swift and decisive—or hostile forces might regroup. Hence the lengthening of the day. The thoroughness of the operation that the miracle permitted foiled the southern threat, and fundamentally changed the military equation.

The nature of the battle of Gibeon makes it a type of earth's final conflict, the battle of Armageddon (see Rev. 16:12-16), in which the evil forces of the entire world—north, south, east, and west—deploy in opposition to the God of heaven and His last-day remnant people. The eschatological Joshua will speak this time, and the powers of the heavens will be shaken. As John puts it, "loud voices in heaven" will announce that "the kingdom of the world has become the kingdom of our Lord and of his Christ, and he will reign for ever and ever" (Rev. 11:15).

## Questions for Reflection
### Joshua 9; 10

1. In their conversations with the Gibeonites, Joshua and the other leaders failed to seek God's direction, probably feeling that the matter was simple enough for them to handle. How, because of your expertise and training, might you face a similar danger?

2. How faithful are you to the commitments you make? Why should you keep your promise even at great inconvenience to

yourself? What are some times that it would be wise not to honor promises or commitments made?

3. Joshua's command that the sun stand still flowed from his deep burden to complete the mission of the day. How strong is your sense of urgency to finish the Lord's work today? How should you demonstrate that urgency?

---

[1] J. M. Miller and G. M. Tucker, *The Book of Joshua,* p. 76.

[2] E. G. White, *Patriarchs and Prophets,* p. 506.

[3] M. H. Woudstra, *The Book of Joshua,* pp. 153, 154.

[4] White, *Patriarchs and Prophets,* p. 506.

[5] P. P. Enns, *Joshua,* p. 83.

[6] G. Mitchell, *Together in the Land,* p. 87.

[7] *The Seventh-day Adventist Bible Commentary,* vol. 2, p. 226.

[8] Martin Noth, *The History of Israel,* 2nd ed. (New York: Harper and Row, 1958), p. 3.

Chapter 7

# The Fighting Over

## Joshua 11; 12

At the end of Joshua 10 the Israelite army has returned to its home base at Gilgal. The southern campaign has ended, and the region is secure.

It would not be a long respite, however, for battle noises, already commenced in the north, would accelerate to fever pitch as Jabin, king of Hazor, summoned the northern wing of the now-defunct pan-Canaanite military confederation to meet at the Waters of Merom, the staging area for the ensuing offensive against Israel.

Scripture does not tell us how Joshua learned about the ominous gathering. But he and the entire Israelite army would surprise the enemy once again. This northern campaign would be the final major struggle for Canaan. At its end, all effective hostile resistance to Israel was eliminated, all general fighting ceased, and the land experienced "rest from war" (Joshua 11:23).

### Northern Coalition Forms

We do not know how events would have developed had the Gibeonites not made their historic visit to Israel at Gilgal (Joshua 9:3-24). But based on subsequent developments, we'd have to say that that strategic visit, with its resulting treaty, was the catalyst that sparked the wider battle for the capture of Canaan. In keeping with the rapid pace of the narrative (as we noted in the introduction), the struggle, begun in earnest in Joshua 10, was all over by the end of Joshua 11. When one considers that these developments constitute the pivotal events in the book of Joshua—and, indeed, constitute the whole purpose of the Exodus movement—one can only be impressed by the economy of detail used in telling the story.

# The Fighting Over

By now we've become familiar with the (more or less) identical literary formula by which our author prepares us for each major struggle in the battle for Palestine. It runs as follows:

Joshua 5:1: "Now when all the Amorite kings west of the Jordan and all the Canaanite kings along the coast heard how the Lord had dried up the Jordan . . ." This sets the backdrop for the battle of Jericho, the account of which begins at verse 13, extending through chapter 6.

Joshua 9:1: "Now when all the kings west of the Jordan heard about these things . . ." The statement anticipates the formation of the ill-fated pan-Canaanite military confederation.

Joshua 10:1: "Now Adoni-Zedek king of Jerusalem heard that Joshua had taken Ai . . ." This gives the background for the attack on Gibeon by the southern coalition—as we've seen, a pivotal development in the struggle for Canaan.

Joshua 11:1: "When Jabin king of Hazor heard [that Joshua had subdued the south] . . ." The passage introduces us to the final massive attempt to thwart Israel's drive for the control of the region.

The language of this repeated literary formula demonstrates clearly that the Israelites had become the top news item in the entire area, the subject of both ordinary conversation and intense military deliberation and planning. The mighty acts of God associated with Israel's advance had struck terror everywhere.

It's noteworthy that in every case the entire Canaanite confederation—whether actually formed or simply contemplated—comprised the nations within the geographical borders of Canaan itself. There was, in other words, no appeal for help outside the region. Nor did a single foreign power attempt to intervene. Any such intervention would have terribly complicated the situation for Israel.

And why, indeed, was there no such intervention? For example, why did the Egyptians not consider it in their best interest to punish and humiliate these former slaves of theirs who'd brought such misery upon them? Had they simply learned the lesson of leaving Israel to itself? Or had they been so thoroughly devastated by the Exodus and the plagues preceding it (see Ex. 10:7) that they couldn't possibly have mounted an effective counteroffensive even if they had wanted to?

Perhaps it was both. By the reign of Amenhotep III (c. 1412-

# Crossing Jordan

1375 B.C.), "the high tide of Egyptian power [had begun] to ebb." With "her military might . . . ending," Egypt found it difficult to intervene in the affairs of Syria and Palestine. "Conditions in Palestine were thus such as to make possible the Israelite conquest, without their having to meet the strength of the Egyptian Empire."[1] At the same time, the Hittite Empire in the north and west of Palestine was just coming into its own and as yet did not have the resources to get involved in foreign interventions.[2] Thus the Lord had timed the conquest of Canaan to occur at a period when "the political world was in a state of flux, and no power from without was in a position to come to the rescue of the peoples of Canaan."[3]

Joshua 11:1-5 describes the formation of a military confederation to defeat the Israelites. I believe that here, as was the case in the south, it was in God's providence that such an alliance should form. It was fortuitous for Israel to be able to engage the bulk of these kings (see the list in Joshua 12:9-24) in just two decisive battles rather than face them in a multitude of exhausting encounters.

All this notwithstanding, the struggle (as the text informs us) took "a long time" (Joshua 11:18), and we can only imagine how much additional time it would have required had the number of major encounters not been reduced to just two. The formation of these coalitions obviated the need for Israel to fight 31 separate battles up and down the area. In the one southern offensive, for example, Israel destroyed at least nine kings (and the cities of eight of them) (see Joshua 10:16-42). And the coalition now forming in the north would bring perhaps as many as 15 kings together in one place. Thus the very developments that at first looked most menacing to Israel would turn out, in the end, to Israel's advantage.

## Where It All Happened

With Joshua 11 the need to consult a map of ancient Palestine increases dramatically. For whereas all the geography required to understand what's happening in Joshua 2-6, for example, was the location of Shittim, Jordan, Gilgal, and Jericho, now in Joshua 11 we can hardly comprehend what's going on without a map of ancient Palestine open in front of us and a Bible dictionary (if possible) by our side. The text comes alive only as one takes the time to tag the location of at least the major places listed.

Of course, we can no longer positively identify all the localities named in the chapter. But a look at those that are known (see Map VI in the *Seventh-day Adventist Bible Dictionary*) gives a good idea of the extensive spread of the northern coalition. From Hazor in the center (just west of the northern stretch of the Jordan River, along the Sea of Galilee) the area reached clear to the Mediterranean coast; and from Naphoth Dor (near the port city of Dor) all the way to Sidon, the northernmost point of Canaan (Joshua 11:1-3).

The list of rulers and territories at the beginning of Joshua 11 moves from specific to general. The author lists Jobab, king of Madan, by name, and also the kings of Shimron and Acshaph. After these, however, the description becomes more vague, with no specific mention of particular rulers. Thus we hear of "the northern kings" (see verse 2) who were

- "in the mountains,"
- "in the Arabah south of Kinnereth," and
- "in the western foothills."

Finally, in a kind of catchall (see verse 3) the passage goes on to indicate that Jabin's call also included

- "the Canaanites in the east and west,"
- "the Amorites, Hittites, Perizzites, and Jebusites in the hill country," and
- "the Hivites below Hermon in the region of Mizpah."

This describes a fairly extensive area. And had all the entities occupying it turned on Israel, as individual states, such a development could have thrown Joshua and his forces into total chaos. Instead (in the providence of God, I believe) they all "joined forces and made camp together" (verse 5).

But why did they gather at the Waters of Merom? The area was about 4,000 feet (1,219 meters) above sea level and extremely inconvenient for chariot maneuvers.[4] It was a location, moreover, that necessitated the dismantling of the chariots so that the armies could carry them up the elevation and reassemble them for battle.[5]

I think we may be justified in assuming that the forces of the confederation had not intended to fight at that location. Why would they expect to meet Israel there? Situated on high ground, the place was more likely a staging area for the combined attack, with the offensive launched from there. Apart from its elevation and the abundance of water, the locality might also have held other strategic advantages unknown to us today.

## The Critical Confrontation

In connection with the southern offensive, the author informs us about the Israelite army's all-night march on the enemy, amassed outside the city of Gibeon (Joshua 10:9). Here, however, we receive no details of the Israelite advance on the northern coalition.

And there are other unknowns. How much time, for example, had elapsed since Joshua and the army returned to Gilgal after defeating the southern kings? How much time did the army have to recoup? And how did Joshua learn the northern kings were gathering against Israel?

On that last point we need to remember the critical importance of Gibeon's defection. For if Gibeon was an important part of the proposed pan-Canaanite loop, it certainly retained reams of valuable intelligence for its new ally, intelligence that might have included the fact that the Waters of Merom would be the staging area for the northern forces. Had Gibeon not compromised the original scheme, Israel would most likely have faced a coordinated attack from the north under Jabin (staged from Merom) and from the south under Adoni-Zedek (probably operating out of the vicinity of Gibeon).

By whatever means, Joshua received information of the ominous gathering and headed north to confront the coalition. The distance between Gilgal and Lake Semechonitis (the Waters of Merom) was considerable—about 70 miles (113 kilometers). Josephus indicates that it was a five-day march.[6]

Therefore, unlike the case with Gibeon, Israel's approach was no overnight affair—it could not be. But given the time it would have taken to cover that distance, why did the allied forces not learn of Israel's advance? How did the Israelites manage to get as far north as the Waters of Merom undetected—and thus come against the enemy "suddenly" (Joshua 11:7)? *The Seventh-day Adventist Bible Commentary* suggests, plausibly, that they probably went north by a route that took them along the eastern side of the Jordan, through friendly territory—territory already subdued by Israel and occupied by the East Jordan tribes.[7] To have taken a route along the west bank of the Jordan would have led the Israelite army through enemy territory, sparking unwanted attention, interference, and resistance.

The forces Israel was about to confront were both numerous and formidable. According to the text, the northern kings assembling at Merom had come out "with all their troops and a large number of horses and chariots—a huge army, as numerous as the sand on the seashore" (verse 4). Josephus states that the combined force numbered 300,000 infantry, 10,000 horsemen, and 20,000 chariots.[8] From a purely military point of view (if Josephus is correct) the Canaanites had an overwhelming advantage—a realization that must have sent Joshua to his knees again, seeking fresh guidance and assurance from the Lord.

What we see here in the book of Joshua is that before every new offensive God comes to His servant with words of encouragement and assurance. It is as if the one declaration of commitment and support given at the beginning (see Joshua 1:9) is not enough. As if, in our humanness, we need repeated pledges of God's unfailing help and guidance, continual reinforcements of His love.

As before (see Joshua 3:7, 8; 5:13-15; 8:1; 10:7, 8), God came to Joshua on the eve of the critical encounter. The Lord said to him, "Do not be afraid of them, because by this time tomorrow I will hand all of them over to Israel, slain" (Joshua 11:6). It is interesting to note here that in the Hebrew, the word "I" is emphatic, God meaning to say "I myself will hand them over" to you within 24 hours. We would have to assume that Joshua and Israel had by that time already arrived in the vicinity of the Waters of Merom.

But just as we have no details as to how Joshua and his forces made their way to Merom, 70 miles away from Gilgal, so we also have no information, unlike the case in previous battles, of the method God used to defeat the allied forces. The battle of Gibeon, for example, included supernaturally generated confusion, a hailstorm, and the halting of the sun in its circuit (Joshua 10:9-14). Here, however, the author has provided very few details and indicates no specific supernatural intervention. The one significant clue we have comes in Joshua 11:7: "So Joshua and his whole army came against them *suddenly* . . . and attacked them."

# Crossing Jordan

The absence of detail regarding this historic encounter has led to some imaginative reconstruction of how events might have developed in this strategic struggle. Garstang, for example, has suggested the following scenario: informed about the amassing of the combined armies at Merom "and realizing the vital importance of forestalling their next move . . . [Joshua] led his troops northward over the hills in a forced march." Caught by surprise, with their chariots disassembled (as they would have been for transport up the mountain), the northern armies found themselves at a terrible disadvantage. A special detail of Israelite soldiers perhaps ran up and down the tethering lines, maiming and liberating the horses. This would have produced "a commotion that could not be quelled, leading to stampede and panic."[9]

Whatever the strategy Israel employed, the text leaves no doubt that the swiftness and unexpectedness of its attack completely threw the allied forces into a panic. And the author makes the additional point that it was "the Lord [who] gave them into the hand of Israel" (verse 8).

The outcome is also clear from the text:

1. Israel pursued the enemy westward all the way to the Mediterranean coast—to Sidon and Misrephoth Maim—and northeastward to the Valley of Mizpah, all above the 33rd parallel (Joshua 11:8; see Map VI, *Seventh-day Adventist Bible Dictionary*).

Troops naturally tend to flee toward their home base, and the direction of the pursuit here probably represented that of the home cities of the fleeing soldiers. It must have stretched Joshua and his forces to the limit to give chase in two (and possibly even three) directions simultaneously.

2. Joshua, as instructed, burned the chariots of the allied forces and hamstrung their horses (verses 6, 9). What's described here in regard to the animals would have inflicted some pain, but did not constitute cruelty as such. The common understanding is that the Israelite soldiers cut the tendons of the legs of the horses so as to make them ineffective for future military purposes. Given the gravity of the situation and the potential danger of these creatures as instruments of war, such action would have been totally justified.

As for the chariots, they were to be burned. Israel was not to confiscate them for future use. It was God's intention that His people should put their confidence not in either horses or chariots (see Deut. 17:16), but in the Lord. Were they allowed to keep these implements of war, they would eventually come to think that their strength lay in such armaments. So the command was given: "You are to hamstring their horses and burn their chariots" (Joshua 11:6).

3. The Israelites captured Hazor, the ringleader of the pact, killed its king and its entire population, and, finally, burned down the city (verses 10, 11).

By all accounts, Hazor was a comparatively large and impressive city in the thirteenth century B.C., the very time when the Israelites were advancing into Canaan. Located some eight miles (13 kilometers) north of the Sea of Galilee and just south of the Waters of Merom, it was situated on the "way of the sea," a road that ran from Egypt across Megiddo to Qatna in the north. "Its size was much larger than that of other prominent cities in Canaan."[10] With such a central location, it could command access to the entire region, north and south and toward the coast.

The other outcomes of the northern campaign—indeed, the whole struggle for Canaan—are not as easy to define as the three results just listed. But in the section that follows, I attempt to grapple with the issue.

### Understanding What Happened

The difficulty we have understanding precisely what happened is not uncommon in the study of ancient historical texts. If, as we have assumed, the account that constitutes the book of Joshua was written fairly close to the events themselves, we would expect the writer to have taken for granted many of the details we now regard as missing. They're absent, perhaps, because they'd been so well known to the writer's contemporaries. Any effort to reconstruct the situation must, therefore, take that element into consideration.

We look now at some of the areas that have given readers trouble through the years:

1. *The extent of the destruction.* The passage indicates that "Joshua took all these royal cities and their kings and put them to the sword.

He totally destroyed them, as Moses the servant of the Lord had commanded" (verse 12).

The first intimation that we should not take the words absolutely at face value comes in the passage itself, which immediately says that Israel, however, "did not burn any of the cities built on their mounds—except Hazor, which Joshua burned" (verse 13). And even in the case of Hazor, we discover that the destruction was not as final as it might appear in the text. For less than probably 100 years later, in the time of the judges, we find the Israelites oppressed by this very entity, under a king by the same name as the one mentioned in our text (Judges 4:1-3). ("Jabin" was perhaps a dynastic title rather than a personal name.)

Did Joshua really comply, then, with the stipulations of the covenant? What did Moses command?

Deuteronomy contains two sets of specifications regarding Israel's treatment of enemy nations in time of war. The first had to do with those far removed from Israel's own borders. In such cases, Israel had permission to extend an offer of peace. Only if the particular nation refused the proposal was Israel authorized to attack it. Upon capturing it, Joshua was to execute the men but save "the women, the children, the livestock and everything else in the city" as plunder for themselves (Deut. 20:14).

The second set of conditions involved those towns and cities physically close to Israel. In those cases, the command was to "not leave alive anything that breathes." Israel was to "completely destroy them—the Hittites, Amorites, Canaanites, Perizzites, Hivites and Jebusites" (Deut. 20:16, 17).

In the face of these last stipulations, L. Daniel Hawk has raised several important questions about the integrity of some of the claims made in Joshua 11. For example, did Joshua and Israel capture "all" the land? Why was Hazor the only city burned? Did Israel and Joshua really obey the requirements of the covenant, as the narrative claims? Was not their failure to completely destroy the Canaanites a violation of the covenant's conditions? Did they really destroy all the fleeing forces, as the record seems to claim?[11]

In other words, how is Joshua different from Saul, who, while clearly violating Yahweh's express command to "totally destroy" the

# The Fighting Over

Amalekites and "everything that belongs to them," greeted Samuel with the words "I have carried out the Lord's instructions" (1 Sam. 15:3, 13)? But if you have indeed carried out the Lord's instructions, Samuel said to him, "what then is this bleating of sheep in my ears? What is this lowing of cattle that I hear?" (verse 14).

So in this case, why, in the face of obvious discrepancies, should we take Joshua's statement at face value—that he had indeed complied with the stipulations of the covenant?

It's a fair question, and brings to the fore the way in which we should understand those very requirements.

In the first place, we would have to say that the covenant stipulations were not quite as simple as the single command given to Saul in one specific case. In the case of Saul, moreover, the king obviously had something to hide and was probably embarrassed by the noisiness of the evidence. In regard to the conquest, however, it is the narrator himself who puts on the table all the cards. The author does not attempt to hide anything. And so we would have to conclude that the biblical writer genuinely regards Israel as being in compliance with the requisites of the Mosaic covenant. And the question then becomes: *How could this be? How did the author of Joshua understand such compliance?*

What seems to be happening, as is common to human experience throughout all time, is that there usually exist written and unwritten understandings that mitigate what might be considered strict, literal compliance to a particular set of commands, regulations, or provisions. In this case, for example, one would have to bring into focus the intimations found in Deuteronomy 7:22. There Moses indicated that "the Lord your God will drive out those nations before you, little by little. You will not be allowed to eliminate them all at once, or the wild animals will multiply around you" (cf. Ex. 23:29, 30).

And the clear implication of Deuteronomy 6:10, 11 is that not all the cities were to be destroyed either. For in that passage Moses speaks, without censure, of Israel living in "a land with large, flourishing cities you did not build, houses filled with all kinds of good things you did not provide, wells you did not dig, and vineyards and olive groves you did not plant." Further evidence that Israel was not to destroy everything, and that the process for the total displacement of the indigenous nations was to be a gradual one, appears in one of the developments in the book of Judges. Angry with His people for violating the covenant, God threatened to "no longer drive out before them any of the nations Joshua left when he died. I will use them," said the Lord, "to test Israel and see whether they will keep the way of the Lord and walk in it as their forefathers did" (Judges 2:21, 22). The text goes on to add that it was "the Lord [who] had allowed those nations to remain; he did not drive them out at once by giving them into the hands of Joshua" (verse 23).

The point, therefore, is that we do not have a cut-and-dried situation before us. The covenant stipulations were complex, and we must assume that, given his proximity to the events, Joshua understood their implications much better than we do today—and indeed, genuinely saw himself as having acted in conformity with them.

2. *The territory captured.* In Joshua 11:16, 17 we have a wrap-up of the territories captured in this vigorous northern drive (cf. Joshua 12:7, 8)—the entire half of northern Palestine west of the Jordan River, reaching above the 33rd parallel and going well beyond the classical "from Dan to Beer-sheba" designation.[12]

The narrative makes it clear that the victory was not an overnight affair. It took "a long time" (Joshua 11:18). Incidentally, verses 6 and 18 are not in conflict. The second reference is to the war as a whole, while the first speaks of the decisive battle of the war that was to take place the following day.

This parallels closely what happened at the battle of Gibeon. That struggle led to the death of all five invading kings (Joshua 10:26). And even though the passage indicates that the Israelite army destroyed the enemy forces "almost to a man" (verse 20), it still did not mark the end of the southern struggle. As we learn from verses 29-39, the Israelite army then pressed the battle to Libnah, Lachish, Hebron, and Debir—an operation that must have taken several days, perhaps even weeks.

## Comparing the Two Campaigns

The northern campaign was certainly not a carbon copy of the southern, but it did have striking similarities. In both cases, one king called the coalition together—Adoni-Zedek in the south (Joshua

10:1); Jabin in the north (Joshua 11:1). Israel was able to come upon the enemy unawares—"by surprise" in the south (Joshua 10:9); "suddenly" in the north (Joshua 11:7). And the enemy forces had amassed in a single locality—on the outskirts of Gibeon in the south (Joshua 10:5) and at the Waters of Merom in the north (Joshua 11:7). On the eve of both offensives Joshua received fresh and direct assurances from the Lord not to be afraid—almost in the identical words (compare Joshua 10:8 with 11:6). Israel routed the enemy in each campaign, with enemy soldiers scrambling to reach their respective home bases (Joshua 10:20; 11:8).

And just as Israel had much work to do after the decisive battle in the south, so also in the north. Following the important initial engagement, Joshua and his forces "turned back and captured Hazor," thus focusing first on the leading city of the coalition (Joshua 11:10). That victory behind them, they then proceeded to take "all these royal cities and their kings and put them to the sword" (verse 12). It took time and suggests that the promise of Joshua 11:6 ("by this time tomorrow") had to do with the outcome of the initial confrontation—the decisive battle—and must not be seen in contradiction to verse 18, which refers to the subsequent struggle for the conquest of the cities and towns of the coalition.

Moreover, the "long time" mentioned in Joshua 11:18 not only refers to the northern campaign but encompasses the southern as well—a conclusion based on the description in verses 16, 17 of the territories conquered, a list that includes much if not all of the areas covered in Joshua 10:40-42. So the "long time" of Joshua 11:18 represents the time taken to execute the total campaign—south and north.

How long was that time? We get a clue from Joshua 14:7-12. Here Caleb reminds Joshua of Moses' promise to give him the hill country of Hebron as an inheritance. That was 45 years ago, Caleb said (verse 10). And since the event to which Caleb was referring (see Num. 14:24) took place two years after the Israelites left Egypt, this means 38 years existed between it and the attack on Jericho, as Israel entered Canaan. Therefore to calculate the time occupied by the conquest, we simply subtract 38 from 45, giving us seven years.

One would assume, however, that Israel spent most of that protracted seven-year period on the northern campaign. The southern victories seemed to have come much more rapidly. Jericho actually came down in one fell swoop—with a shout (Joshua 6:20). Ai, as soon as Israel was spiritually ready, fell within a matter of hours (Joshua 8:9-26). The decisive battle of the southern campaign terminated in one extended day, with some additional time—weeks at the most—for the complete subjugation of the surrounding cities (Joshua 10:7-43).

Yet another factor made the southern campaign disproportionately shorter. In that conflict the five invading kings made the mistake of fleeing in the same direction and then hiding together—a most convenient arrangement for their pursuers (see Joshua 10:16-18). Apparently determined to avoid a repetition of that tragic blunder (Joshua 11:1 seems to indicate that Jabin and the others had received a full report of what had happened in the south), the northern kings escaped in different directions. And we have to assume that many (if not all) of them made it safely back to home base, there being no direct intimation that any of them had been killed or captured at the Waters of Merom.

We'd have to say, then, that the divine assurance to Joshua on the eve of the battle (that within 24 hours God will hand "all of them over to Israel, slain" [Joshua 11:6]) does not specifically refer to the assembled kings. In the context it can apply equally to the rest of the army. We clearly see this in the verses immediately following, which tell us that Joshua and the army "came against *them* suddenly," that "the Lord gave *them*" into Israel's hands, and that Israel "defeated *them* and pursued *them*" (verses 7, 8). So while the assembled kings would obviously have been Israel's chief targets, it's quite clear that the "them" in the passage is much broader than the kings themselves.

That last detail points to yet another factor that made the northern campaign more protracted than the southern. In the south Joshua destroyed the invading forces "completely—almost to a man," and only the "few who were left reached their fortified cities" (Joshua 10:20). The situation in the north was much more complex. Clearly Israel had struck a decisive blow on the first day of battle when it attacked and defeated the enemy, as we have noted (Joshua 11:7, 8). But we need not assume that verse 8 (Israel pursued the enemy "until no survivors were left") implies that Israel destroyed the entire allied army. It means, rather, that the Israelite army did not slacken the attack until it had eliminated as many fleeing enemy soldiers as possible.

The clear indication of the narrative is that many military personnel—not "few," as in the southern campaign—escaped, however bruised and battered, back to their own home bases. And we may be sure that the respective kings, learning well from what happened in the south, had beaten hasty retreats back to their own cities. Joshua would from then on encounter them, one at a time, "for a long time" (verse 18). In the process, Israel would learn the lesson that victory is not always swift, nor does it always come easily.

## Another Major Milepost

The content and structure of Joshua 12 indicates that, insofar as the book is concerned, we have come to a major milepost in the history of Israel, namely, the culmination of Israel's military campaign for the occupation of Canaan (and certain adjunct territories). Joshua treats this whole operation as a unit, as evidenced by the fact that he reaches back more than 40 years into the past (under Moses' leadership) to begin his listing of Israel's conquest: Sihon, king of the Amorites, and Og, king of Basham (Joshua 12:2-5)—both in Transjordan. And he gives the extent of their territories: "From the Arnon Gorge to Mount Hermon, including all the eastern side of the Arabah" (verse 1; cf. Num. 21). As you locate this area on the map (see Map VI, *Seventh-day Adventist Bible Dictionary*), between the 31st and 34th parallels, you will notice that it's quite extensive. And it's remarkable that this large area east of the Jordan had never been part of God's original promise to Abraham. Instead, Israel seized it only when its rulers, refusing Israel's harmless request to pass through their territories, initiated unprovoked, hostile action.

The conquest on the eastern side was not, however, without major gaps. The territory of Moab, for example, remained untouched, as well as Edom to the south. And as Israel pressed north against the Amorites, they halted at the fortified border of Ammon (Num. 21:24). Thus the territories of Ammon, Moab, and Edom remained intact. God forbade Israel to engage those nations in war or seize their territories because of close blood ties and because of commitments God had made to their ancestors (see Deut. 2:4-6, 9, 18, 19). In succeeding centuries they would become a threat to Israel and an offense to God (see, for example, Judges 10:17, 18; 11:4-32; 1 Kings 11:33; Jer. 9:25, 26).

The rest of Joshua 12 lists the kings defeated by Joshua and his army west of the Jordan—31 in all, a number meant to indicate, among other things, that the military mission west of the river was much more extensive and complicated than that on the east.

Joshua 12 also gives the boundaries of this newly acquired territory: the northern boundary was Baal Gad in the Valley of Lebanon (verse 7); the southern was Mount Halak, near Seir (verse 7). Between these two points lay "the hill country, the western foothills, the Arabah, the mountain slopes, the desert and the Negev" (verse 8). This territory coincided, of course, with that of the now-dispossessed nations that had intended to form the pan-Canaanite alliance against Israel—the "Hittites, Amorites, Canaanites, Perizzites, Hivites and Jebusites" (verse 8).

You will notice that Deuteronomy 7:1 had listed seven nations to be expelled from Canaan, whereas Joshua 12 mentions only six, the Girgashites being omitted. "It has been suggested that the Girgashites had by now either been incorporated with some of these other nations or, according to the tradition of the Jews, had withdrawn into Africa on the approach of Israel under Joshua." Previously they had inhabited an area to the north of the Sea of Galilee.[13]

But of the whole conquest, perhaps the part that must have given Joshua and Israel the greatest satisfaction was the victory over the Anakites. After all, they were the people who'd struck such terror into the hearts of the spies, leading to the crisis at Kadesh (see Num. 13:26-14:25). Their mention comes at the end of chapter 11: "At that time Joshua went and destroyed the Anakites from the hill country: from Hebron, Debir and Anab, from all the hill country of Judah, and from all the hill country of Israel. Joshua totally destroyed them and their towns. No Anakites were left in Israelite territory" (Joshua 11:21, 22).

Despite this strong statement, some of the Anakites still survived "in Gaza, Gath and Ashdod" (verse 22) and would resist the Israelites in later years—the most spectacular occasion being the confrontation between the young David and Goliath of Gath (1 Sam. 17). But their back had been broken, so to speak, and the dreaded race of giants that had struck fear into the hearts of Israel was in retreat.

The entire land of Canaan is now subdued and effectively brought under Israel's control. God's people have put down all significant resistance. And "the land [experiences] rest from war" (Joshua 11:23).

As Joshua and the rest of Israel reflect upon the amazing accomplishment, their thoughts must have paralleled that expressed hundreds of years later by an Israelite sage: "There is no wisdom, no insight, no plan that can succeed against the Lord. The horse is made ready for the day of battle, but victory rests with the Lord" (Prov. 21:30, 31).

### Questions for Reflection
Joshua 11; 12

1. Again and again God came to Joshua with words of encouragement and assurance. How keenly do you sense a daily need for God?

2. After defeating the coalition forces at Merom, Joshua pursued the fleeing armies "until no survivors were left." What spiritual lessons might you draw from that experience? What does it say about the need to gain complete victory in the struggle with evil?

3. Throughout the mission of the conquest Joshua was careful to follow the divine stipulations, as handed down through Moses. How concerned are you to adhere to God's directives in the affairs of your personal life?

---

[1] *The Seventh-day Adventist Bible Commentary,* vol. 2, p. 171.

[2] *Ibid.*

[3] *Ibid.*

[4] M. H. Woudstra, *The Book of Joshua,* p. 191.

[5] See John Garstang, *The Foundations of Bible History: Joshua, Judges* (New York: R. R. Smith, 1931), p. 196.

[6] *Antiquities* 5. 1. 18.

[7] See the map entitled Israel's Last Campaign West of the Jordan (*The Seventh-day Adventist Bible Commentary,* vol. 2, p. 230), showing Israel's possible route north.

[8] *Antiquities* 5. 1. 18.

[9] Garstang, p. 196.

[10] Woudstra, p. 187.

[11] See L. Daniel Hawk, *Every Promise Fulfilled: Contesting Plots in Joshua* (Louisville, Ky.: Westminster/John Knox Press, 1991), pp. 44-52, in which the author grapples at length with this issue.

[12] J. A. Grindel, *Joshua, Judges,* p. 35.

[13] *The Seventh-day Adventist Bible Commentary,* vol. 2, p. 237.

Chapter 8

# Taking Human Life:
# The Character of God in Joshua

## Joshua 6-12

*If we're to bear an effective Christian witness in the world, it's essential that we have a correct perception of God's character. We cannot have, nor can we convey to others, a sense of assurance and worth unless we are ourselves persuaded that the One in whom it all centers is loving and just and good. Accordingly, we must take in all seriousness any concerns that call into question God's compassion and justice.*

*The present chapter grapples with just such concerns arising from the book of Joshua. Against the background of certain critical passages in the document, it attempts to draw out the implications for the character of God. Many Christians, embarrassed by what they see as a bloodthirsty God in the Old Testament, have virtually abandoned that part of Scripture, preferring instead to dwell on the New Testament, with its emphasis on Jesus and His love.*

*Yet we find not the slightest hint in the life and teachings of Jesus Himself that would suggest any discomfort whatsoever with the God revealed in the Old Testament. Indeed, if God is one, we may even go so far as to say that Jesus is, in fact, the God depicted within those very pages.*

*We cannot escape the issue raised by God's treatment of the Canaanites (or, for that matter, God's actions in the Old Testament as a whole) simply by fleeing to the New Testament. If the "gentle Jesus, meek and mild" who blessed little children 2,000 years ago in Palestine is, indeed, the same God who ordered Israel to "leave no survivors" (including children) among the ancient inhabitants of that same land, then we must come to grips with it.*

141

# Crossing Jordan

## An Angry God?

Many see the God of the Old Testament as an angry deity. A bloodthirsty God. Even a wicked God. And they find it difficult, if not impossible, to reconcile that Person with the God revealed in Jesus Christ.

The period of the conquest of Canaan, in particular, has given rise to the greatest difficulty, for here the "anger" of God seems utterly unprovoked.[1] On the face of it, one sees a group of peaceful nations calmly engaged in their own affairs, only to be rudely invaded by a horde of runaway slaves from the desert wreaking death and destruction everywhere—in the name of Yahweh and at His command.

Here, in all their starkness, is a listing of some of the offending passages in Joshua:

- "Then [the Israelite army] burned the whole city [of Jericho] and everything in it" (Joshua 6:24).
- "When Israel had finished killing all the men of Ai in the fields and in the desert . . . , all the Israelites returned to Ai and killed those who were in it. Twelve thousand men and women fell that day—all the people of Ai" (Joshua 8:24, 25).
- "The city [of Libnah] and everyone in it Joshua put to the sword. He left no survivors" (Joshua 10:30).
- "They captured [Eglon] . . . and totally destroyed everyone in it" (verse 35).
- "They left no survivors. Just as at Eglon, they totally destroyed [Hebron] and everything in it" (verse 37).
- "They took the city [of Debir], its king and its villages, and put them to the sword. Everyone in it they totally destroyed. They left no survivors" (verse 39).
- "But all the people [of those royal cities] they put to the sword until they completely destroyed them, not sparing anyone that breathed" (Joshua 11:14).
- "For it was the Lord himself who hardened their hearts to wage war against Israel so that he might destroy them totally, exterminating them without mercy" (verse 20).

Altogether 31 kings (Joshua 12:24) and scores of thousands of their people seem to have been eliminated in this way.

Now, if you're on Israel's side—or if you have no interest in the

# Taking Human Life: The Character of God in Joshua

philosophical problems of justice and human suffering—then you probably see no difficulty in these accounts. But the graphic and violent incidents before us here have given rise to some of the harshest criticism of Old Testament faith and religion through the centuries. It's what led the second-century religious activist Marcion, for example, to condemn the Old Testament and its God.

"Haunted by the problem of evil and suffering, [Marcion] came to espouse a sharp dualism which contrasted the god of [the Old Testament] with the God of mercy revealed in Jesus."[2] Though none of Marcion's writings have survived, historians have been able to piece together his major concerns through the writings of Tertullian and other prominent second- and third-century Christians who opposed him. For Marcion the Old Testament God (whom he referred to as the Demiurge—an inferior deity of temporary duration) was "at best . . . just, at worst, capricious, wrathful and violent. Although not in himself the principle of evil, he was not the principle of good."[3] This apparently unmerciful aspect of God, which Paul Volz called "das Dämonische in Jahve" ("the demonic element in Yahweh"),[4] has continued to disturb many in our times.

Herbert Muller, for example, commenting on Yahweh's covenant with Israel, saw only wanton cruelty on the part of God, who, according to him, "fulfilled his share of the [covenant] bargain by showing no concern whatever for the rest of mankind except to slaughter them when they got in the way of his own people."[5] "Joshua touches a raw nerve in most modern readers," says Richard D. Nelson. They "recoil," he says, "from its chronicle of a brutal conquest of an indigenous population, deliberate acts of genocide against them, and the colonization of their ancestral land." In addition, he indicates, "the concept of a Divine Warrior who fights the battles of one nation at the expense of others seems incompatible with enlightened notions of religion."[6]

In their commentary on Joshua, J. Gordon Harris, Cheryl A. Brown, and Michael S. Moore note that many readers have trouble "with God's sanctions and commands of violence and the way in which God gives territory to a favored nation that exterminates the inhabitants of its land." According to these scholars, "God's brutality upsets readers who expect the God of the Old Testament to love enemies as Jesus commanded."[7]

Old Testament scholar Jerry A. Gladson says that "even if we consider the Bible a progressive development of faith and ethics, it remains morally offensive to think of God approving of such wholesale slaughter, even if only for a time. Murdering entire populations in the name of God seems incredibly barbaric and cruel."[8]

One of the strongest recent voices against violence in the Old Testament is that of John J. Collins of Yale University. His presidential address to the Society of Biblical Literature in Toronto, Canada, in November 2002 began with a quote from Professor Meike Bal of the University of Amsterdam. "The Bible, of all books," Bal had written, "is the most dangerous one, the one that has been endowed with the power to kill."[9] Damning with faint praise (if I may borrow an expression from Alexander Pope), Collins says that Bal's statement "is not quite true." And why not? "The Qur'an is surely as lethal," he says.[10] Yet Bal has a point, he goes on. "The Bible appears to endorse and bless the recourse to violence."[11] "When it became clear," he said, "that the terrorists of September 11, 2001, saw or imagined their grievances in religious terms, any reader of the Bible should have had a flash of recognition." And even though "the Muslim extremists drew their inspiration from the Qur'an rather than the Bible . . . both Scriptures draw from the same wellsprings of ancient Near Eastern religion."[12] It is not hard, he said, "to find biblical precedents for the legitimation of violence."[13] For him, the injunction of Deuteronomy 20:16-18 amounts to a prescription for "ethnic cleansing."[14]

So what are we to say about Israel's action in the conquest? How do we justify killing in God's name?

## God's Preferred Plan

The biblical record hints that God's original plan for the conquest of Canaan—His preferred plan—was markedly different from what actually transpired. When God addressed the Israelite people in Egypt, for example, He made no mention of warfare or bloodshed: "And I will bring you to the land I swore with uplifted hand to give to Abraham, to Isaac and to Jacob. I will give it to you as a possession. I am the Lord" (Ex. 6:8). And as Pharaoh's army advanced to pin the Israelites down in a death trap, God's command through Moses was: "Do not be afraid. Stand firm and you will see the deliverance the Lord will bring you today. The Egyptians you see today you will never see again. *The Lord will fight for you; you need only to be still*" (Ex. 14:13, 14).

The point here is that He did not intend for the people to take up arms, even in self-defense. In fact, they had no weapons to use, even if they wished—nothing, at any rate, to match what they faced. "The Lord will fight for you," Moses told the people. "[Just] be still."

The earliest instructions concerning the actual method for conquering Canaan, so far as we know, came at Sinai: "I will send my terror ahead of you and throw into confusion every nation you encounter. *I will make all your enemies turn their backs and run. I will send the hornet ahead of you* to drive the Hivites, Canaanites and Hittites out of your way" (Ex. 23:27, 28).

Having just seen the miracle at the Red Sea and, even more recently, the awesome presence of Yahweh on Sinai, the people were mentally and psychologically prepared for such a plan. The nations of Canaan also were duly impressed that the army of the most powerful nation in the region had been supernaturally wiped out at the Red Sea by Yahweh in behalf of His people, the same ones now headed their way.

In the midst of the ensuing panic and confusion, the hornets would descend, setting off pandemonium everywhere. Given the novelty of the situation, the prevailing superstition of the people, and the general breakdown of morale, the nations of Canaan would easily have taken to their heels in the face of the Israelite advance. Israel would literally have driven them out (see Ex. 23:31).

In fact, we find evidence of this terror even 40 years later. You'll recall, for example, that Joshua found Jericho under a complete shutdown—no one entered or left the city "because of the Israelites" (Joshua 6:1). And from a woman in a position to feel the pulse of the nation, the spies had earlier learned the reason for the state of panic: "I know," she said, "that the Lord has given this land to you and that a great fear of you has fallen on us, so that all who live in this country are melting in fear because of you. We have heard how the Lord

145

dried up the water of the Red Sea for you when you came out of Egypt, and what you did to Sihon and Og, the two kings of the Amorites. . . . When we heard of it, our hearts melted and everyone's courage failed because of you, for the Lord your God is God in heaven above and on the earth below" (Joshua 2:9-11).

We may conclude, therefore, that God's original plan did not envision the carnage and bloodshed of war. As He spoke at Sinai, the people of Israel stood before Him practically defenseless in terms of weapons of war. *Evidently God intended to settle them in Canaan no less miraculously than He had brought them out of Egypt.* It's a terrible mistake to overlook this point.

### Yahweh's Adjusted Plan

Israel's 40-year delay in the desert was not according to God's plan. He had brought the people out of Egypt at the optimum time for accomplishing His will. We have indications that His preferred plan, frustrated only by Israel's faithlessness, would have been for them to travel as the crow flies, northward into Canaan, passing right through Philistine territory (Ex. 13:17, 18).

Though they took the longer route, they were still within the optimum window for effortless conquest (so to speak) when they came to the border of Canaan from the southeast. However, demoralized by the spies' (majority) report (see Num. 13; 14), they lost faith. At the command of a disappointed God, they turned back into the wilderness (Num. 14:22-25).

Upon their return to Canaan's border some 38 years later, the entire military and psychological situation had changed. "When they were at first preparing to enter Canaan, the undertaking was attended with far less difficulty than now. . . . The fears of the nations had not been generally aroused, and little preparation had been made to oppose their progress. But when the Lord now bade Israel go forward, they must advance against alert and powerful foes, and must contend with large and well-trained armies that had been preparing to resist their approach." [15]

The new realities required an altered strategy, and it's only now that we find explicit direction to Israel to destroy the nations of Canaan: "However, in the cities of the nations the Lord your God is giving you as an inheritance, do not leave alive anything that breathes" (Deut. 20:16). For what it's worth, we should note at this point that this command involved specific nations. Israel was not to attack indiscriminately. The peoples marked for destruction were seven in number: "the Hittites, Girgashites, Amorites, Canaanites, Perizzites, Hivites and Jebusites" (Deut. 7:1).

## Slated for Destruction

Why did God target these particular nations? Was it an arbitrary decision on His part?

In Genesis 15:13-16 God informed Abraham that his descendants would be "strangers in a country not their own." "And afterward," said the Lord, "they will come out with great possessions. . . . In the fourth generation [they] will come back here [that is, to the land of Canaan], *for the sin of the Amorites has not yet reached its full measure.*"

The obvious implication of the prophecy is that the Amorites (or Canaanites—the two terms, as we have seen, are often interchangeable and serve as a catchall for the nations in focus here) were driven out on account of their "sin"—in particular, the sin of idolatry. Speaking to Israel, God says: "If you ever forget the Lord your God and follow other gods and worship and bow down to them, I testify against you today that you will surely be destroyed. Like the nations the Lord destroyed before you, so you will be destroyed for not obeying the Lord your God" (Deut. 8:19, 20). The Lord made it clear to Israel that the divine favor it enjoyed came, not because of its righteousness, but because of "the wickedness of these nations" (Deut. 9:4-6).

The broad-brush approach taken by the Pentateuch does not provide us sufficient detail as to what constituted "the wickedness of these nations." Thus we probably lack a considerable part of the evidence needed to put the conquest into proper perspective and understand better the reasons for the drastic actions prescribed.

I remember awaking from deep sleep during a trans-Pacific flight just in time to see a character from the in-flight movie pushed off a multistory building to the applause of passengers all around me. *How could they cheer such a ghastly deed?* I wondered. The answer was that they'd been following the plot—I hadn't. I was not aware of the role that particular character had played in the drama; I had no idea what horrible atrocities he might have committed. And without that knowledge, I was in no position to understand—let alone appreciate—the applause of otherwise decent fellow passengers. Today, as we look back at the period of the conquest from our historical and cultural distance, God frequently comes across in negative light. And the reason probably has much to do with our ignorance of the plot and the role played by the principals.

But we're not totally unaware as to what constituted the "wickedness" of these nations. We get a hint from one of the Mosaic stipulations: "When you enter the land the Lord your God is giving you, do not learn to imitate the detestable ways of the nations there. Let no one be found among you who sacrifices his son or daughter in the fire, who practices divination or sorcery, interprets omens, engages in witchcraft, or casts spells, or who is a medium or spiritist or who consults the dead. Anyone who does these things is detestable to the Lord, and because of these detestable practices the Lord your God will drive out those nations before you" (Deut. 18:9-12).

The warnings and prohibitions directed to Israel should be seen in the context of the customs, attitudes, and practices of the surrounding cultures—and, in particular, the targeted nations of Canaan. Indirectly the language contained in the covenant curses pointed to a Canaanite lifestyle degenerate in the extreme. From the proscriptions of the covenant we know that the people of Canaan made and worshipped graven images, dishonored parents, violated property rights, and perverted justice. Incest was common. And they even practiced sexual intercourse with animals (see Deut. 27:15-25). Hundreds of years later, at a time when the postexilic Israelite community faced the danger of social absorption among the surrounding peoples, Ezra called their attention to God's warnings to their ancestors: "The land you are entering to possess is a land polluted by the corruption of its peoples. By their detestable practices they have filled it with their impurity from one end to the other" (Ezra 9:11).

And we have external confirmation of the biblical evidence. The discovery of the mythological texts at Ras Shamra (ancient Ugarit) in 1929 has shed much light on Canaanite religion and culture. It is the general scholarly consensus that Canaanite religion was utterly depraved: "The more I studied pre-Israelite religion," said U. Oldenberg, "the more I was amazed with its utter depravity and wickedness. Indeed, there was *nothing* in it to inspire the sublime faith of Yahweh. His coming is like the rising sun dispelling the darkness of Canaanite superstition."[16]

G. Ernest Wright, noting the appeal of Canaanite religion to "the baser aspects of man," concluded that "religion as commonly practiced in Canaan . . . must have been a rather sordid and degrading business."[17] And the same evidence led John Bright to the conclusion that Canaanite religion was "an extraordinarily debasing form of paganism."[18]

Historians and archaeologists have cited the following practices as constituting significant elements of Canaanite mythology and religion:

1. *Sacred Prostitution.* "The chief emphasis in Canaanite religion . . . was upon fertility and sex. . . . It is probable that many of the mythological stories were acted out in the religious festivals, and that some of them, at least, would have been every bit as sensuous in the acting as in the telling. . . . In any event, we know that sacred prostitution, both male and female, was exceedingly common, practiced in the name of religion at the various centers of worship."[19]

2. *Homosexuality and Sex Orgies.* "Numerous debasing practices, including sacred prostitution, *homosexuality*, and various *orgiastic rites,* were prevalent."[20] In the context of this general sordidness, we also find evidence of *transvestism.* An ancient text describes the goddess Anath as "a manlike woman, dressed as a man but girded as a woman."[21]

3. *Rape.* "The most striking of the Canaanite myths of Anath preserved in Egyptian dress runs as follows: Anath was bathing on the shore of the sea, at Hamkat. Baal . . . went for a walk and *raped her,* 'leaping her as the sacred ram (of Amun) leaps, forcing her.'"[22] When Baal fell ill, as a result, the god Re, Anath's father, claimed that his sickness was "punishment for his folly, since he had . . . intercourse with [Anath] in fire and raped her with a chisel."[23]

4. *Incest.* "Both in Egypt and Canaan the notion of *incest* scarcely existed. In fact, Phoenicia and Egypt shared a general tendency to use 'sister' and 'wife' synonymously. . . . Baal was closely associated with two other goddesses. The relations between him and the goddesses Anath and Astarte were very complex. For example, Anath

was not only Baal's virgin . . . sister, but also his consort. While she was in the form of a heifer, he raped her in an epic myth '77—even 88 times.'"[24]

5. *Human Sacrifices.* "From numerous biblical and Roman allusions we know also that child sacrifice was occasionally practiced, the story of the Moabite king Mesha (2 Kings 3:27) immediately coming to mind."[25] In succeeding centuries Israel itself fell into this dangerous practice. The chronicler cites, among others, Ahaz, who "sacrificed his sons in the fire, following the detestable ways of the nations the Lord had driven out before the Israelites" (2 Chron. 28:3). Ahaz paid for the sacrilege, as the rest of the chapter demonstrated. And so also did Manasseh, king of Judah. The record lists a litany of atrocities committed by this miscreant, including child sacrifice. Eventually the Assyrians seized him, and dragged him away with a "hook in his nose" (2 Chron. 33:6, 11).

6. *Cannibalism.* The action of Anath upon finding the body of Baal, as revealed in an Ugaritic tablet, has given rise to the suspicion of cannibalism:

> "While Anath walked along, lamenting (?)
> The beauty of her brother . . .
> The charm of her brother—how seemly!
> She devoured his flesh without a knife
> And drank his blood without a cup."[26]

Commenting on this text, William F. Albright says: "Apparently she was carrying her gruesome burden as she devoured it. . . . The practice of *omophagia,* eating sacrifices raw, is well known. Legend pointed to Zagreus, a form of Dionysus, who was torn to pieces and devoured by the Titans. . . . (It must be remembered that cannibalism is said in early Hittite historical inscriptions to have been practiced in Armenia about the sixteenth century B.C.)"[27]

7. *Wanton Brutality.* The Baal Epic graphically portrays the goddess Anath as the agent in a general, senseless massacre: "'With might she hewed down the people of the cities, she smote the folks of the seacoast, she slew the men of the sunrise (east).' After filling her temple (it seems) with men . . . 'she hurled chairs at the youths, tables at the warriors, footstools at the men of might.' The blood was so deep

that she waded in it up to her knees—nay, up to her neck. Under her feet were human heads, above her human hands flew like locusts. In her sensuous delight she decorated herself with suspended heads, while she attached hands to her girdle. Her joy at the butchery is described in even more sadistic language: 'Her liver swelled with laughter, her heart was full of joy. . . .' Afterwards Anath 'was satisfied' and washed her hands in human gore before proceeding to other occupations." [28]

What effect would this kind of morality among the gods produce in their devotees? To what depths of depravity will a nation descend that has no higher ethical norms than that depicted among such degenerate deities? And when behaviors such as prostitution, homosexuality, and child sacrifice become acts of worship (cf. 1 Kings 14:24), then their potential to warp and debase human society does take on new and frightening dimensions.

If the egregiousness of these conditions fails to impress us; if our response to such a sordid litany of evil and debasement is a shrug of the shoulder; if in our mind such sacrilegious willfulness does not provide sufficient reason for divine action; then we're not in a position to understand the divine outrage. We can become so acclimatized to evil, and in a permissive culture so well adjusted to the abnormality of sin, that we grow callous to immorality and wickedness and wonder why God gets worked up about them.

But, says the Lord, "my thoughts are not your thoughts, neither are my ways your ways. . . . As the heavens are higher than the earth, so are my ways higher than your ways and my thoughts than your thoughts" (Isa. 55:8, 9). Regardless of our limited understanding of them, God's actions are always for the ultimate good not only of those immediately involved but the universe as a whole.

It's clear from both biblical and extrabiblical evidence that the Canaanites were totally debased and unredeemably corrupt. They had become a polluting contagion in the midst of the nations. And the order to destroy them, after hundreds of years of merciful probation, was an act of divine judgment.

## Understanding God's Actions
### 1. God Is Sovereign Creator
It's impossible to understand God's actions (or that of Israel

under His direction) apart from the concept of His role as sovereign Creator. That's the fundamental starting point. And that's why the Bible begins the way it does: "In the beginning God created the heavens and the earth" (Gen. 1:1). The ringing declaration echoes across the centuries, finding voice in all the prophets:

"The Lord is God; besides him there is no other" (Deut. 4:35).

"Yours, O Lord, is the greatness and the power and the glory and the majesty and the splendor, for everything in heaven and earth is yours. Yours, O Lord, is the kingdom; you are exalted as head over all" (1 Chron. 29:11).

"Turn to me and be saved, all you ends of the earth; for I am God, and there is no other. By myself I have sworn, my mouth has uttered in all integrity a word that will not be revoked: Before me every knee will bow; by me every tongue will swear" (Isa. 45:22, 23).

"Seven times will pass by for you until you acknowledge that the Most High is sovereign over the kingdoms of men and gives them to anyone he wishes" (Dan. 4:32).

The fact that God is sovereign Creator gives Him the intrinsic and inalienable prerogative of ownership and government. He has absolute right to receive obedience, allegiance, and worship from the whole universe of creatures, who owe their existence to Him. This right is incontrovertible and incontestable. Yahweh has absolute jurisdiction over the affairs of the universe, to direct and rule according to His inscrutable will and wisdom.

It's in this context that He addresses humanity: "I make known the end from the beginning, from ancient times, what is still to come. I say: My purpose will stand, and I will do all that I please" (Isa. 46:10).

This is reality. There is no getting around it. Job came to understand this fact when God confronted him: " 'Will the one who contends with the Almighty correct him? Let him who accuses God answer him!' Then Job answered the Lord: 'I am unworthy—how can I reply to you? I put my hand over my mouth'" (Job 40:2-4).

Job's response should serve as a deterrent to our arrogance. Proud of our ethical high ground, we tend to forget how we got there. Whence came those lofty moral principles we espouse? Did they self-generate? Were they original with us? Did our society invent them? Or do they have their source in God? The nineteenth-century poet had it right: "Every virtue we possess, and every victory won, and every thought of holiness are His alone."[29]

## 2. God Is Owner of All Creation

Once one establishes God's sovereignty, His ownership of the land comes without saying. It's incredible, however, that this point has so often been forgotten—or at least ignored by those who take exception to the Israelite conquest. That He was the real proprietor of the land God taught Israel in a most tangible way—through the sabbatical year and the year of jubilee (see Lev. 25).

It was eminently legal for Yahweh, as supreme owner of the land, to expel the Canaanites who defied Him and expropriate their land. God might have taken the same action anywhere else on this planet, but Palestine was the focus of His attention here, for reasons that we will mention below.

## 3. The Seriousness of Idolatry

Notwithstanding His ownership, God does not arbitrarily disturb or displace peoples from their homelands and settlements. But there comes the moment when His patience is exhausted and He takes action. That was the case with the Canaanites, the root cause being idolatry.

So what about idolatry makes it so odious to Yahweh?

The answer is that it represents a direct and conscious insult to God, a challenge to His right as sovereign in His own universe. It's a revolt against Yahweh, an attempt to dethrone and belittle Him. An act of cruel and willful insubordination, it represents the most egregious crime that God's creation can commit against Him. By its very nature, it invites destruction upon itself and upon its perpetrator. If we get away with it today, it's only because of God's long-suffering mercy.

Idolatry—brazen, willful, and defiant—is the sin above all sins that provokes the anger of a righteous God. Ancient Israel meted out the death penalty for it (Deut. 13:6-17), and the first of the covenant curses focused on it (Deut 27:15). To the modern mind, ancient idolatry may represent just so much superstition, but to Yahweh it was the worship of demons (Deut. 32:17; Ps. 106:36, 37), a crime that almost never failed to provoke His wrath (Deut. 32:21; Ex. 32; 1 Cor. 10:14; 2 Thess. 2:3-12).

## 4. The Use of Israel as an Instrument

We come now to perhaps the most difficult and sensitive aspect of the issue before us. Why did God employ Israel to take human life?

The resentment toward God's use of Israel as an instrument of judgment centers on three fundamental issues: the sixth commandment, the sanctity of human life, and the problem of suffering.

a. *The Sixth Commandment.* This commandment says: "Thou shalt not kill" (Ex. 20:13, KJV). But the question is: Does it forbid all killing? W. J. Harrelson thinks so. "The commandment against taking human life is not to be limited to willful homicide or murder; the Hebrew word *[ratsach]* means either to kill or to murder, without distinction."[30]

But however strongly one may defend this idea from a linguistic standpoint, the context of the command shows this position to be untenable. We see this in the fact that immediately following the proclamation of the Ten Commandments, Moses received instructions from God Himself that "anyone who strikes a man and kills him shall surely be put to death" (Ex. 21:12)—by legally constituted human authority, of course. Thus the sixth commandment is not an absolute proscription of all human killing. Rather, it forbids murder and any other form of killing not according to the will of God. In the words of Angel Rodríguez, it refers to "culpable homicide," "illegal killing."[31]

It's curious to watch what happens when high principles confront reality. Reflecting, for example, on Ecclesiastes 3:3, 8, the violence-opposing Collins (cited previously) concedes that "not all violence is necessarily to be condemned." However, he says that "few will disagree that violence is seldom a good option, and that it can be justified only as a last recourse."[32]

Precisely. And how does Collins know that the period of the conquest was not one of those "seldom" times when violence could be "justified . . . as a last recourse"? One of those "seldom" times when violence was not "necessarily to be condemned"? Collins's caveats help us understand why God might be exonerated for finally taking action after giving the Canaanites (depending on how one calculates the time) more than two centuries of probation.

Moreover, as Collins defines it, violence is "the killing of others without benefit of judicial procedure."[33] Again, precisely. And if God is, as Abraham expressed it, "the Judge of all the earth" (Gen 18:25), then shouldn't that settle the issue of the legality of the conquest?

It's not as if we're trying to get God off the hook—He doesn't need mortals to come to His rescue. Our struggle here is to understand reality as it is, not invent it.

During the conquest Israel was acting under Yahweh's express command and as His special agent. It was an extraordinary situation, to be sure—unique in Old Testament history. And it would be wholly unwarranted and dangerous to look for parallels today. The entire concept hangs, moreover, on a view of revelation that accepts the intervention of God in human affairs; that believes that God could and did communicate His will to Moses, and to Joshua, Moses' immediate successor—the insane excesses of modern fundamentalist extremists notwithstanding.

Yes, the sixth commandment is important. But it is disingenuous to use it to condemn the actions and directives of the very God who gave it.

b. *The Sanctity of Human Life.* To understand the sixth commandment as described above does not in any way detract from the sanctity of human life. Rather, it establishes an equally important principle, namely, *that that sanctity is not absolute.* In other words, human life is not so sacred that even God Himself cannot take it or order that it be forfeited. It must remain the inherent right of the One who gave life in the first place to take it back (see Deut. 32:39-41). And by extension, the One who has this inherent prerogative would also have the right to delegate that responsibility—or He would no longer be sovereign.

All this said, it's important to remember that what we're dealing with here is a case of war. It's not as though Israel went out and wantonly slaughtered innocent, defenseless populations. That image of the conquest, however widespread, is false. This was not genocide. As the record makes clear, Joshua and his forces encountered sophisticated nations, armed to the teeth for combat and ready to use their united strength to liquidate this nomadic horde (as they saw Israel) from the desert. Thus the vast majority of the adult deaths during the conquest happened in the "normal" course of hostilities.

We may debate the issue as to whether the war was just or unjust, but it would be grossly incorrect to speak about genocide. In fact, one recent student of Joshua has even argued that the killing may not have been as extensive as we often conclude from a cursory reading of the text. It would be incorrect, he contends, to take such expressions as "no survivors," for example, as meaning "that the only people left in Canaan were Israelites [and that] all others were dead." But the Israelites did not kill "until there was no one left to kill," he insists.[34] Rather, at the onset of battle, as he sees it, "both the opposing warriors on the field of battle and the population in the cities fled from the reach of the Israelites," with only those killed who'd stayed behind to fight or resist. It is thus possible to interpret the account in Joshua to mean that "everyone in the cities was killed but the majority of the people were not killed. They had run away."[35]

The question of the children is quite another matter, however—sensitive and difficult to handle. But painful as it is to express, it would have been both impractical and dangerous under the circumstances of the conquest to preserve alive the younger members of the Canaanite population. If the long memory and the element of revenge we see among contemporary peoples provide any guidance, such a course could have resulted only in widespread future ugliness, defeating the very purpose of the divine placement of Israel in that particular geographical region.

Those of us who live in secure democracies today are apt to forget the price paid for the freedoms we enjoy. That cost has not always been pretty. I often need to make a conscious effort to remember that the air I breathe now has not always been free of bomb smoke, of cannon fire, and of the smell of human blood. We cannot understand the Civil War in the United States, for example, without a conception of the horrific injustice that preceded it. Nor can the carnage of World War II make any sense to us apart from the historical precedents.

The time of Joshua and the emerging Israelite nation was one of those rough periods in human history. And a practical God equipped His people to function within the context of that situation. Even so, it bears reiterating that the conquest was a unique occurrence, an event never repeated in the whole history of Israel.

# Taking Human Life: The Character of God in Joshua

The sanctity of human life means that absolutely no one has the right to tamper with it, except He who gave it, or someone acting expressly on His behalf and at His bidding (see Rom. 13:2-4). No other issue affecting the human person can be of greater consequence. And notwithstanding the difficult questions raised by the present discussion, the overwhelming impression we get from the Old Testament as a whole is that human life is not cheap. Taking it unlawfully leads to heavy consequences.

c. *The Problem of Suffering.* In regard to the conquest, the imagination pictures multitudes of human beings *suffering* under the onslaught of Israel's sword. But is that the only way to picture it? The issue is a sensitive one, and we should handle it with appropriate care.

The first thing to notice is that in no case do we find any hint of torture on the part of Israel. Judging from the general tenor of the accounts, the Canaanites were put to death in the most humane and expedient way possible.

A second point to keep in mind is our natural tendency to be impressed by numbers. If God had ordered the death of just one incorrigibly wicked Canaanite, we'd not be discussing this issue. But we become exercised about it because large numbers of Canaanites were involved—as if that fact means, by itself, that the pain and suffering were somehow multiplied. But as C. S. Lewis once said—and in this respect I cite him guardedly—"we must never make the problem of pain worse than it is by vague talk about the 'unimaginable sum of human misery.' . . . There is no such thing as a sum of suffering, for no one suffers it. When we have reached the maximum that a single person can suffer, we have, no doubt, reached something very horrible, but we have reached all the suffering there ever can be in the universe. The addition of a million fellow-sufferers adds no more pain."[36]

Lewis's statement can easily come across as cold and heartless—almost crass. I use it here, however, only in an attempt to put matters in perspective. The primary question is not how much suffering the Canaanites (or anyone else) have had to undergo, but whether such suffering was justified. If what we have shown above about the Canaanites is correct, then their destruction certainly fell within the ambit of justice. And if the act was just, then the Israelites, under God, participated in the execution of justice.

That's an extraordinary statement, I know. Taken out of context, its philosophical and practical implications could be downright frightening. What if a contemporary political or religious entity, for example, should decide it had a similar mandate. That's why it's utterly critical to remember that in the thousands of years of Old Testament history the strategy we see in the conquest was adopted only once. It did not repeat—it was unique.

As Yahweh's agents in the fulfillment of the divine purpose in the conquest, Israel received a graphic (we may even say gruesome) window into the seriousness of idolatry and the tragic cost of rebellion. And it's notable that the particular group of Israelites involved in the conquest never succumbed to idolatry. The record says that "Israel served the Lord throughout the lifetime of Joshua and of the elders who outlived him and who had experienced everything the Lord had done for Israel" (Joshua 24:31).

Nor, remarkably, were they brutalized by the experience. On the contrary, they developed a deep sense of reverence—for God and for human life. That was the standing message conveyed by the "cities of refuge" concept (Joshua 20).

Ultimately, the issue before us boils down to the question of revelation and inspiration. If it was not God who ordered Israel into battle and decreed the execution of the Canaanites, then the Scriptures are in error, and we are looking at a horrible atrocity. *But if the Almighty did so order it* (and we can hardly exaggerate the significance of this point), *then we are looking at judgment.* Put bluntly, that's the difference between the two. If we do not make a radical distinction between atrocity and judgment, then we have before us an insoluble philosophical problem.

## 5. The Conquest of Canaan and God's Overall Purpose

Incredibly, some scholars who condemn the bloodshed of the conquest do not actually believe it really happened. Collins, whose views we cited above, is among them. It's generally recognized today, he says, "that the biblical texts are not historically reliable accounts of early Israelite history but ideological fictions from a much later time." "The archeological evidence does not support the view that marauding Israelites actually engaged in the massive slaughter of Canaanites, either in the thirteenth century or at any later time."[37]

# Taking Human Life: The Character of God in Joshua

But, he argues, such accounts "project a model of the ways in which Israel should relate to its neighbors," and, as such, shape the moral climate for a large segment of the human race. Therefore, however fictional they may be, we cannot ignore them.[38]

I believe, on the contrary, that we're dealing here with real historical events—events, moreover, that have everything to do with human salvation. The central focus of God's plan in the Old Testament was the preservation of a "remnant" through whom the Messiah might come into the world.

To refer to Israel as the "remnant" is to imply two fundamental things: (1) that all the nations had, at one time, been God's people, with Noah as their common progenitor; and (2) that there had been mass apostasy on the part of the overwhelming number of them. And it was in an attempt to rescue the situation and bring about the salvation of all people that God chose Israel as His agent.

It was a "scandalous" choice, to be sure. "The Lord your God has chosen you," Moses explained to the nation on the verge of the Promised Land, "out of all the peoples on the face of the earth to be his people, his treasured possession," not because "you were more numerous than other peoples. . . . But . . . because the Lord loved you and kept the oath he swore to your forefathers" (Deut. 7:6-8).

The statement is enough to provoke outrage on the part of the rest of us—unless we take the time to understand it. For notwithstanding such apparently radical favoritism, the remarkable phenomenon one discovers from reading the Old Testament is the almost complete absence of jingoism on the part of the inspired leaders of Israel—the prophets, in particular. A brutal honesty characterizes the text, an objectivity that does not sugarcoat the rebellious history of the nation. Israel's dirty rags—all its shameful foibles and misbehavior—hang out in the open for all to see. And again and again, like any other nation, it pays the heavy price for insubordination.

Through it all, however, God holds the feet of His special remnant to the fire—for their own good and for the wider good of the nations. And as He envisioned the ultimate fulfillment of the divine plan (notwithstanding the repeated failures of the remnant people), Jesus uttered what for the Jews would have been an astonishing comment: "I say to you that many will come from the east and the west, and will take their places at the feast with Abraham, Isaac and Jacob in the kingdom of heaven. But the subjects of the kingdom [the remnant] will be thrown outside, into the darkness" (Matt. 8:11, 12).

Strong stuff indeed! But it points to the reason God wanted Israel established in Palestine, the central commercial crossroad of the ancient world (see Map III, *Seventh-day Adventist Bible Dictionary*). Palestine lay in the midst of the overland traffic between Europe, Asia, and Africa, thus furnishing Israel "with every facility for becoming the greatest nation on earth."[39] God's ultimate intention was that through Israel He would communicate the message of His salvation to foreign ambassadors, commercial traders, and ordinary travelers passing through Israelite territory. Those visitors, in turn, would spread His message of grace to the ends of the earth (see Gen. 12:1-3; 18:18; 22:18; 26:4; Isa. 2:1-5; 56:3-8; 61:9, 10; 66:19-21).[40]

It was this plan that, wittingly or unwittingly, the Canaanites were doggedly determined to sabotage. The archenemy who goaded them in that direction knew that "the entire development of Israel's history in the land, the coming of Jesus, and the formation of the Christian church all hinged on Joshua's response to God's imperative."[41]

"To many these commands [such as those in Deuteronomy 7:2] seem to be contrary to the spirit of love and mercy enjoined in other portions of the Bible, but they were in truth the dictates of infinite wisdom and goodness. God was about to establish Israel in Canaan, to develop among them a nation and government that should be a manifestation of His kingdom upon the earth. They were not only to be inheritors of the true religion, but to disseminate its principles throughout the world. The Canaanites [once part of the people of God] had abandoned themselves to the foulest and most debasing heathenism, and it was necessary that the land should be cleared of what would so surely prevent the fulfillment of God's gracious purposes."[42]

The problem of reconciling God's "anger" with His love is insoluble only as long as we attach a trivial, sentimental meaning to the concept of love. But God's love is neither trivial nor sentimental. It's anchored in infinite wisdom. And guided by that inscrutable intelligence, He ordered drastic action against an incorrigibly degenerate and rebellious people, so as to remove the source of a spreading "cancer" that ultimately would have frustrated His gracious purpose for the rest of the nations.[43]

Are there incidents in the Old Testament I find puzzling? Yes— even troubling. But I have found that simplistic condemnation of divine action does not work. Our vision is limited, and we do not see all the evidence. Here I need to move beyond philosophy, to experience; beyond the head, to the heart.

That thought came to me during a Bible lesson on Jonah. I'd asked the class how they'd explain the fact that the same God who showed such incredible mercy to Nineveh (even expressing concern for the animals in the place—see Jonah 4:10, 11) could order Saul to "attack the Amalekites" and "put to death men and women, children and infants, cattle and sheep, camels and donkeys" (1 Sam 15:1-3). As if she'd long since resolved that troubling question in her mind, one woman in the class spontaneously gave the following answer: "When I consider the goodness of God in my own personal experience, I have no doubt whatsoever that He would never give such an order without having pretty good reasons for it."

Marcionism is not dead—in fact, it's very much alive. The temptation is strong to think that we're somehow more righteous—*more ethical*—than the God of the Old Testament. But I would say that if the New Testament did not exist, and all we had was the Old Testament, we'd still be facing, in regard to the Old Testament's fundamental teachings, a standard of morality and justice unparalleled anywhere in the world, a code of ethics that still would leave us moral dwarfs, notwithstanding all our pretensions.

God's revelation of Himself to Moses remains unsurpassed in the history of human literature: "compassionate and gracious . . . , slow to anger, abounding in love and faithfulness, maintaining love to thousands, and forgiving wickedness, rebellion and sin" (Ex. 34:6, 7). And in those immortal lines that have come down the centuries to our times, the eighth-century prophet Micah captures the shining summit of Old Testament faith: "He has told you, O mortal, what is good; and what does the Lord require of you but to do justice, and to love kindness, and to walk humbly with your God?" (Micah 6:8, NRSV).

Can the bar be raised any higher?

The overriding impression left by the inspired sources and by history is that God is far from arbitrary in His dealings with us, a point made most eloquently in Abraham's extraordinary dialogue with his divine Visitor just before the fall of Sodom. "Far be it from you," Abraham said to the Lord, "to do such a thing—to kill the righteous with the wicked, treating the righteous and the wicked alike. . . . Will not the Judge of all the earth do right?" (Gen. 18:25).

The ensuing conversation revealed that with regard to Sodom God was, indeed, doing right. Sadly, there were not to be found even 10 righteous persons—perhaps not even one—in Sodom, apart from Lot (see Gen. 18:26-32). And the implication of the story is that God does not ever destroy people without good reason. There is absolutely no capriciousness with Him.

H. H. Rowley had it right: "The wrath of God and his love are not to be set over against one another. His wrath was the expression of his love, no less than his justice was. For love is not soft indulgence; nor is the wrath of God a display of temper. [Rather], it is his holy intolerance of that which is not merely antithetical to his own character, but also hostile to man's deepest interest. His justice visits man's iniquity upon him, because that iniquity is man's own worst foe. The words rendered *righteousness* and *justice* are often used forensically in Hebrew. Their use in relation to God means that he is utterly blameless, and that if there were a court before which he could be arraigned, his acts would stand the utmost scrutiny."[44]

## It Will Happen Again

The actions of Yahweh in the conquest were meant for the ultimate good of the human race. And we cannot understand them except in the context of what Seventh-day Adventists call "the great controversy between Christ and Satan." We're in the midst of a cosmic conflict. The whole human race finds itself participants in it. And the struggle, as the apostle would put it hundreds of years after Joshua, "is not against flesh and blood, but against . . . the powers of this dark world and against the spiritual forces of evil in the heavenly realms" (Eph. 6:12).

We stand today on the borders of the heavenly Canaan. Theologically, the situation is more complex and involved, but the main outlines are clear. Like the land of Canaan for ancient Israel, this earth is to become the (eternal) home of God's people. The meek will inherit it, Jesus said (Matt. 5:5).

It means that history, in a sense, will repeat itself. *The land will be cleared again.* As the antitypical Joshua gets ready to make His move, the rulers of neo-Canaan, like their ancient counterparts thrown into panic and confusion, will hide "in caves and among the rocks," calling on inanimate nature to veil them "from the face of him who sits on the throne and from the wrath of the Lamb" (Rev. 6:15, 16). As the rebels against God's government are dispossessed, great voices in heaven will announce that "the kingdom of the world has become the kingdom of our Lord and of his Christ, and he will reign for ever and ever" (Rev. 11:15).

It's a mistake to paint a contrast between the so-called God of the Old Testament and that of the New. The entire Bible is one. "These things happened to them as examples and were written down as warnings for us, on whom the fulfillment of the ages has come" (1 Cor. 10:11). No judgment that ever took place in the Old Testament is more terrifying than what's predicted in the New. In Noah's time, Jesus observed, sinful, rebellious men and women were going about their normal activities. "Then the flood came and destroyed them all" (Luke 17:27). The sinners of Sodom were doing the same, He said, "but the day Lot left Sodom, fire and sulfur rained down from heaven and destroyed them all" (verse 29). "It will be just like this," He said, "on the day the Son of Man is revealed" (verse 30).

In the end, Paul says, the Lord Jesus will be "revealed from heaven in blazing fire with his powerful angels. He will punish those who do not know God and do not obey the gospel of our Lord Jesus. They will be punished with everlasting destruction and shut out from the presence of the Lord and from the majesty of his power" (2 Thess. 1:7-9). "It is a dreadful thing," declares the author of Hebrews, "to fall into the hands of the living God" (Heb. 10:31).

And though the book of Revelation is filled with the most awe-inspiring descriptions of heaven and the singing of the redeemed, it also contains some of the most hair-raising depictions of the final judgment found anywhere in Scripture. "A third angel followed them and said . . . : 'If anyone worships the beast and his image and receives his mark on the forehead or on the hand, he, too, will drink of the wine of God's fury, which has been poured full strength into the cup of his wrath. He will be tormented with burning sulfur in the presence of the holy angels and of the Lamb" (Rev. 14:9-11). In the end, it says, "death and Hades were thrown into the lake of fire. The lake of fire is the second death. If anyone's name was not found written in the book of life, he was thrown into the lake of fire" (Rev. 20:14, 15).

Even if we say that not all of this is literal, it should still be obvious that what's being described here is not a slap on the wrist. Jesus, fielding a rare question on the subject of human calamity and suffering, answered His interrogators with the same calm authority we find in Job when God appears—no protracted argumentation, no defensive posturing, no highfalutin philosophy. Simply this: "But unless you repent, you too will all perish" (Luke 13:3).

The Bible contains violence because it's about life—life in the real world. We find love in the Bible, but it's tough, unblinking love— love girded for an ugly world. And the salvation in the Bible comes with a heavy cost. Those married to the political correctness of a particular generation, arrogantly refusing to recognize the realities of the ancient world, will forever find the Old Testament an impediment to faith. "As you do not know the path of the wind," said the wise man, "or how the body is formed in a mother's womb, so you cannot understand the work of God, the Maker of all things" (Eccl. 11:5).

We are not to become the creators of our own God. In all humility, we must come to terms with the God the Bible reveals. In our limited knowledge, supported by personal experience of His goodness, we may do so now. Or we may wait, at our eternal peril, until all the evidence is in—until the entire universe of rebels, saints, and angels join in one united testimony:

> "Great and marvelous are your deeds,
> Lord God Almighty.
> Just and true are your ways,
> King of the Ages" (Rev. 15:3).

The day approaches when the universal blight we know now will vanish and the vision of the ancient prophet will become reality:

# Taking Human Life: The Character of God in Joshua

"They shall not hurt nor destroy in all My holy mountain, for the earth shall be full of the knowledge of the Lord as the waters cover the sea" (Isa. 11:9, NKJV). No more pain; no more crying; no more death. An entire universe without tears. That's what God wants.

## Questions for Reflection
### Joshua 6-12

1. How comfortable are you with God? How do you feel deep down inside about His actions in the Old Testament? And how has the present chapter affected the issue for you?

2. What thought patterns do you need to develop in order to maintain objectivity in your interpretation of Scripture? How willing are you to take all the relevant facts into consideration and not be influenced by your own shortsightedness or that of others?

3. You accept the mercy of God, but how ready are you to accept His justice also? How does God's goodness in your personal life inform your understanding of His justice and judgment?

---

[1] Curiously, few if any call the character of God into question for the plagues on Egypt or the drowning of the Egyptian army. Nor is it usually faulted for the destruction of the antediluvians. Somehow these events come across as legitimate acts of God. It's the conquest that creates the greatest outrage.

[2] Williston Walker, *A History of the Christian Church* (New York: Charles Scribner's Sons, 1959), p. 54.

[3] S. L. Greenslade, "Marcionites," *Encyclopaedia Britannica* (1961), vol. 14, pp. 869, 870.

[4] In E. Jacob, *Theology of the Old Testament* (New York: Harper and Brothers, 1958), pp. 114, 115.

[5] Herbert J. Muller, *Freedom in the Ancient World* (New York: Harper and Brothers, 1961), p. 117.

[6] Richard D. Nelson, *Joshua: A Commentary* (Louisville, Ky.: Westminster John Knox Press, 1997), p. 2.

[7] J. Gordon Harris, Cheryl A. Brown, and Michael S. Moore, *New International Biblical Commentary: Joshua, Judges, Ruth* (Peabody, Mass.: Hendrickson Publishers, Inc., 2000), p. 3.

[8] Jerry A. Gladson, "The Moral Outrage of Holy War," *Spectrum,* June 1995, pp. 16, 17.

[9] Mieke Bal, ed., *Anti-Covenant: Counter-Reading Women's Lives in the Hebrew Bible* (Sheffield, Eng.: Almond, 1989), p. 14.

[10] John J. Collins, "The Zeal of Phinehas: The Bible and the Legitimation of Violence," *Journal of Biblical Literature* 122, no. 1 (2003): 4.

[11] *Ibid.*

[12] *Ibid.,* p. 3.

[13] *Ibid.*

[14] *Ibid.,* p. 7.

[15] E. G. White, *Patriarchs and Prophets,* pp. 436, 437.

[16] U. Oldenberg, *The Conflict Between El and Ba'al in Canaanite Religion* (Leiden, Netherlands: E. J. Brill, 1969), p. x.

[17] G. Ernest Wright, *Biblical Archeology* (Philadelphia: Westminster Press, 1957), p. 113.

[18] John Bright, *A History of Israel* (Philadelphia: Westminster Press, 1959), p. 108.

[19] Wright, p. 113. Cf. 1 Kings 14:24.

[20] Bright, p. 109. (Italics supplied.)

[21] William F. Albright, *Archaeology and the Religion of Israel* (Baltimore: Johns Hopkins Press, 1956), p. 129. (Italics supplied.)

[22] *Ibid.* (Italics supplied.)

[23] *Ibid.*

[24] *Ibid.*, p. 128.

[25] Wright, p. 112.

[26] William F. Albright, *Yahweh and the Gods of Canaan: A Historical Analysis of Two Contrasting Faiths* (Garden City, N.Y.: Doubleday, 1968), pp. 131, 132.

[27] *Ibid.*, p. 132.

[28] Albright, *Archaeology and the Religion of Israel,* p. 77.

[29] Harriet Auber, "Our Blest Redeemer" (1829).

[30] W. J. Harrelson, "Ten Commandments," *The Interpreter's Dictionary of the Bible,* ed. George A. Buttrick (Nashville: Abingdon, 1962), vol. 4, p. 571.

[31] Angel Rodríguez, "Is Killing Murder?" *Adventist Review,* Dec. 11, 2003, p. 14.

[32] Collins, p. 18.

[33] *Ibid.*, p. 4.

[34] David Merling, Sr., *The Book of Joshua: Its Theme and Role in Archaeological Discussions* (Berrien Springs, Mich.: Andrews University Press, 1997), pp. 188, 189.

[35] *Ibid.*, p. 192.

[36] C. S. Lewis, *The Problem of Pain* (New York: Macmillan, 1962), pp. 115, 116.

[37] Collins, p. 10. A similar point is made in Nelson, p. 2.

[38] *Ibid.*

[39] Ellen G. White, *Christ's Object Lessons* (Washington, D.C.: Review and Herald Pub. Assn., 1900), p. 288.

[40] Also see *The Seventh-day Adventist Bible Commentary,* vol. 4, p. 29.

[41] E. John Hamlin, *Inheriting the Land: A Commentary on the Book of Joshua* (Grand Rapids: William B. Eerdmans, 1983), p. 4.

[42] White, *Patriarchs and Prophets,* p. 492.

[43] Though he argues the case from a different perspective, the thoughts of Walter Brueggemann are worth noting on this score. Brueggemann sees Israel as a marginalized people fighting for survival against great odds and not prepared to give way to further oppression (such as they'd undergone in Egypt). It's a notion in keeping with the struggle of oppressed peoples in the modern world. See Walter Brueggemann, *Revelation and Violence: A Study in Contextualization* (Milwaukee: Marquette University Press, 1986), pp. 9, 32-35.

[44] H. H. Rowley, *The Faith of Israel: Aspects of Old Testament Thought* (London: SCM Press, 1956), p. 65.

Chapter 9

# Establishing Boundaries

## Joshua 13-22

With Joshua 13 we come to the beginning of the second half of the book. From here on, the author will make the point at every turn that Israel had accomplished its mission to conquer Canaan. The apportioning of the land, a most sacred transaction, will take place, and the Transjordan tribes will return at last to their adopted homeland across the river.

The section now before us is chock-full of geographical details, requiring (if one were to pursue each item) an extensive mastery of ancient history and archaeology to comprehend it all fully. For the purposes of the present work, however, we focus primarily on the broad outlines and implications of the text, standing over the shoulders of its first readers, as it were, and trying to understand its meaning for our times.

Regardless of its geographical and historical complexity, this segment will bring us to the fundamental point of the entire book—or, to say it differently, to the basic goal and purpose of the whole Exodus movement, namely, the settling of the people in the Land of Promise in fulfillment of the ancient covenant. It's the one big item missing in the Pentateuch, and without which (as we said at the beginning) those five books of Moses, with all their vast coverage of the period, would be incomplete.

### The Major Themes

In the segment before us (Joshua 13-22) the author takes up six major topics:

1. The land remaining to be taken (Joshua 13:1-7).
2. The allotment of the land in Transjordan (verses 8-33).
3. The partial distribution of the land at Gilgal (Joshua 14-17).

4. The distribution of the rest of the land at Shiloh (Joshua 18; 19).
5. The allotment of cities of refuge and the designation of Levitical towns (Joshua 20:1–21:42).
6. The return of the eastern tribes (Joshua 22).

For convenience, the material below will follow this basic outline (Joshua 21:43-45, omitted here, will be included in the final chapter).

### The Land Remaining to Be Taken (Joshua 13:1-7)

Joshua 13:1-7 speaks of the territory not yet captured. This is not simply unoccupied territory or land repossessed by its previous inhabitants. Rather, it refers to regions never conquered or occupied by Israel. The areas specified are very difficult to define on a map, one reason being that scholars, in many cases, have never positively identified the exact location of some areas. The Geshurite territory, for example, or the Shihor River. Also, it's not quite clear what the author exactly means by "the region of the Amorites" and "the area of the Gebalites." But locations like Gaza, Ashdod, Ashkelon, Gath, and Ekron are well known. The Lebanon region also is clear. (Try to pinpoint these latter areas on Map VI, *Seventh-day Adventist Bible Dictionary*).

Broadly speaking, "three separate areas seem to be indicated: (1) the territory southwest of the Shephelah [the foothill regions near the Judean highlands] inhabited by the Philistines, Geshurites, and Avvites; (2) the Sidonian territory between the Lebanon . . . Mountains and the Mediterranean Sea; and (3) the territory east of the Lebanon Mountains."[1]

Joshua receives assurance that *the Lord Himself* (the pronoun in the text is emphatic) will drive out the inhabitants of these regions, and that he should thus feel free simply to go ahead and include these territories in the general distribution of the land to the tribes of Israel (Joshua 13:6, 7).

At first glance verses 1-7 seem utterly disconnected from what follows it—namely, the allotment of the land in Transjordan. Upon closer inspection, however, the situation becomes clear. Joshua is here preparing to record a legal document of the most profound importance to Israel: the division of the land. If it is to be complete, it must start with the allotments in Transjordan and must include all the territory west of the Jordan.

# Establishing Boundaries

And that's where Joshua 13:1-7 comes in. It lists those areas in the west not yet under Israel's control (but areas considered an essential part of Canaan—see verses 3, 4), and it directs Joshua not to exclude them when he parcels up the land. "The whole land, both the parts already conquered and that which was yet unsubdued, was to be apportioned among the tribes. And it was the duty of each tribe to fully subdue its own inheritance."[2]

An interesting item in Joshua 13:1-7 is the reference to Joshua's age. Verse 1 refers to this detail three times, telling us that Joshua is (1) "old," that he is (2) "well advanced in years," and that he is (3) "very old." So when exactly did this vision take place?

The wording of the text sounds so similar to Joshua 23:1, 2, describing the closing days of Joshua, that some have tried to link the two passages. It would seem evident, however—given the fact that Joshua was to include the territories listed in Joshua 13:1-7 in the allotment of the land—that the vision described in that passage must have taken place *prior* to the land distributions at Gilgal and Shiloh mentioned in chapters 16-19. And thus Joshua 13:1-7 and 23:1, 2 are not chronologically connected.

But if, as we must conclude, the transaction of the land began not long after the northern campaign, then how could the author have described Joshua as "very old" and "well advanced in years"? In Joshua 10 he had been strong enough to lead his forces on an all-night march against the southern coalition (verse 9) and then pursue the battle all the next day and much beyond. As regards the war in the north, all the evidence suggests that he had been at the head of his army in their 70-mile (113-kilometer) trek to the Waters of Merom—and, we may assume, during the six or seven years of fighting that followed.

We will have occasion to return to the point of Joshua's age when we deal with Joshua 23:1 in the following chapter. For the time being, let's just say that the reference to his age in Joshua 13:1 probably served to indicate that the recent prolonged campaigns had taken their toll on the vitality of the intrepid leader. If we take Josephus' word for it, Joshua worked as Moses' aide for 40 years and then led Israel 25 years on his own until his death at 110.[3] It would mean, when you stop to calculate it, that he was 45 years at the time of the Exodus, 85 years when entering Canaan, and now, after some seven years of fighting (see below under "Return of the Eastern Tribes"), he'd have been 92 years old.

It was not an age at which Joshua would want to undertake another military mission approaching the intensity of those he'd just completed. Had he been a Levite, at 92 he'd have been 42 years past retirement age (see Num. 8:25).

## The Allotment in Transjordan (Joshua 13:8-33)

The author is about to record the distribution and allotment of land. He begins with Transjordan, a detail he'd already covered briefly in Joshua 12:1-6. But for good reasons it belongs here as well. First, the record about to be created would be a formal instrument, having legal standing and serving as a reference source for all future generations in Israel. It must, therefore, be exhaustive and complete. Every Israelite would have a personal stake in its provisions. A second reason for the merging of the record of the eastern allotments with that of the west was to show the vital continuity between the mission of Moses and that of Joshua. Both were part and parcel of the one whole, under the one divine Commander. A third reason was to make it clear, both to the surrounding nations and to Israel itself, that the whole nation—east and west—was one. It was a recognition that on whichever side of the Jordan an Israelite lived, they had received the land from the one heavenly Proprietor.

We might see the significance of these points in the sheer panic that struck Joshua and the entire nation west of the river when they received reports that the departing eastern tribes had built what appeared to be a rival altar for worship (see Joshua 22:10-33). The reaction of Joshua and the western tribes suggests that what we have in Joshua 13:8-32, far from being a redundant addition to the text, was a vital and indispensable part of its completeness.

## Partial Distribution of the Land at Gilgal (Joshua 14-17)

The war was over. The struggle for the subjugation of Canaan had come to a successful end. The army had returned to Gilgal. And the eastern tribes were itching to depart.

But before that much-anticipated event, it was necessary that they witness the fulfillment of the fundamental purpose of the Exodus, the goal for which they'd risked their lives in the west—namely, the allotment of the land. It was to be the next item on the agenda—and a most sacred one. "Without land," as someone has noted, "a people remains a nomadic tribe; it has no roots and no base, and it has little chance of surviving as a group against the power of historical forces."[4] Now, at last, the promise made to their ancestors was about to meet its tangible fulfillment.

The transaction of distributing the land would take place at the tent of meeting (the sanctuary) in the presence of all the top leaders of Israel: "Eleazar the [high] priest and Joshua" and the heads of the tribal clans of Israel, all of whom Moses had designated by name (Num. 34:17-29).

It is significant that the text mentions the high priest, the representative of God in the nation, first. This was in keeping with the theocratic system of government established in Israel, in which the priest, as God's representative, legislated, while the judge, representing the people, administered the government. Here again, as in the crossing of the Jordan (Joshua 3) and in the siege of Jericho (Joshua 6), we have an example of the prominence given to the priestly role in the book of Joshua.

In the allotment of the land the function of Eleazar, the high priest, was pivotal. Israel's inheritance was "assigned by lot" (Joshua 14:2)—a process, in that period of Israel's history, centered on the Urim and Thummim, those special stones carried on the breastplate of the high priest's garment. "When questions were brought for decision before the Lord, a halo of light encircling the precious stone at the right was a token of the divine consent or approval, while a cloud shadowing the stone at the left was an evidence of denial or disapprobation."[5]

Old Testament scholars are at a loss to explain why there would be two separate occasions for dividing the territory among the tribes—at Gilgal (Joshua 14:6) and at Shiloh (Joshua 18:1). My surmise is that it had something to do with Caleb.

Though still full of vitality, as he indicates in Joshua 14:11, Caleb was not getting any younger. And after waiting all those years in the wilderness (unnecessarily, from his standpoint, since he fully believed that Israel, under God, was ready to take Canaan 45 years before [see Num. 13:30]), he naturally felt the time had come to take possession of his inheritance. Had events developed in a normal way, the entire transaction of dividing the territory would, undoubtedly, have occurred at the sanctuary's new location in Shiloh. But Joshua probably had his plan interrupted by an urgent request from the fearless Caleb, whose patience had now run the full limit.

And so it was that Joshua convened a special meeting before dismantling the sanctuary at Gilgal. It would be a preliminary allotment made for Caleb and for the rest the tribe of Judah. And while they were at it, they would also include in this first round of allotment the tribes of Ephraim and the western half of Manasseh, perhaps out of deference for the fact that the latter had crossed the Jordan to fight in behalf of the rest of Israel.[6]

Given the courage and faith Caleb manifested during the crisis at Kadesh-barnea (see Num. 13; 14), it was most fitting that he should be the first to receive his inheritance. The 85-year-old veteran (see Joshua 14:7, 10), citing his courage and vigor after 45 years of struggle, put forward his bold request on the basis of a promise and commitment made to him by Moses 45 years before (see Num. 14:24; Deut. 1:36). "Now give me this hill country that the Lord promised me," he said to Joshua (Joshua 14:12).

Caleb appears several times in the book after this point (see Joshua 14:13, 14; 15:13, 14, 16, 18; 21:12), but this is the first reference to him in the document. One suspects, however, that his presence must have been a continuing source of inspiration and strength to Joshua and the rest of the nation. Those who were older would have remembered his resoluteness and loyalty during the Kadesh rebellion. All during the subsequent years of desert wanderings (which came upon the nation through no fault of his) he had stood by Moses—and, after Moses' death, by Joshua. At 78 years of age he had gone out with the rest of the army to fight the battles of the Lord, and now at 85 he stood ready to do the same to secure a personal inheritance for his family (Joshua 14:7-12). And Joshua apparently felt that nothing must delay the fulfillment of his request.

The Anakites, the very group whose stature had struck such terror in the hearts of the people 45 years earlier (Num. 13), inhabited the territory Caleb requested. He had stood firm then, and he was just as resolute now. Thus he demonstrated that his stance at the Kadesh-barnea face-off was no attempt to gain points or curry Moses' favor. Rather, it was the expression of a genuine conviction that the Anakites could be defeated, a confidence that the passage of time did not erase.

Caleb's action was not a landgrab—after all, the territory he sought was not yet secure (Joshua 14:12). Instead, it was an attempt to validate the position he and Joshua had taken 45 years earlier. "Then Joshua blessed Caleb . . . and gave him Hebron as his inheritance" (verse 14). And to indicate the implications of that allotment, the text adds, parenthetically, that "Hebron used to be called Kiriath Arba [see Gen. 23:2] after Arba, who was the greatest man among the Anakites" (Joshua 14:15).

Even though the book earlier reported that Joshua had "destroyed the Anakites" (see Joshua 11:21), it would appear that it was not complete, and that later they had regrouped. Moreover, Caleb "did not mean the city of Hebron alone . . . , but he included, in his request, all the adjacent country, including the caves and strongholds to which the Anakim had retired, and where they were now abiding in considerable force."[7] Thus Caleb marched against the whole area, including Kiriath Arba (Hebron), driving out Sheshai, Ahiman, and Talmai, the three Anakite leaders descended from the giant Anak (Joshua 15:13-15).

I've dwelt at length on the Caleb story because of the powerful contribution it makes to the theme of the book of Joshua. In the first place, it shows the importance of obedience and loyalty, qualities mentioned three times in Joshua 14 (verses 8, 9, 14). Caleb was successful and had lived to see the fulfillment of the promise because he had "followed the Lord wholeheartedly." "The words give the idea of a traveler, who, intent upon following his guide, walks so closely in his steps as to leave hardly any space between."[8]

The Caleb story also highlights the need to keep our promises. Joshua did not hesitate to comply with Caleb's bold request. He gave him Hebron (Joshua 14:13)—a gift that, in turn, shows that God is faithful to His covenant. In fact, we may say that the fundamental message of the Caleb story is that human faithfulness is possible only because God's faithfulness is a reality. As He promised their fathers (see Gen. 12), God had now brought His people into the land. And He had been faithful to Caleb personally, keeping him alive and well for 45 years to experience and inherit the land promised (Joshua 14:10, 11).

And there is yet one thing more about the Caleb story—something significant and special. It centers on Caleb's genealogical relationship to Israel. While several Old Testament passages identify him as belonging to the tribe of Judah (e.g., Num. 13:6; 34:19), the passage before us describes him as "Caleb son of Jephunneh the Kenizzite" (Joshua 14:6; cf. Num. 32:12). We have no information on the lineage of Jephunneh, but the Kenizzites were the descendants of Kenaz, son of Eliphaz, the firstborn son of Esau (Gen. 36:11; 1 Chron. 1:36). They were, therefore, an Edomite tribal group (see Gen. 36:15, 40-43). It would mean, as some have suggested, that "Caleb was a proselyte, one of the mixed multitude who had joined himself to Israel."[9]

So what we probably have before us is a fascinating story of God's acceptance and grace. For here a person who was not a natural-born Israelite—or, at least, one who could not, like Paul, describe himself as "a Hebrew of Hebrews" (Phil. 3:5)—had managed to become one of only two persons (among those who left Egypt as adults) to make it to the Promised Land. *And now he had become the first to receive territory in Canaan!*

This is nothing short of astonishing. And it shows that we have a God who is no respecter of persons. Not only can He accept the shady lady of Jericho (see Joshua 6:22, 23) and the conniving Gibeonites (Joshua 10:6-14; 11:19, 20); He can also put someone who was not a full-blooded Hebrew first in line for territory in the Promised Land.

It is a powerful lesson for us all, one that Jesus tried to drive home to the religious pretenders of His day: "I say to you that many will come from the east and the west, and will take their places at the feast with Abraham, Isaac and Jacob in the kingdom of heaven. But the subjects of the kingdom will be thrown outside, into the darkness, where there will be weeping and gnashing of teeth" (Matt. 8:11, 12).

Having appointed the inheritance of Caleb, the leaders then proceeded to distribute the rest of Judah's territory—and also that of Ephraim and half Manasseh (Joshua 15:1-17:13).

One development in regard to the allotment for Manasseh deserves mention at this point: that of the daughters of Zelophehad (Joshua 17:3, 4). The fact that they had no brothers (Num. 26:33) made theirs a special case in regard to the laws of inheritance. A culture in which land inheritance and ownership were the right of males only had no precedent as to how to treat the daughters.

At a complete loss on how to proceed when first approached on the issue, Moses had taken the matter to the Lord for guidance. God's unequivocal response flew smack in the face of the prevailing norms: "What Zelophehad's daughters are saying is right. You must certainly give them property as an inheritance among their father's relatives and turn their father's inheritance over to them" (Num. 27:7). Henceforth, this was to be the law in Israel (verses 8-11).

It was against that background that the women now approached Eleazer, Joshua, and the other allotment officers to claim their inheritance. With the stipulations already in place, the path ahead was clear: "So Joshua gave them an inheritance along with the brothers of their father, according to the Lord's command" (Joshua 17:4).

This story has implications for the way we deal today with new situations that arise in which we have no biblical precedent on how to proceed. Moses might easily have informed the women that God in His great wisdom had not chosen to include such matters when He descended on Sinai in blazing fire. Had He, in His omniscience, considered their concern valid, He would certainly have made provision for it in the regulations handed down at that time.

But that was not how Moses handled the case. Common sense led him to see merit in the women's concerns, that it was the sort of thing that would likely come up again. So Moses took up the matter with the Lord. And God answered him.

How should we approach similar situations today, situations that have no biblical precedent? Our response should be exactly that of Moses. And though our access to God may not be as direct as his (nor God's answer as clear), we should move forward, after we've prayed, guided by the Spirit of God and sanctified common sense. Where the merit of the case is clear and compelling, *the one thing we must not do* is hide behind a lack of biblical precedent. Had Moses done that, he'd not only have denied the women their basic rights, but would also have done a great disservice to all succeeding generations. The case of Zelophehad's daughters, reminiscent of the developments we find in Acts 15, stands as an eternal beacon for serious Christians trying to forge a way through uncharted theological waters.

Dealing with the territorial designations in Joshua is a challenge. Just going through the boundary points of the allotment of Judah alone—a catalog of interminable and unfamiliar place names—can thrust one into mental overload. Where is the contemporary reader who can possibly comprehend it all? The elaborate geographical details that would have given the first readers of the document no trouble at all throw the typical modern reader for a loop.

"In a study of the role of cities in Joshua, M. Ottosson points out that of the 746 city names listed in the Hebrew Bible, 358 [or nearly 48 percent] occur in the book of Joshua, and that of these 199 are *hapax legomena* [words that occur only once in the Bible]." [10]

A further difficulty for the modern reader is that Bible scholars have not been able to identify positively a considerable number of landmark towns and cities mentioned in the book. This makes for a high degree of frustration as one tries to follow the already difficult demarcation points in a Bible atlas. We might note also that new renderings, such as "Scorpion Pass" (Joshua 15:3), can be tricky to locate if one is using a Bible dictionary or atlas based on the King James Version, which uses a completely different term—in this case, "Maaleh-acrabbim."

Yet another complexity might arise from trying, unnecessarily, to identify certain transient geographical points such as "the stone of Bohan" (verse 6), "the waters of Jericho" (Joshua 16:1), or "the large tree in Zaanannim" (Joshua 19:33). One would simply have to use good judgment as to when to pass over certain details.

Difficult as it is for us now to follow these boundary points, it was enormously more complicated to do the initial location and identification. It took a vast amount of diligent, painstaking work on the part of biblical scholars, archaeologists, cartographers, and others—working hundreds of years—to bring us even to what we do know today. Map VI, in the *Seventh-day Adventist Bible Dictionary,* represents a part of these results. On it you can see the territories of the respective tribes. "The tribal inheritances included four main geographical regions: (1) Canaan south of Jebusite Jerusalem (Judah and Simeon); (2) Canaan north of Jerusalem (Benjamin, Ephraim, and half of Manasseh); (3) Galilee (Zebulun, Issachar, Asher, Naphtali, and Dan); and (4) Transjordan (Reuben, Gad, and half of Manasseh)."[11] (For the sheer challenge—and fun—of it, take a few minutes to trace the outlines for the tribe of Judah, going back and forth from Bible to map.)

In the present chapter I do not seek (nor do I ask the reader) to reinvent the wheel. We have to admit in all frankness that for most people the boundaries of the territories of the tribes of Israel, together with their list of towns, cities, and other geographical details, are purely academic, with very little spiritual or practical significance.

So although the details should not be ignored, the intention of the present chapter is to have the reader grasp the underlying message of all this geographical and historical minutiae and the important role of the reality they describe in the whole scheme of salvation history. What we need to remember, as John L. McKenzie reminds us, is that "the gift of the land is a great token of Yahweh's fidelity to his promises. It comes second only to the recital of the Exodus as a statement of Israel's faith."[12]

Through Israel's conquest and settlement of Canaan God placed His people at the crossroads of ancient civilization. Thus positioned, they had the opportunity and privilege of shedding a saving influence on the entire world by way of the international commercial traffic moving through their borders. Any attention to the details of geography should occur in the context of this broad salvation-historical scheme.

Such records exist, then, not for memorization or mastery, but rather to give us assurance that the stories of the Bible are based on real places, real events, real people. This means that however difficult or unfamiliar or inaccessible they may appear to us, they belong in the Sacred Canon. They exist not only to share their secrets with the researcher who needs them, but also to confirm the faith of God's people in every generation as to the veracity of the sacred text.

## The Allotments at Shiloh (Joshua 18; 19)

For reasons not mentioned in the text, Israel's national religious (and probably also political) center now moved to Shiloh (Joshua 18:1). Shiloh was "near the center of the land, and was easy of access to all the tribes. Here a portion of country had been thoroughly subdued, so that the worshipers would not be molested."[13] The ark would remain in Shiloh for 300 years, until captured by the Philistines in an ill-fated battle that saw the death of the two sons of Eli, apostate priests who'd presumptuously carried the sacred symbols into the conflict (see 1 Sam. 4). It would be at Shiloh that the second and final phase of the allotment of the land west of the Jordan would take place.

"The country was brought under their control, but there were still seven Israelite tribes who'd not yet received their inheritance" (Joshua 18:1, 2). And why not? One source suggests that having led a nomadic life for 45 years, they were reluctant to settle down. "They had been enriched with the plunder of the Canaanites and were living in plenty. They seemed to be more intent on present ease and indulgence than upon obtaining their inheritance."[14]

Whatever the reason, Joshua felt that the time had come for these seven tribes to make a move. "How long will you wait before you begin to take possession of the land that the Lord . . . has given you?" (verse 3). The question suggests that some time had elapsed since the end of the northern campaign and the first apportionment of the land, at Gilgal. And it also gives evidence of a certain impatience on Joshua's part—understandable in view of the desire of the eastern tribes to return to their homes across the river.

A survey team immediately came into being, consisting of three leaders from each tribe (verse 4)—perhaps only from the seven that had not yet received their portions, though we cannot be sure. The written description they would bring back to Shiloh was to be submitted to Joshua, who, after casting lots, would distribute the territory among the seven remaining tribes (verses 6, 8-10)—Benjamin, Simeon, Zebulun, Issachar, Asher, Naphtali, and Dan (see Joshua 18:11-19:46).

Were all the tribes satisfied with their territorial allotments? Or might dissatisfaction and jealousy have surfaced among them? After all, the question of land rights is potentially one of the most contentious issues in the history of human society. The distribution of the land must have been a matter that took a considerable degree of sensitivity. What tribe in Israel would not have opted for territory that would give it access to the Mediterranean Sea or to some other body of water—if their preferences were anything like ours today?

But they could not all have such a privilege. Some, like Ephraim and Zebulun, would need to make do with landlocked territory (see Map VI, *Seventh-day Adventist Bible Dictionary*). Simeon would have to be content with being located totally within the territory of Judah (see Joshua 19:1, 9). And Manasseh would have to put up with some of its towns and settlements within the territories of Issachar and Asher (Joshua 17:11).

Given all this, we can better appreciate the wisdom of dividing the land through the medium of the lot, mediated by the high priest, who, not up for tribal inheritance himself, had no vested interest in the outcome. Only the impartiality of the divine will (which the high priest represented) could provide the kind of confidence that would make for peaceful territorial coexistence.

Even so, at least one tribe (following the partial division of the land at Gilgal) found reason for complaint. "The people of Joseph," calling attention to their large size, appealed for more land (see Joshua 17:14). Joshua's response to them (see verses 15-18) combined wisdom, generosity, and toughness. Meeting them with their own argument, he challenged them to use their large number and their military strength to increase their territory.

That response smoked out their real concern: "All the Canaanites who live in the plain have iron chariots," they said (verse 16). But Joshua was not to be swayed from his decision: "Though they are strong," he said to them, "you can drive them out" (verse 18). Given the fact that Joshua was himself a member of the tribe of Ephraim (part of the united tribe of Joseph), his handling of the situation demonstrated impeccable impartiality.

We may also note that Joshua showed appropriate self-denial in putting himself at the end of the allotment line (Joshua 19:49, 50). As the leader of Israel, he did not lord it over God's people, a point that perhaps comes through even in the language that couches the bestowal of his inheritance. It says that "the Israelites *gave Joshua* . . . an inheritance among them" (verse 49). The entire account shows a most commendable humility on his part. It's a lesson for those of us living today in cultures that operate on a "me first" philosophy—in which the subtle (and sometimes not-so-subtle) advice is to "take care of number one!" The story of Joshua is one of self-denial, of putting others first.

The final verses of chapter 19 indicate that the territorial allotments had come to an end. And once again the text names the principal leaders involved, cites the place of the historic transaction, and describes the procedure followed. This formal summation is further evidence that what we have before us is a legal document of enormous importance. It puts the divine seal of approval and authenticity on the transaction. It suggests that no human authority should call the document into question. The highest power in the universe stood behind it.

"And so they finished dividing the land" (verse 51).

### Levitical Towns and Cities of Refuge (Joshua 20:1-21:42)

"But to the tribe of Levi he gave no inheritance" (Joshua 13:14).

This observation runs like a refrain throughout the account of the division of land. And the reasons offered, however varied, probably amounted to the same thing: "The offerings made by fire to the Lord . . . are their inheritance" (Joshua 13:14); "The Lord . . . is their inheritance" (verse 33); "Because the priestly service of the Lord is their inheritance" (Joshua 18:7).

The suggestion seems to be that everything belongs to the Lord. All that the people of Israel possess is His. And since Yahweh has chosen the Levites as His special representatives in Israel, then to them belong all the tithes and voluntary gifts of the nation that pertain to Him (see Num. 18:20-24).

Thus the Levites were to receive no inheritance, as such, "but only towns to live in, with pasturelands for their flocks and herds" (Joshua 14:4; cf. Num. 35:2-5). And now that all the tribes had received their allotments, the time had come for each to assign a certain number of towns from their territory to the Levites.

The formula for the municipal donations to the Levites was to be "in proportion to the inheritance of each tribe: . . . many towns from a tribe that has many, but few from one that has few" (Num. 35:8). Following the divine stipulations to the letter, the Israelites assigned to the Levites exactly 48 towns (Joshua 21:41), distributing them by lot among them. Here, between their assigned courses at the tabernacle/temple and following retirement at 50 (see Num. 8:25), they would live and, perhaps, continue serving in various capacities—spiritual, educational, and administrative.

The six towns designated "cities of refuge" appear in Joshua 20:7, 8: Kedesh, Shechem, and Kiriath Arba on the west: and Bezer, Ramoth, and Golan on the east. (See Map VI, *Seventh-day Adventist Bible Dictionary*, for those whose location is known.) The purpose of these cities has been stated at length in Numbers 35:6-34 and Deuteronomy 4:41-43. They were places of safety for the one who, with no malice aforethought, accidentally caused the death of another human being. Until the case could come to trial, the city of refuge provided the fugitive with protection from the avenger (usually some close relative of the deceased [see Joshua 20:1-6]).

"The cities of refuge were so distributed as to be within half day's journey of every part of the land. The roads leading to them were always to be kept in good repair; all along the way signposts were to be erected bearing the word 'Refuge' in plain, bold characters, that the fleeing one might not be delayed for a moment. Any person—Hebrew, stranger, or sojourner—might avail himself of this provision." [15]

Evidently the idea of asylum was not unique to the Hebrew people. Among the Phoenicians, Syrians, Greeks, etc., "certain shrines or sacred precincts were regarded as providing absolute security for fugitives. Innocent and guilty, criminals, runaway slaves, debtors, and political fugitives passed beyond the reach of revenge and justice alike upon attaining sacred ground and claiming the protection of the deity." [16] (It would be instructive to investigate what differences, if any, existed between the Israelite asylum and that practiced by other nations.)

The author of Hebrews alludes to this ancient practice when he spoke of those who had "fled for refuge to lay hold upon the hope set before us," the hope anchored in Jesus (Heb. 6:18, KJV). It's as if the apostle pictures the entire human race as fugitives under a death sentence, needing to flee for refuge in Jesus, our great high priest and mediator, our "city of reguge."

The urgency that characterized the ancient fugitives should characterize us who realize our danger today. "He who fled to the city of refuge could make no delay. Family and employment were left behind. There was no time to say farewell to loved ones. His life was at stake, and every other interest must be sacrificed to the one purpose—to reach the place of safety. Weariness was forgotten, difficulties were unheeded. A fugitive dare not for one moment slacken his pace until he was within the wall of the city." This is the kind of response that should characterize our flight from the threat of eternal death, until we find "a hiding place in Christ." [17]

One significant bit of information in the rest of chapter 21 (which, up to verse 42 catalogs the contribution of the various tribes to the Levitical allotments), comes in verses 10, 11: in the distribution of towns, Kiriath Arba (Hebron) went to the Kohathite Levites. It's an important detail, for it shows that that this prized town, the one for which Caleb had fought so vigorously, ended up as a possession of the Levites.

The text does not inform us how Caleb took it. It says simply that "the fields and villages around the city [of Hebron] they had given to Caleb . . . as his possession" (verse 12). But based on the spirit displayed by this loyal veteran throughout his life, one would hazard that he would have had no hesitation offering the best for God's consecrated servants, the Levites. If this surmise is correct, then Caleb, in addition to teaching us lessons of courage, loyalty, and faith, also shows us the meaning of self-denial and sacrifice.

And it's significant that the city he gave up (Hebron) became one of the six cities of refuge (Joshua 21:13; cf. Joshua 20:7-9), thus turning history full circle. For the city that had struck such terror in the heart of Israel had now been transformed into a place associated with protection, safety, and security for those facing deadly peril.

## Return of the Eastern Tribes (Joshua 22)

The agreement that allowed the two and a half tribes to take up residence on the eastern side of the Jordan (contrary to the original plan for all Israel to settle in the west) called for them to meet two important nonnegotiable conditions: (1) a portion of their fighting men—40,000 strong, as it turned out (Joshua 4:12, 13)—were to cross over with the rest of Israel, fully armed for combat in the struggle for Canaan (see Num. 32:17, 21; Joshua 1:14); and (2) they were to remain with the effort until Israel had routed the Canaanites and subdued the land (Num. 32:18, 22; Joshua 1:15).

The end of hostilities and the distribution of the land signaled the completion of the task for which they'd crossed the Jordan. Their mission had ended. Now they could return to their homes and families. When they assembled before Joshua to receive their official farewell (Joshua 22:1), he called attention to two factors: their solid term of service in Canaan and their faithfulness to duty. "For a long time now—to this very day—you have not deserted your brothers but have carried out the mission the Lord . . . gave you" (verses 1-3).

I believe that the period referred to here includes the "long time" of Joshua 11:18. Its length, as best as we can calculate it from Joshua 14:7, 10, 11 (see comments in chapter 7 of this work), was about seven years. Obviously we'd have to allow time, following the cessation of hostilities, for the eastern tribes to return to Gilgal, to recoup, and then to round out their affairs and duties in the west before departing.

It would almost certainly have involved helping to relocate the religious and political headquarters of Israel from Gilgal to Shiloh (see Joshua 18:1, 8-10; 22:9). They'd also have waited for the survey teams (Joshua 18:4-9) to complete their work. If we allow between one and three years for all of this to take place, then we're probably looking at a total period of some eight to 10 years that the eastern tribes would have remained in the west.

This means that the "long time" mentioned in Joshua 22:3 is not to be added to that of Joshua 11:18, but rather *includes it*. It would have been unconscionable to keep these tribes away from their families and loved ones a single moment longer than was absolutely necessary. In fact, given the momentum of the conquest in the east, the Transjordanian tribes might even have anticipated a much shorter stay in the west. We probably see some evidence of this when they vowed "not [to] return to our homes until every Israelite has received his inheritance" (Num. 32:18).

However—at least on the face of it—the farsighted Moses did not hold them to that strict pledge, but instead modified it. Their obligation would end, he said, when the Lord had "driven his enemies out" and "the land [had been] subdued" (Num. 32:21, 22). On the eve of the crossing Joshua reiterated, in substance, the injunction of Moses to them: "You are to help your brothers until the Lord gives them rest . . . and until they too have taken possession of the land that the Lord, your God, is giving them. After that, you may go back" (Joshua 1:14, 15).

On the basis of the less-stringent condition laid down by Moses (and repeated by Joshua), the tribes probably could have been free to leave immediately following the northern campaign when "the land [at last] had rest from war" (Joshua 11:23). But it would appear that they wanted to hold themselves to their (stricter) original pledge.

Eventually, however, it must have become apparent to them that it would be a very long time before "every Israelite [had literally] received his inheritance." In fact, it would be a long time before even every tribe would achieve that much. Way down in the time of the judges, for example, we hear that the Danites are still "seeking a place of their own where they might settle, because they had not come into an inheritance among the tribes of Israel" (Judges 18:1).

However, the broad conditions, as laid down by Moses and Joshua, having now been met, the eastern tribes stood poised to leave, now much wealthier than when they crossed over. They were returning home with "great wealth—with large herds of livestock, with silver, gold, bronze and iron, and a great quantity of clothing" that Joshua advised them to share with the members of their tribes that had to remain in the east (see Joshua 22:8).

The men, all veterans, had seen so much that one would think they'd have no further need for admonition. Yet in his farewell address to them Joshua felt it necessary to remind them to "keep the commandment and the law that Moses" gave to them, namely (see verse 5):
1. "To love the Lord."
2. "To walk in all his ways."
3. "To obey his commands."
4. "To hold fast to him."
5. "To serve him with all . . . [the] heart and . . . soul."

# Establishing Boundaries

The future history of Israel—one filled with backsliding and insubordination—would reveal how appropriate Joshua's words were to them (see 1 Chron. 5:23-26).

In these parting admonitions Joshua was making clear that though separated by distance and by the Jordan, Israel was still one nation, one people, and subject to the same laws and stipulations emanating from the one God. He would make clear that for all Israel the secret of success would always be *obedience*.

## The Crisis Averted

The departing tribes had not been gone very long when word arrived that left Joshua and the rest of Israel in a state of shock. Before crossing the Jordan, they had "built an imposing altar" at Geliloth near the Jordan on the western side of the river (Joshua 22:10). What did it all mean? Had they so quickly abandoned their allegiance to Yahweh?

The war cry sounded as the western tribes gathered at Shiloh to take up arms against those with whom they had for so many years fought side by side (verses 11, 12). But cooler heads prevailed, and Joshua instead dispatched a 10-person delegation headed by the formidable Phinehas to conduct an inquiry into the incident (verses 13, 14).

It was not the first time the eastern tribes had been misunderstood or their motives questioned. Moses had been quite stern with them when they first broached the idea of settling in the east. In downright stinging language he'd accused them of abandonment, of acting to bring discouragement to the rest of Israel, and of rebellion (Num. 32:6-8). It was, Moses suggested, what had caused God to sentence the entire nation to 40 years in the desert. "And here you are," he'd concluded, "a brood of sinners, standing in the place of your fathers and making the Lord even more angry with Israel" (Num. 32:14). If you abandon the rest of Israel now, that would be like calling down a death sentence on their heads, and of course you'd be held responsible (see Num. 32:13-15).

But Moses had misunderstood them (as Numbers 32:16-22 shows). And here again their brothers had misjudged them. One would think that the eastern tribes, learning from experience, ought to have known better than to erect such an object without first (or even subsequently) briefing Joshua on its meaning and purpose. But they'd failed to do so, and a western delegation arrived in Gilead with the mighty Phinehas at its head, bearing a message from "the whole assembly of the Lord" (Joshua 22:13-16).

Accusing the eastern tribes of breaking faith with Yahweh, the delegation, as had Moses many years before, recounted a few select chapters of Israel's painful past, among them the events following the sin of Peor and of Achan (verses 15-20; cf. Num. 25; Joshua 7). In response, the leaders of Gad, Reuben, and the half tribe of Manasseh offered the most emphatic denial that could be expressed in words. One can almost feel the deep anguish in the voice of their appointed spokesman: "The Mighty One, God, the Lord! The Mighty One, God, the Lord! He knows! And let Israel know! If this has been in rebellion or disobedience to the Lord, do not spare us this day" (Joshua 22:22).

No, they said, we have not built the altar either to turn away from the Lord or institute our own system of worship. To the contrary, we have built it as a witness to coming generations of your descendants in the west who might someday attempt to deny our common heritage with the rest of Israel, point to the Jordan as a separating boundary between us, and "cause [our children] to stop fearing the Lord" (verse 25; cf. verses 26-29).

Phinehas and his fellow emissaries "were pleased" with the explanation. "Today," he said, "we know that the Lord is with us, because you have not acted unfaithfully toward the Lord in this matter" (verse 31). That too was the reaction of the entire nation upon receiving the report from the delegation. "They . . . praised God" and abandoned all plans of invasion (verse 33). Diplomacy, we might say, had paid off.

How many conflicts might come to peaceful endings today if we followed the same procedure! Nothing can take the place of face-to-face contact in times of difficulty and misunderstanding.

To forestall any future misgivings, the eastern tribes now attached an inscription to their altar, reading: "A Witness Between Us that the Lord is God" (verse 34).

And so this protracted segment comes to an end. It had been a long and dangerous journey from Jericho to this juncture. At Jericho everything looked so uncertain. The entire mission lay before the people. Now the task is done, the tribes have received their inheritance, the sanctuary has found a permanent home, vital infrastructure has been established, and the Transjordan tribes have returned to their homes in the east. The land is at peace. The nation is secure.

But how solid was the peace? How strong the security? Have we not read, again and again, that one tribe or another could not drive out the native population from its territory? And did not the present segment begin with a declaration from the Lord Himself that "there are still very large areas of land to be taken over" (Joshua 13:1)? How are we to reconcile such apparent conflicts? We will give some space to this problem in the final chapter.

## Questions for Reflection
### Joshua 13-22

1. An aging Joshua had to face up to the fact that "there are still very large areas of land to be taken over" (Joshua 13:1). How do you deal with unfinished business in your personal life? Do you become frustrated and depressed? Or do you, after you've done your best, leave the rest in the hands of God?

2. How can you, like Caleb, keep passion and hope alive through the passage of time? Do you choose the easy road? Or do you, like him, demand the challenge of the hills? Explain.

3. How can you know when your desires are as selfish and as cowardly as that of the tribe of Joseph? And how do you respond to wise counsel in those times?

4. How can you avoid building "altars" that create misunderstanding between you and fellow Christians? And in what attitude should you approach others whom you think have built such offending "altars"?

---

[1] J. M. Miller and G. M. Tucker, *The Book of Joshua,* pp. 105, 106.

[2] E. G. White, *Patriarchs and Prophets,* p. 511.

[3] See *Antiquities* 5. 1. 29.

[4] John L. McKenzie, *The World of the Judges* (Englewood Cliffs, N.J.: Prentice-Hall, 1966), p. 15.

[5] White, *Patriarchs and Prophets,* p. 351.

[6] Another probable reason for the priority given here to these three tribes has been sug-

gested by *The Seventh-day Adventist Bible Commentary:* "Judah and Joseph [Joseph being the father of Ephraim and Manasseh] were the two sons of Jacob on whom Reuben's forfeited birthright devolved. Judah had the dominion given to him and Joseph the double portion" (vol. 2, p. 251; cf. Gen. 35:22; 49:3, 4, 8-10, 22-26). See also Gen. 48:21, 22; 1 Chron. 5:1, 2.

[7] *The Seventh-day Adventist Bible Commentary,* vol. 2, p. 248.

[8] *Ibid.*

[9] *Ibid.,* p. 247.

[10] Cited in G. Mitchell, *Together in the Land,* p. 100.

[11] Larry G. Herr, "The Role of Law in the Book of Joshua," *Spectrum,* June 1995, p. 13.

[12] McKenzie, p. 14.

[13] White, *Patriarchs and Prophets,* p. 514.

[14] *The Seventh-day Adventist Bible Commentary,* vol. 2, p. 265.

[15] White, *Patriarchs and Prophets,* p. 515.

[16] M. Greenberg, "City of Refuge," *The Interpreter's Dictionary of the Bible,* vol. 1, p. 638.

[17] White, *Patriarchs and Prophets,* p. 517.

# Chapter 10

# Laying Down the Mantle

## Joshua 23; 24

The book of Joshua opened with a new era in the life of Israel. Moses was dead. Joshua had taken over the reins. And the nation stood poised to enter upon a most ambitious—and dangerous—mission: the conquest of Canaan.

In the ensuing years the nations of Canaan, with their 31 kings, would witness a frightening blitzkrieg by a previously inconsequential people, who put down every opposition raised against them.

Some 25 years have now passed. The war is over. The new nation is at peace. And their lionhearted leader, now feeble, is ready to lay down his heavy mantle.

The chapters now before us (23; 24) will depict Joshua's last meetings with Israel's leaders and capture his final admonition and challenge to a nation for whose welfare and destiny he's devoted his entire life. As he dismisses the people assembled at historic Shechem, it would be for the last time. He would never see them again. And yet another new era will have begun.

### Measuring Time in Joshua

If I tell a Western audience about what happened on my visit to China, the first question it would raise (if I failed to include the detail in my talk) would almost certainly be the following: *"When* did you go there?"

Westerners consider three aspects of a story to be fundamental: the *what,* the *where,* and the *when.* And often they consider the answer to the first suspect if the response to the other two is missing or inadequate.

189

# Crossing Jordan

It would appear, however, that for the typical ancient Near Eastern mind, the big interest lay with the first question (the *what*) and only secondarily with the other two. And herein lies a great deal of the trouble Westerners have had trying to figure out the sequence and chronology of many ancient Near Eastern stories.

The book of Joshua is no exception. One struggles, for example, to know the chronological relationship between the events described in Joshua 11 and 12 and that of 13:1-7. Or between Joshua 13:1 and 23:1, both of which refer to Joshua's advanced age. And though no weighty theological outcome hangs upon it, it would have been nice to know the exact chronological and other relationships between the two meetings described in chapters 23 and 24. Were they back-to-back convocations, for example? Did they gather in the same place? How exactly did the audience for the two differ, and how were they the same? However, the answers to such questions are not directly forthcoming from the narrative.

But it will do no good to quarrel with the text. Apparently it worked just fine for those who first received it. And it's up to us, recognizing its limitations—as well as our own cultural distance— simply to take it as it comes and make the best of it.

So how, then, do we understand the opening words of chapter 23? What does the statement "after a long time had passed" mean? What's the point of reference? Long after what?

This is the second occasion that the book of Joshua has referred to the idea of "a long time." The first occurred in Joshua 11:18, referring to the period of general mobilization in Canaan. The one before us now clearly has in mind a new period with a new starting point.

But what is that starting point? The translation in the New International Version ("after a long time had passed *and* the Lord had given Israel rest" [Joshua 23:1]) leaves the answer to that question somewhat ambiguous. The starting point becomes obvious, however, if we translate the word "and" in the section just quoted as "since." This would make the sentence read, as in *The New English Bible:* "A long time had passed *since* the Lord had given Israel security from all the enemies who surrounded them" (a similar translation occurs in the KJV).

This rendition (which reflects the intent of the passage, I believe) clearly identifies the starting point here as the end of the northern campaign when, after years of hostilities, "the land had rest from war" (Joshua 14:15). Now we can understand why the biblical author would describe Joshua as "old and well advanced in years" if the point referred to is "a long time" *after* the northern campaign.

But why would Scripture apply the same description to him at a point *just following that same campaign?* (See Joshua 13:1.)

Here again, we see the need to understand the text within its own Near Eastern milieu. We cannot fully comprehend the ancient narrative unless we're prepared, from time to time, to set aside the rigidness of our Greco-Roman perspectives of time and space and enter the biblical *Sitz im Leben* (life situation).

The story of Abraham is a good illustration of what's happening here. When the Lord first intimated to him that his wife would conceive, Sarah (who'd been eavesdropping) laughed, and—from the human point of view—for good reason. For both she and Abraham "were already old and well advanced in years" (Gen. 18:11; cf. verse 12)—Abraham was 99 at the time, and she was 89 (Gen. 17:1, 15-17). The following year, Abraham being 100 and Sarah 90, Isaac was born (Gen. 21:5; 17:17).

More than 37 years later (see Gen. 23:1; 24:67), when Isaac had come to marriageable age, Genesis will again describe Abraham as "old and well advanced in years" (Gen. 24:1).

In respect, then, to the issue before us (the reference to Joshua's age) several points are significant. After the narrator had depicted Sarah at 89 as "old and well advanced in age," she lived another 38 years, dying at the age of 127 (Gen. 17:17; 18:11; 23:1). And not only did Abraham, for his part, live 76 years after being similarly described, but he also remarried following Sarah's death and fathered at least six children with his new wife, Keturah (Gen. 25:1-4, 7).

So we ought not to understand Joshua 13:1 as suggesting that Joshua was then feeble and helpless. No, he still had much vitality left. The author made the observation, rather, against the background of the strenuous task that still lay ahead for Israel—"very large areas of land [yet] to be taken." In other words, God was saying to Joshua that he was not going to be the one to lead Israel into those new undertakings.

# Crossing Jordan

The case of Abraham and Sarah also makes it easier to understand why the identical terminology ("old and well advanced in years") could be used to portray Joshua in Joshua 13:1 and also "a long time" later in Joshua 23:1. The descriptions are obviously relative, and the one in Joshua 23:1 referred to a much later point in the life of the veteran leader. This is shown by the ominous line a little further down in the passage in which Joshua announces that he is "about to go the way of all the earth" (verse 14), a euphemism, of course, for his impending death.

Thus we may say in summary that in Joshua 13:1 Israel's leader is too old to lead another military campaign, whereas in Joshua 23:1 he is too old to live much longer. Joshua's statement that he was "about to go the way of all the earth" may well indicate that he was in the final year of life when he convened the two meetings reported in chapters 23 and 24.

The description of those summoned is not quite as precise as we might wish. The text of Joshua 23, while stating that "all Israel" had been summoned, seems to define that group as comprising "elders, leaders, judges, and officials." Joshua 24:1 says that he "assembled all the tribes of Israel." The text then goes on to say that he "summoned" all "the elders, leaders, judges, and officials"—in other words, all those mentioned in Joshua 23:2.

The general consensus—to which I concur—is that there were two separate meetings, the first (Joshua 23:2) presumably taking place at Shiloh (or, perhaps, in Joshua's own hometown of Timnath Serah) and the second at Shechem (Joshua 24:1). And they probably took place back-to-back, so that those gathered for the first did not have to return to their homes before attending the second.

But how inclusive was the attendance at both meetings? What does the expression "all Israel" in Joshua 23:2 mean? This is an intriguing question in the light of the use of the expression in the book of Joshua itself. God's spectacular works, performed through the medium of Joshua, were to exalt the military leader in the eyes of "all Israel" (Joshua 3:7), a clear reference here to the whole nation (cf. Joshua 4:14). The priests were to stand in the middle of the Jordan until "all Israel" (the whole nation, obviously) had passed over (Joshua 3:17). And the covenant renewal ceremony at Mount

# Laying Down the Mantle

Ebal involved "all Israel, aliens and citizens alike, with their elders, officials and judges" (Joshua 8:33). Again, we have a clear reference to the nation as a whole. Thus a case might be made that these two convocations included a group as comprehensive as that referred to in the texts just cited—the whole Israelite nation.

Two factors, however, seem to argue against such an inclusive understanding of the expression at this point: 1. By this time ("a long time" after the end of hostilities) the various tribes had dispersed to their own territories, and it is hard to imagine that Joshua would have summoned the entire nation back to Shiloh or Shechem for the two meetings. That would have entailed a major and complicated undertaking, involving, in the case of the eastern tribes, the crossing of the Jordan with women, children, and all kinds of bulky provisions for the journey. 2. The form of the expression, both in Joshua 23:2 and 24:1, seems to point to a less-inclusive group than the foregoing texts would suggest. In Joshua 23:2 the groups listed (elders, leaders, etc.) seem to stand in apposition to "all Israel," and not in *addition* to, as in Joshua 8:33, for example. The same kind of construction appears in Joshua 24:1, in which the assembling of all the tribes seems to parallel (and not add to) the summoning of the four groups of officials named.

If we are correct thus far, then we are really looking at a representative group of leaders who appear before Joshua in behalf of the nation. One envisions him convening the first meeting at either Shiloh or Timrath Serah, and then, as happened once before (see Joshua 8), journeying with Israel's leaders to Shechem for a final, solemn renewal of the covenant.

The foregoing arguments, however, do not preclude the attendance at the Shechem meeting of all available Israelites in the immediate vicinity. It's entirely conceivable that ordinary men, women, and children from the surrounding regions swelled the number of those attending the Shechem convocation.

## Joshua's Burden

As Joshua shared his final burden with the assembled leaders, four important elements stood out:

1. *A review of the past.* Said Joshua to the people: You yourselves

have seen the exploits of the Lord—what He has done to the nations "for your sake" (Joshua 23:3).

Israel had now come into possession of Canaan—land that once belonged to others. Not a single nation had been able to withstand the invaders, a truly extraordinary phenomenon in the history of warfare for a group the size of Israel and with the same level of preparation and competence. Those "nations that [still remained]" (Joshua 23:4) in Canaan were all in a defensive posture, none being in a position to launch an offensive against Israel. God had fought for Israel, just as He had promised.

One sees here another evidence of faithfulness to covenant that characterizes the book. Again and again in the chapter Joshua attributes victory to the power and faithfulness of the Lord: "One of you routs a thousand because the Lord your God fights for you, just as he promised" (Joshua 23:10; cf. verses 3, 9, 13).

2. *A reminder of the unfinished task.* While the Lord had accomplished great things for Israel, there were still "nations that remain" (verse 4). Thus it's clear that what Israel had accomplished did not amount to a total annihilation of the people of Canaan. Some of the original inhabitants still remained among them (verse 7; cf. verse 12).

3. *A survey of the qualities needed by Israel's leaders:*

    a. Courage: "Being strong" (verse 6).

    b. Unswerving obedience: "Be careful to obey" (verse 6).

    c. Disassociation from the surrounding peoples (verse 7).

    d. Loyalty to Yahweh (verse 8).

In this survey of the qualities, one notices parallels to God's own commissioning of Joshua in Joshua 1:3-9. For example, Joshua said to the people that "to this day no one has been able to withstand you" (Joshua 23:9), paralleling God's promise in Joshua 1:5 that no one will be able to stand up against Joshua. When Joshua commanded the leaders to "be very strong" (Joshua 23:6), it echoed God's admonition to him: "Be strong and courageous" (Joshua 1:6; cf. verse 7). Joshua warned the people to "be careful to obey all that is written in the Book of the Law of Moses" (Joshua 23:6), reflecting God's command to him "to be careful to obey" all things written in "this Book of the Law" (Joshua 1:7, 8). You are to move forward "without turning to the right or to the left" (Joshua 23:6),

# Laying Down the Mantle

Joshua said to the people—just as God had said earlier to him, "Do not turn . . . to the right or to the left" (Joshua 1:7).

Are the parallels simply accidental? Or are they meant to send a message? I think the latter. Just as God's charge to Joshua in chapter 1 had come at the end of the Mosaic era, just so Joshua's charge to the collective leadership that was to succeed him (Joshua left no individual successor) occurred in the final days of the Joshuarian era.

Using, in many instances, the identical sentiments employed by the Lord in His own commissioning in chapter 1, Joshua now vests in the national leadership gathered before him collective authority and responsibility and holds out to them a challenge similar to that he'd received from the Lord some 25 years before. It's as if we should see chapter 23 as bringing to maturity the promises and commitments found in Joshua 1:3-9 and, at the same time, opening up the door to a new era before the nation.

4. *A summary of the consequences of disobedience.* These would be as follows:

> a. Israel would be unable to withstand its enemies (Joshua 23:12, 13).
>
> b. The nations that remain would imperil Israel's safety, well-being, and its very existence (verses 15, 16).

But if God placed Israel in its central location to be a blessing to the world, then how do we explain the command not to associate with the very nations that were closest to them? Was it divinely sanctioned snobbery?

I think the answer is that the prohibition in question contained quite specific references. Israel was not to invoke the name of the gods of its neighbors or swear by them (verse 7). Nor was Israel to serve or bow down to their gods (verse 7). Instead, Israel was to hold unswerving allegiance to Yahweh only (verse 8). Furthermore, His people were not to form alliances with such peoples (verse 12)—alliances that, in the custom of the times, would have been ratified by mutual recognition of the gods of the nation(s) involved. And finally, the Israelites were not to intermarry with other peoples (verse 12).

Such restrictions may look antiquated to people living in an age of ecumenism and inclusiveness. But we must never lose sight of the fact that the Israelite adherence to these injunctions involved the destiny of the human race. No one who has studied the results of the violation of these strictures in the subsequent history of Israel would deny their vital importance. God designed the guidelines to preserve a faithful remnant in the earth through whom the Messiah would eventually come to bless all nations (see Gen. 3:15; 12:1-3; 18:18; 22:18; 26:4; 28:14; Rom. 4:16, 17; Gal. 3:8, 9).

### Every Promise Fulfilled

We come now to the most controversial—and at the same time most beautiful—statement in Joshua 23: *"Now I am about to go the way of all the earth. You know with all your heart and soul that not one of all the good promises the Lord your God gave you has failed. Every promise has been fulfilled; not one has failed"* (verse 14).

This text is the last of a series in the book of Joshua on this theme, and thus I've waited until now to focus on the important issue raised by it and the others. Earlier statements were equally specific—Joshua 21:43-45, for example. There, as one expositor noted, the author demonstrates the comprehensiveness of the fulfillment through the six-fold use of *kol,* the Hebrew word for *all.*[1] The translation of the text in the King James Version (though it omits one of the *kols* in verse 43) brings out the point clearly: "And the Lord gave unto Israel *all* the land which he sware to give unto their fathers. . . . And the Lord gave them rest round about, according to *all* that he sware unto their fathers: and there stood not a man of *all* their enemies before them; the Lord delivered *all* their enemies into their hand. There failed not ought of any good thing which the Lord had spoken . . .; *all* came to pass" (Joshua 21:43-45, KJV; cf. Joshua 11:12, 14; 11:18-20; 11:23; 14:15).

Critics of the book of Joshua have had a field day pointing out what L. Daniel Hawk calls "jarring inconsistencies,"[2] especially in the area of promise-fulfillment. "Taken as a whole," Hawk says, "the text's repeated juxtaposition of contrary reports and assertions can be baffling. How much of the land does Israel actually take?"[3]

The issue is crucial. For with the whole book anchored on the concept of faithfulness and integrity, a blow in this area, if sustained, is fatal.

The basic problem is that running side by side are two sets of apparently conflicting statements in regard to the conquest and settlement of the land. On the one hand, we seem to hear that God has fulfilled the promise made to Israel's forebears, that not one promise had failed. On the other hand, however, we learn that the native inhabitants still dwell in the midst of Israel, and that one tribe or another had failed to drive them out from its allotted territory. Here are a few examples of the latter statements:

- "When Joshua was old and well advanced in years, the Lord said to him 'You are very old, and there are still very large areas of land to be taken over" (Joshua 13:1).
- "Judah could not dislodge the Jebusites, who were living in Jerusalem; to this day the Jebusites live there with the people of Judah" (Joshua 15:63).
- "They did not dislodge the Canaanites living in Gezer; to this day the Canaanites live among the people of Ephraim" (Joshua 16:10).
- "But Joshua said to the house of Joseph—to Ephraim and Manasseh—'You are numerous and very powerful. . . . Though the Canaanites have iron chariots and though they are strong, you can drive them out'" (Joshua 17:17, 18).
- "But the Danites had difficulty taking possession of their territory" (Joshua 19:47).
- "Do not associate with these nations *that remain among you*" (Joshua 23:7).

In view of such passages, how could Joshua claim that God had fulfilled the promise and that not a word had failed? After all, not only was the tribe of Judah, for example, unable to dislodge the Jebusites, but the latter remained put until the time of David, some 400 years later (1 Chron. 11:4, 5; cf. Judges 1:8, however). And in the book of Judges we hear that "the Amorites [had] confined the Danites to the hill country, not allowing them to come down into the plain" (Judges 1:34). Even some 200 years later the Danites were still "seeking a place of their own where they might settle, because they had not yet come into an inheritance among the tribes of Israel" (Judges 18:1). And in 1 Kings 9:20, 21 we learn that Amorites still remained in the land, together with Hittites, Perizzites, Hivites, and Jebusites.

So what's going on here? How are we to understand these (apparent) discrepancies?

The first thing to note is the openness of the narrative with regard to the two sets of claims. In other words, it's quite evident that the text has nothing to hide. Joshua 23, for instance—the very chapter that ends with a ringing declaration that "every promise has been fulfilled"—first warns Israel about intermingling "with these *nations that remain* among you," worshipping their own heathen gods (Joshua 23:7, 8). It would seem that the author purposefully means to make both sets of statements and evidently sees no conflict between them. So it's up to us to try to figure out how *the narrator* understands the fulfillment of the promise.

This pulls us back to a consideration of what the divine promise was in the first place. As we look back to Genesis, we find that God made it to Abraham on at least five separate occasions:

The *first* occasion comes in Genesis 12 as Abraham arrives in Canaan. God appears to him and says: "To your offspring I will give this land" (verse 7). No designation of boundaries appears here. It's simply the land where Abraham stood, the land he could see all around him.

The *second* promise appears in Genesis 13. Here we find an allusion to its geographical extent: "Lift up your eyes from where you are and look north and south, east and west. All the land that you see I will give to you and your offspring forever" (verses 14, 15). It's the land of Canaan, of course (verse 12), seen from a lookout spot in the vicinity of Ai. Following this last promise, Abraham moves his tent to Hebron, at that time named Kiriath Arba (the city of Arba), named after Arba, the greatest of the Anakites (verse 18; Joshua 14:15).

The area promised here seems comparatively limited, one that Abraham—from high ground, presumably—could see with the naked eye. Still a considerable amount of property, one might observe. But probably not equal to the extensive reach described in later passages.

Genesis 15 presents the *third* promise. The context has now changed slightly. Abraham is becoming concerned about the fact that he is childless. How, then, could the promise (verses 1-5) possibly be fulfilled? Accordingly, God moves to reassure him. He will both have an abundant seed (verses 14-16) and will possess the land: "I am the Lord who brought you out of Ur of the Chaldeans to give you this land to take possession of it" (verse 7).

But Abraham presses the Lord: How can I know these things will be? (See verse 8.) Then follows a divinely directed covenant ceremony, a twilight vision, and a recitation of the promise (verses 9-17) that now turns out bigger than ever described previously, bigger than Abraham had imagined: "To your descendants I give this land, from the river of Egypt to the great river, the Euphrates—the land of the Kenites, Kenizzites, Kadmonites, Hittites, Perizzites, Rephaites, Amorites, Canaanites, Girgashites, and Jebusites" (verses 18-21).

One notices that whereas the first two promises (more limited in scope) were made specifically to Abraham (as if to be realized in his own lifetime), this third promise not only broadens out to include his descendants, but also expands the territory in question. No way could Abraham's eyes see that far—not at ground level, anyway.

The promise now mentions a 400-year gap that includes the sojourn in Egypt of Abraham's descendants, a factor that, by itself, clearly broadens its scope and perspective.

The *fourth* declaration finds Abraham at age 90. Still feeling alien in the land, he falls facedown before the Lord, seeking reassurance. God then repeats the pledge to give to him and his descendants "the whole land of Canaan" "as an everlasting possession" (Gen. 17:8).

The *fifth* promise (in Gen. 22:17) includes a new twist, suggesting that Abraham's descendants "will take possession of the cities of their enemies," a description implying the displacement of settled populations rather than simply the taking over of vast areas of previously unoccupied territory, the picture we might receive from the earliest promises and from the division of the territory with Lot, for example (see Gen. 13:9).

We may quibble about the exact extent of the borders of the territory promised to Abraham. The descriptions are not always as precise as we might wish. The northern border, for example, variously appears as Sidon (Gen. 10:19); the Euphrates River and Lebanon (Deut. 11:24); the Euphrates (Gen. 15:18); Baal Gad below Mount Hermon in the Lebanon Valley (Joshua 11:17); and Lebo Hamath (Num. 13:21).

# Crossing Jordan

But at the end of the day, and for all practical purposes, we're talking about what's commonly known as the land of Canaan, that portion of Palestine west of the Jordan River, south of the Lebanon Mountains, and north of the river of Egypt. It is the home of the seven nations mentioned in Deuteronomy 7:1: "The Hittites, Girgashites, Amorites, Canaanites, Perizzites, Hivites and Jebusites."

And the essential question now is whether Joshua overstated the case when he declared that "every promise had been fulfilled" and that "not one has failed" (Joshua 23:14; cf. Joshua 21:43-45). Did he not know that Israel's northern border did not yet extend to the Euphrates, as Genesis 15:18 and Deuteronomy 11:24 indicated it would? Of course he did. But he knew also that certain aspects of the promise would yet be for the more distant future and were also dependent upon Israel's subsequent relations to Yahweh. But as far as Joshua was concerned, the critical task, the one that mattered for all practical purposes, was complete: the seven nations of Canaan (Deut. 7:1) had been overthrown (see Acts 13:19). And whereas the eastern border of Israel was to have been the Jordan (see Num. 34:10-12), Israel now possessed (as detailed in the previous chapter) vast regions not included in the ancient promises—the territories in Transjordan.

At the risk of sounding repetitive, I have to say again that the way to come to grips with the issue is to put oneself into the *Sitz im Leben* (the life setting) of Abraham, trying to see things the way he would have had he been raised from the dead at the point Joshua spoke and been called upon to give a testimony after seeing a replay of the Exodus and the ensuing experiences of Israel that Joshua had witnessed.

I would suggest that this is the kind of thinking that ought to inform our assessment of Joshua's declaration. In his mind's eye he saw where Israel had been since that day when their ancestor, a bewildered household in tow, first entered the land west of the Jordan. He witnessed how God's providences had operated in behalf of His people, thwarting the wicked schemes and conniving of the enemy. As Joshua looked back he saw before his mind's eyes the devastating plagues on Egypt, the stupendous victory at the Red Sea, the mysterious providences in the desert, the miraculous crossing of the Jordan at harvesttime, the fall of Jericho and Ai, and the overthrow of the powerful military confederations of Canaan by a comparatively small and insignificant people—the descendants of slaves, in fact, with no formal training to speak of in the art of warfare.

Where is that person who, having taken the time to put himself or herself in Joshua's place, would not have uttered, with profound wonder, the same ringing testimony?

The fact that remnants of Canaan's native inhabitants still remained in the land or that some territory still needed conquering was completely overwhelmed in Joshua's mind by the stupendous reality of what God had wrought for a once homeless and defenseless people. We do not get it if we fail to see it from Joshua's eyes. God had been mighty good to Israel. Not a single nation could stand up against it. And apart from the Ai fiasco (resulting from Israel's own culpability), we hear of no Israelite casualties throughout the whole conquest. In fact, so sure was he of God's protection of his people through the period of conquest *that Moses could actually name those leaders who, nearly a decade later, would assist Joshua and Eleazar in the allotment of the land* (see Num. 34:16-29)—and presumably they were all alive to perform that function (see Joshua 14:1).

As Joshua spoke, the tribes of Israel in their thousands had spread out, unchallenged, across the land of Canaan, the very place where Abraham had been a stranger and an alien, and where the only property deeded to his name was a small plot of land bought from Ephron the Hittite to bury Abraham's dead (Gen. 23). How can we, from the mere presence here and there of remnants of the original population, reach the conclusion that Joshua had overstated the case? It seems to me that he is simply expressing here an incontrovertible fact: namely, that as the document that constitutes his book is being written, there is no sign of organized hostilities anywhere within the borders of Canaan. The nation faces no significant threat from its enemies. *The land as a whole belongs to them!*

Three indisputable, objective facts confirm these points:

1. *The change of agenda.* Whereas Israel's energies in chapters 6-11 "are devoted almost entirely to the eradication of the occupants of the land," it seems clear that "from ch[apter] 13 onward, the accounts of the destruction of the enemy are no longer dominant." In other words, Israel has moved into "a new state of affairs."[4] A new agenda is in force—a peacetime agenda, if you please.

2. *Freedom of movement.* The survey teams commissioned to map the territory still unallotted (Joshua 18:4-9) apparently traveled freely, with no military escorts through the land. A clear sign that Israel had put down all significant resistance.

3. *The return of the Transjordan tribes.* In Joshua 1, as you may recall, Joshua had emphasized the critical condition for the return of the tribes living beyond the Jordan. That event was not to take place, all parties agreed, until the Lord brought peace to the west bank of the Jordan—until the rest of Israel had "taken possession of the land that the Lord . . . is giving them." "After that," said Joshua, "you may go back and occupy your own land" (Joshua 1:15).

So the fact that the tribes had now received clearance to return to Transjordan offered a clear indication that the condition had been met—that Canaan was secure. We must take the words of Joshua 22:4 with all seriousness, for the security of all Israel depended on their validity: "Now that the Lord your God has given your brothers rest as he promised, return to your homes . . . on the other side of the Jordan." Israel's leader would not have spoken those words lightly. They constitute incontrovertible evidence of the veracity of Joshua's declaration in Joshua 23:14.

Let's also keep in mind the following points:

a. The evidence indicates that from the start it had not been God's intention to drive out the native inhabitants all at once. And the reason: "Because the land would become desolate and the wild animals too numerous for you" (Ex. 23:29). "Little by little," said the Lord, "I will drive them out before you, until you have increased enough to take possession of the land" (Ex. 23:30).

b. Just about everything God promises to do for us involves our personal or corporate response and participation. And we have evidence that the response of the tribes was not always adequate. At one point Joshua needed to urge several of them to get moving. "How long will you wait before you begin to take possession of the land . . . given you?" (Joshua 18:3). In another case the tribe of Joseph shamelessly complained about not being able to take control of all their allotted territory because "the Canaanites who live in the plain have iron chariots" (Joshua 17:16), as if that were a problem for the Lord.

In such instances particular tribes had indeed failed, but the nation as a whole did not. And more important, God did not fail. Under His outstretched arm, Joshua had conquered the ruling powers of Canaan and rendered their armies virtually impotent in the face of Israel. But he certainly did not exterminate the population from every part of the country. That was not in the plans.

c. Finally, we need to remember—and this point is exceedingly important—that the promise was not simply in respect to land, but also included the prospect of a numerous posterity.

When Abraham came out of Ur, the total number of his household and retainers together probably did not exceed 500 persons (see Gen. 14:14), with Isaac, the seed of the promise, still unborn (see Gen. 15:1-6; 16:1, 3). By contrast, when Moses counted the people in the desert following the Exodus, the fighting men alone numbered 603,550 strong (Num. 1:46). And after a whole generation had perished in the desert, the number was still at 601,730 (Num. 26:51). Even with the possibility that our translation of these figures may be incorrect (since large biblical numbers can be extremely difficult to decipher with complete accuracy), we can be sure that we're talking about a rather large group of people, especially when we add women, youth, and children.

It was an absolutely astonishing development, one that the forces of evil could not thwart. Not the Egyptian government, with its program of infanticide (Ex. 1:15-22). Not Balak, with his fiendish attempt to wipe out the nation through sorcery (Num. 21; 22). And not all the kings and chieftains east or west of the Jordan.

Thus as Joshua gave his final address to the representatives of Israel gathered before him in their thousands, he could say with all integrity, ignoring the insignificant details over which we sometimes needlessly stumble: "Every promise has been fulfilled. Not one has failed" (Joshua 23:14).

## Time for Renewal

More keenly aware each day that his strength was fading, "Joshua assembled all the tribes of Israel at Shechem" (Joshua 24:1; cf. Joshua 23:14). It was most fitting that his final meeting with the people should convene here. Shechem was the place where Abraham, upon arriving in Canaan, built an altar to the God who had thus far guided him (Gen. 12:6, 7). At Shechem Abraham first received the covenant (verses 6, 7). Here Jacob purchased a parcel of ground and, like Abraham before him, built an altar for worship (Gen. 33:18-20). Here at Shechem Jacob put away the foreign gods of his family (Gen. 35:2-4), the event that probably inspired Joshua's appeal to the nation to "throw away the foreign gods that are among you and yield your hearts to the Lord" (Joshua 24:23). And when it says in verse 26 that as a witness to the covenant, "[Joshua] took a large stone and set it up there under the oak near the holy place of the Lord," one wonders whether it might be the same oak tree where Jacob had buried his family's gods.

And so, for his final farewell convocation, Joshua, seeking to impress the strongest and most lasting memories on the minds of Israel's leaders, called them to this sacred spot in the shadows of Mount Ebal and Mount Gerizim, a site rich with ancient memories and traditions reaching all the way back to patriarchal times.

Human society moves forward on the basis of agreements and treaties—or *covenants,* as people often called them in the ancient world. Only fragmentary evidence remains, however, of the actual form such covenants took—with at least one notable exception: the suzerainty treaties of the ancient Hittite Empire, which exhibit the actual sequence of the agreements between these ancient rulers (or suzerains) and the vassal nations who depended on them for military protection or economic support. The basic treaty pattern[5] ran as follows:

First came a *preamble,* identifying "the king who gives the treaty, his titles, appellatives, and genealogy." Second, the *historical prologue,* describing the previous relationship between the king (the suzerain) and the vassal with whom the treaty is being made, and all that the king had done in behalf of the vassal in previous years. Thus it lays out "the foundation of the vassal's obligations" to the king. Third came the *stipulations,* prescribing the vassal's obligations to the king under the terms of the covenant or treaty. The fourth element included *arrangements for the deposit* of the treaty document and for its *periodic public reading.* The fifth aspect consisted of a list of *witnesses* to the treaty. Finally, the document concluded with the *proclamation of blessings and curses* for compliance or violation, respectively, of the treaty.

In many respects Joshua 24, though arranging some of the elements in a slightly different sequence, largely conforms to this ancient covenant pattern. That should not surprise us when we remember that God always communicates with us within our own cultural milieu. He couches the sublime message from heaven within the thought forms of our particular civilization. The *preamble* of the covenant in Joshua 24 comes in verse 2, which identifies the one giving the covenant: "The Lord, the God of Israel."

Next comes the *historical prologue* (verses 2-13), relating how God plucked Abraham from his pagan roots and brought him to the land of Canaan (verses 2-4). In a few sweeping strokes it recounts the history of Israel to the present:

- The journey of Jacob to Egypt (verse 4)
- The Exodus rescue (verse 5)
- The destruction of the Egyptian army (verses 6, 7)
- The wanderings in the wilderness (verse 7)
- The conquest in Transjordan (verse 8)
- The Balak-Balaam fiasco (verses 9, 10)
- The crossing of the Jordan (verse 11)
- The capture of Jericho (verse 11)
- The defeat of the Canaanites (verses 11, 12)

And the point of it all comes in verse 13: "So I gave you a land on which you did not toil and cities you did not build; and you live in them and eat from vineyards and olive groves that you did not plant."

Having laid the basis of Israel's obligations to Yahweh, Joshua 24 now presents the *stipulations* (verses 14, 15). In one of the most powerful challenges to loyalty and faithfulness in all the Bible, Joshua calls upon Israel to abandon the gods of Mesopotamia and Egypt: *"But if serving the Lord seems undesirable to you, then choose for yourselves this day whom you will serve, whether the gods your forefathers served beyond the River, or the gods of the Amorites, in whose land you are living. But as for me and my household, we will serve the Lord"* (verse 15).

What we find here is not a dry, formal rehearsal of the barren formularies of the regular Near Eastern treaty. Not a cowering vassal signing on to a document under duress. But here, instead, is a person whose heart virtually glows with the fire of fervent love for Yahweh, the divine Suzerain, and who, against all the world, is ready to stand up for his God.

# Crossing Jordan

In the annals of ancient treaties and covenants no vassal had ever spoken more passionately or with deeper conviction. With all the earnestness of one who had personally experienced the awesome presence and power of God, Joshua called on the people to make a decision: "Choose for yourselves this day whom you will serve" (verse 15).

I find it extraordinary that Joshua would feel the need for such an appeal to his compatriots after all they'd experienced together. Were his words simply pro forma? Or did they describe current problems in the community? How is it possible that after going through some of the most spectacular events human beings can imagine, some in Israel could still be leaning toward "the gods [their] forefathers worshiped beyond the River and in Egypt" (verse 14)? When Joshua asked the people to "throw away" the gods of their ancestors, did he mean that literally? Did they actually have such gods among them still?

There is certainly a sense in which Joshua was following a liturgical formula, which included certain stipulations as part and parcel of the covenant formalities. But it is, nevertheless, true that the deceptive pull of idolatry had begun to have its effect once more upon the people. "The worship of idols was still to some extent secretly practiced [among them], and Joshua endeavored now to bring them to a decision."[6]

Joshua could say: "But as for me and my household, we will serve the Lord." How was he able to speak with such confidence about his household? Was there a measure of coercion involved in the practice of religion in ancient times? Or was he simply speaking from personal knowledge regarding the commitment of his family? Maybe, in a sense, it was both, if we understand "coercion" in terms of strong moral leadership. For in those days political correctness was on the side of the husband-father who, like Abraham, could "direct his children and his household after him to keep the way of the Lord" (Gen. 18:19).

The book of Joshua has portrayed the idea of family solidarity at strategic times, both positively and negatively. The case of Rahab (Joshua 2:12, 13, 18, 19; 6:22-25) exemplifies positive solidarity— her entire family being saved because of her surrender to Yahweh. That of Achan, on the other hand, stands as an example of negative solidarity—Achan's entire family becoming involved in his crime and in the disaster that followed (Joshua 7:24, 25). And in Joshua

17:3, 4 we find the daughters of Zelophehad standing together in family solidarity to change the social status quo in Israel. Joshua's statement in Joshua 24:15 was in line with this principle.

What is our reaction to this notion? How many heads of household today can speak like Joshua? Indeed, do we even consider such talk politically correct anymore? Do we not live in more democratic times? Indeed we do—for better or for worse. And the time may have arrived when we can no longer say: "As for me *and* my household." But we'd be absolutely done for if the day ever dawns when we cannot even say: "But as for *me!*" That would be the ultimate tragedy.

At this point the Shechem ceremony turned to the matter of *witnesses*. For this occasion, there'd be two sets of *witnesses,* the first being the people themselves (Joshua 24:16-24), whose testimony comes in the form of a formal antiphonal liturgy, in which, Joshua having already spoken (verses 2-15):

(1) the people respond (verses 16-18);

(2) Joshua speaks (verses 19, 20);

(3) the people respond (verse 21);

(4) Joshua speaks (verse 22);

(5) the people respond (verse 22);

(6) Joshua speaks (verse 23);

(7) the people respond (verse 24).

In their first response (verses 16-18) the people declared their allegiance to Yahweh, citing, as Joshua had already done in the historical prologue, many of God's mighty acts in their behalf. But just when we expect Joshua to glow at their ringing testimony, he takes a tack that surprises us: "You are not able to serve the Lord." And why? Because God is "a holy God" and "jealous" (verse 19). Then Joshua adds: "He will not forgive your rebellion and your sins" (verse 19).

What's happening here? After urging the people to serve the Lord, Joshua seems to be discouraging them from their decision to do precisely that. How are we to understand his unexpected response?

It would appear that we must take the whole statement as a package. It's as if Joshua is saying: "You cannot serve God halfheartedly. He is both holy and jealous and requires that those who serve Him be wholly committed to Him, with undivided hearts. If, then, you make a pretense of serving Him fully while clinging to the gods of Mesopotamia and Egypt, then God will certainly fall upon you, not forgiving your rebellion and your sins until you are destroyed." Joshua's intention was to make the people fully aware of the seriousness of their decision.

Finally, the *blessings* and *curses* are drastically abbreviated here when compared to the unabridged version in the Pentateuch (see Deut. 28). As to the curse, Joshua simply says: "If you forsake the Lord and serve foreign gods, he will turn and bring disaster on you and make an end of you" (verse 20). And for the blessings, we find only the faintest echo at the tail end of the curses: "after he has been good to you" (verse 20).

The people agree, and once more pledge their allegiance (verse 21). Then driving the point home, Joshua notes for the record that the people had thereby become their own witnesses in respect to the solemn covenant just agreed to. "Yes," they said, "we are witnesses" (verse 22).

The ceremony ends by noting the place of the covenant— Shechem—and citing *arrangements for its permanent deposit* (verses 25, 26). The *final (inanimate) witness* to the entire transaction—and an impartial one (unlike the people)—is a stone monument set up by Joshua "under the oak near the holy place of the Lord," undoubtedly in the vicinity of Mount Nebo and Mount Gerizim, site of the covenant renewal ceremony after the defeat of Ai. "See!" Joshua said to all the people. "This stone will be a witness against us. It has heard all the words the Lord has said to us. It will be a witness against you if you are untrue to your God" (verse 27).

Surrounded by history and tradition, it was a most solemn ceremony. Its profound impression on the people would last for a long time to come, as the epilogue of the book would show. And as Joshua bade farewell to Israel (verse 28), he knew that it would be for the last time. He would never see them again.

---

[1] G. Mitchell, *Together in the Land*, pp. 104, 105.
[2] L. D. Hawk, *Every Promise Fulfilled*, p. 19.
[3] *Ibid.*, p. 15.
[4] Mitchell, p. 99.
[5] See G. E. Mendenhall, "Covenant," *The Interpreter's Dictionary of the Bible*, vol. 1, pp. 714, 715.
[6] E. G. White, *Patriarchs and Prophets*, p. 523.

# Chapter 11

# Where It All Comes Down

## Joshua 24:29-33

Joshua 24:29-33, written, of course, by a later hand, records several items of deep significance for the theme of the book of Joshua. For convenience, I would mention first the observation made in verse 31: "Israel served the Lord throughout the lifetime of Joshua and of the elders who outlived him and who had experienced everything the Lord had done for Israel."

This is the most impressive legacy of any spiritual leader. It's not a sign of a leader's importance or indispensability when things fall apart after their departure. To derive satisfaction from the fact that things go to shambles since our leadership of a particular enterprise ended is totally misguided and vain. Quite the opposite: the evidence of a good leader appears when things not only *do not* fall apart upon their departure, but instead—all other things being equal—become better, because of the solid foundation laid.

It was to Joshua's everlasting credit that "Israel served the Lord" throughout his lifetime, an occurrence that must have brought him immense satisfaction. But more significant, in a sense, is the indication that his influence continued beyond his death. It was "the noblest testimony of [Joshua's] character as a public leader."[1] Even the great Moses himself did not see such national loyalty or stability.

But those positive words of verse 31 also reflect a darker side to Israel, anticipating (or—depending on when they were written—remembering) the despicable spiritual decline in the time of the judges and beyond. For the centuries following Joshua's time would see Israel turn its back on Yahweh and, totally ignoring every memorial erected to the sovereignty and providence of God (whether at Gilgal or Shechem or Geliloth), embrace the culture, practices, and worship of the surrounding nations. Thus they persisted in their rebellion and insubordination until, with their country and its institutions in ruins, they found themselves led in chains to Babylon (2 Chron. 36:11-21).

If God ever gets frustrated, then our human penchant for forgetting must be one of the primary causes. "Can the church remain faithful after the eyewitnesses are gone? . . . Although we ourselves have not seen the cutting off of the Jordan and the crumbling of Jericho, can we still cling to the God who did these acts?"[2] These are disturbing questions for any religious group that has arrived at the third or fourth generation—or beyond.

Another important detail in the epilogue has to do with the mention of deaths and burials. Joshua dies (at 110) and is buried in the place allotted to him as an inheritance—Timnath Serah in the hill country of Ephraim (Joshua 24:29, 30). And Eleazar the high priest also dies (age unknown) and, like Joshua, is buried in the same hill country—but at Gibeah, on the property of his son Phinehas (verse 33). Then the text mentions Joseph. His bones, carried from Egypt, are now buried at Shechem "in the tract of land that Jacob bought for a hundred pieces of silver from the sons of Hamor, the father of Shechem" (verse 32).

Why these morbid references to deaths and burials to end the book? I think it has something to do with a fundamental theme of the book of Joshua, namely, the importance of keeping promises, of faithfulness to covenant. In regard to Joseph's bones, the element of faithfulness flows simultaneously on two levels. On the first level are the Israelite people—they keep their promise. On the higher level is God—He keeps His covenant. And the people's faithfulness, on the lower level, could be kept only because God, on the higher level, is faithful.

Before he died (like Joshua, at 110), Joseph had prophesied to his brothers that "God will surely come to your aid and take you up out of this land to the land he promised on oath to Abraham, Isaac and Jacob" (Gen. 50:24). Swear to me, he said, that you will carry my bones up with you from here (verse 25).

# Where It All Comes Down

And all through the wilderness wandering, the descendants of those brothers carried those bones of Joseph in fulfillment of the oath taken by their forefathers. As they crossed the Jordan, and through all their movements and activities in Canaan, someone made sure that those bones remained secure. And now in the epilogue of the book we learn that the people were faithful in carrying out the pledge made to Joseph.

Thus the three burials advance the theme of faithfulness to covenant. For the ancients, one of the most sacred privileges imaginable is to be buried in one's own native soil, on one's own property, among one's own ancestors. And thus it is a matter of deep significance that whereas all three of the patriarchs (Abraham, Isaac, and Jacob) had to be buried on land bought from others (see Gen. 23; 25:9, 10; 35:27-29; 49:29-32), the burials of all three leaders mentioned in the epilogue could take place on Israelite soil and on their own tribal properties.

Thus the recording of these burials at this point may be seen as "theological obituaries,"[3] deliberately placed here to underscore the book's major theme: God is faithful. His followers can be laid to rest in their own land. He has kept the promise offered to their ancestors.

The book began by announcing the death of Moses, the great champion of the passing era—a death only recently preceded by that of Aaron (Num. 33:38), Moses' counterpart in leadership. Now the book ends by reporting the death of the two most prominent leaders through the whole period of the conquest—Joshua and Eleazar. In this way it wants to signal the passing of yet another era. At the same time, though, it holds out the hope that just as God had weathered Israel through the tempests behind them, so He would lead them through the storms ahead—if they remained faithful to Him.

And so Joshua lays down the mantle he'd taken up some 25 years before. Faithfulness, integrity, and courage had marked his life. And though his lot was to follow the stellar "performance" of Moses, he had passed nevertheless with flying colors. Under his direction Israel had executed a most perilous mission whose results would be felt clear down to the end of time.

Unlike his great predecessor, who now abides in the heavenly Canaan (see Matt. 17:1-3), Joshua now rests with Abraham in the grave, their remains mingled with the soil of the Land of Promise. But in Jesus Christ, God has guaranteed a better plan for them, and for us— a plan the ancient patriarch grasped by faith, a reality far beyond the transitory things of time and space. "For he looked for a city which hath foundations, whose builder and maker is God" (Heb. 11:10, KJV).

The book of Joshua is about covenants, about keeping promises, about inheritance. And its message for modern Christians is that these covenants, these promises, are real; that the inheritance is sure; that the hope held out before us is not founded on the wishful thinking of religious dreamers and romanticists, the deluded concoctions of unbalanced minds; that we're dealing here with reality, not fiction.

When it comes to the fundamental questions of human origiin and destiny, the postulates of modern science and philosophy are utterly bankrupt. But in the Bible we have a book that synchronizes with what I call deep reality. And it's from the dateless wisdom of this book that we learn that one day God's faithful people in all ages will gather in the heavenly Canaan around the throne of God. In the immortal words of the ancient prophet: "The ransomed of the Lord shall return and come to Zion with songs and everlasting joy upon their head: they shall obtain joy and gladness, and sorrow and sighing shall flee away" (Isa. 35:10, KJV).

It will be a new world order (and here I merge heaven and the new earth in one); a planet transformed; perfect climate; plenty of room; plenty of water; no bloodshed; no pain; no sickness; no disappointment; no poverty; no exploitation; no jails; no hospitals; no war (or those who make them); no terrorists (or those who harbor them); no killings. And no more death!

But best of all, "Joshua" will be there—the eschatological Joshua, whom we call Jesus. He's the center of our fondest hopes. As someone wrote somewhere:

"Oh, heaven without my Savior
Will be not heaven to me."

As I immersed myself in the book of Joshua, with its fast-moving accounts of victory and territorial triumph, I was at the same time reading through the historical and prophetic books of the rest of the Old Testament. From the perspective of the conquest, it was like being able to see the future. It meant that I was witnessing, on the one hand, the most spectacular exploits of an emerging nation; and on the other, watching the specter of failure and defeat in succeeding centuries because of disobedience and insubordination. On the one hand, I saw a nation rising up from slavery, full of promise. On the other, a divided people, saturated with idolatry and willfulness and headed back to foreign bondage.

The contrast was stark, arresting, frightening.

Will history repeat itself? It need not. Like Joshua, we may turn our backs on the gods of the nations among whom we dwell. And like Abraham, we may set our sights on the shining city that lies ahead, on a heavenly future bright with hope, our faith anchored deep in God's unfailing promise.

## Questions for Reflection
Joshua 23; 24

1. The people of Israel were admonished not to associate with the pagans in their midst. How can you be *in* the world, but not *of* it? How can you be "social to save" without being dragged down by those you seek to save?
2. How have you experienced the faithfulness of the Lord? On what basis can you, like Joshua, bear testimony that every promise of God to you has been fulfilled?
3. How often do you take time to recount and reflect upon God's blessings in your life and in that of others close to you?
4. What secret idols might you be cherishing, notwithstanding God's spectacular blessings in your life? How does that hinder the flow of even greater blessings?
5. For his final farewell Joshua assembled Israel at Shechem, a spot filled with memories of God's past blessings and providences. What places or objects have featured in your experience with God? How might you appropriately use such symbols to deepen your walk with Him?

---

[1] E. G. White, *Patriarchs and Prophets,* p. 524.
[2] D. R. Davis, *No Falling Words,* p. 23.
[3] *Ibid.,* p. 21.

# Index

# Index

# Index